Map 1   Southern Scandinavia

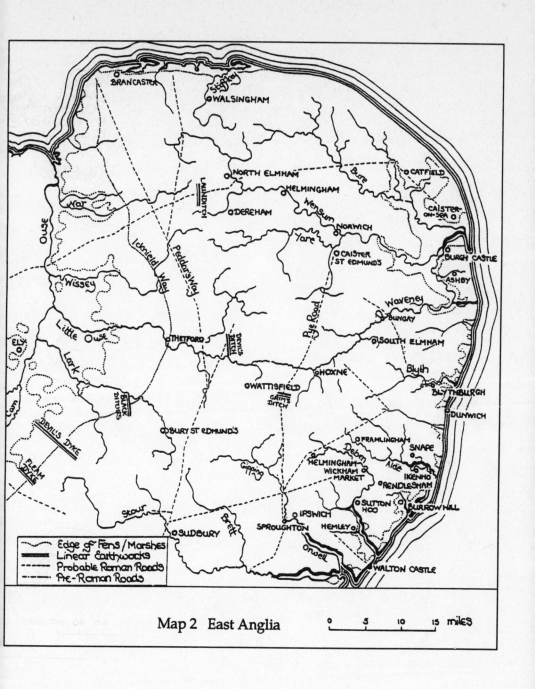

Map 2 East Anglia

Legend:
- Edge of Fens/Marshes
- Linear Earthworks
- Probable Roman Roads
- Pre-Roman Roads

Scale: 0   5   10   15 miles

Place names and features shown on map:

BRANCASTER, WALSINGHAM, Stiffkey, NORTH ELMHAM, HELMINGHAM, Bure, CATFIELD, CAISTER-ON-SEA, Wensum, DEREHAM, LAUNDITCH, NORWICH, Yare, CAISTER ST EDMUND'S, BURGH CASTLE, ASHBY, Wor, Ouse, Icknield Way, Peddars Way, Wissey, Little Ouse, Lark, Waveney, BUNGAY, SOUTH ELMHAM, THETFORD, DEVIL'S DITCH, Pye Road, Blyth, BLYTHBURGH, HOXNE, WATTISFIELD, GRIM'S DITCH, ELY, Cam, BLACK DITCHES, DUNWICH, DEVIL'S DYKE, FLEAM DYKE, BURY ST EDMUND'S, Gipping, FRAMLINGHAM, SNAPE, Deben, HELMINGHAM, WICKHAM MARKET, Alde, IKENHO, RENDLESHAM, SUTTON HOO, BURROW HILL, Stour, Brett, SUDBURY, SPROUGHTON, IPSWICH, HEMLEY, Orwell, WALTON CASTLE

THE ORIGINS OF
BEOWULF
AND THE
PRE-VIKING KINGDOM
OF EAST ANGLIA

Where did the unique Old English epic of *Beowulf* come from? In whose hall did the poem's maker first tell the tale? *Beowulf* is preserved on a single surviving manuscript, probably itself a copy, but a long and careful study of the literary and historical associations reveals striking details which lead Dr Newton to claim a specific origin for the poem.

The fortunes of three early sixth-century Northern dynasties feature prominently in *Beowulf*. Taking this as a probable reflection of the genealogical traditions of a pre-Viking Anglo-Saxon aristocracy claiming descent from one or more of these dynasties, Dr Newton further suggests that references in the poem to the various heroes whose names are listed in Anglo-Saxon royal genealogies indicate that such Northern dynastic concerns are most likely to have been fostered in the kingdom of East Anglia. He supports his argument with evidence drawn from East Anglian archaeology, hagiography and folklore, bringing life to a vanished age with his sympathetic interpretation of the few records that have survived. His argument, detailed and passionate, offers the real and exciting possibility that he has discovered the lost origins of the poem in the pre-Viking kingdom of eighth-century East Anglia.

SAM NEWTON graduated with a first in English literature from the University of East Anglia, Norwich, where he was awarded his Ph.D. for work on *Beowulf* in 1991.

The first folio of the *Beowulf* manuscript (British Library, Cotton Vitellius A.XV: by permission of the British Library). The opening lines read, *HWÆT WE GARDEna in gēardagum þēodcyninga þrym gefrūnon*, "Hwæt, we have heard of the renown of the spear-Danes' folk-kings in days of yore".

THE ORIGINS OF
BEOWULF
AND THE
PRE-VIKING KINGDOM
OF EAST ANGLIA

Sam Newton

D. S. BREWER

First published 1993 by D. S. Brewer, Cambridge
Reprinted in paperback and hardback 1994
Reprinted in paperback 1999

D. S. Brewer is an imprint of Boydell & Brewer Ltd
PO Box 9, Woodbridge, Suffolk IP12 3DF, UK
and of Boydell & Brewer Inc.
PO Box 41026, Rochester, NY 14604–4126, USA

ISBN 0 85991 361 9 (hardback)
ISBN 0 85991 472 0 (paperback)

British Library Cataloguing-in-Publication Data
Newton, Sam
  Origins of "Beowulf" and the Pre-Viking
  Kingdom of East Anglia
  I. Title
  942.601
  ISBN 0–85991–361–9

Library of Congress Catalog Card Number: 92–36873

The paper used in this publication meets the minimum requirements
of American National Standard for Information Sciences –
Permanence of Paper for Printed Library Materials, ANSI Z39.48–1984

Printed in Great Britain by
Athenæum Press Ltd, Gateshead, Tyne & Wear

CONTENTS

LIST OF FIGURES

ACKNOWLEDGEMENTS

On the long road which has led to the making of this book I have received invaluable guidance and support from the following: Professors Michael Lapidge (University of Cambridge) and Malcolm Andrew (Queen's University of Belfast); Dr Jane Martindale (University of East Anglia); Mr Paul Bibire (University of Cambridge); my wife and family; Micronising (U.K.) Ltd.; Dr Rupert Bruce-Mitford (to whom special thanks are due for his encouragement and permission to use his figures); Dr Hilda Ellis Davidson; Dr William Filmer-Sankey and the Snape Historical Trust; Dr Stanley West and the Suffolk Archaeological Unit; Professor Martin Carver and the Sutton Hoo Research Project; Mr Norman Scarfe and the Scarfe Trust; The British Academy; Suffolk County Council Education Department; Dr David Dumville; Mr Chris Sturman; Mr Peter Goodsir; Dr David Corker; Mr George Hyde; Mrs Ann Wood and the UEA Library; and the many scholarly colleagues with whom I have discussed the matter of *Beowulf*.

ABBREVIATIONS

Chronicle	*The Anglo-Saxon Chronicle* (various editions for which references are given in text and bibliograhy);
HE	B. Colgrave and R. Mynors (ed.), *Bede's Ecclesiastical History of the English Peoples* (Oxford, 1969);
Klaeber	F. Klaeber (ed.), *Beowulf and the Fight at Finnsburg*, 3rd edition, with 1st and 2nd supplements (Boston, 1950) – unless otherwise stated, all line references are to this edition of the poem;
OE	Old English;
ON	Old Norse;
Sawyer	P. Sawyer (ed.), *Anglo-Saxon Charters: an Annotated List and Bibliography* (London, 1968);
SHSB	R. Bruce-Mitford, *The Sutton Hoo Ship-Burial*, 3 vols (London, 1975, 1978, 1982).

PREFACE

In this book, which is based on my doctoral dissertation (University of East Anglia, 1991), I have sought to reconsider the question of the origins of our first great work of English literature, the Old English alliterative verse epic of *Beowulf*. Nearly all scholars regard its single surviving manuscript as a copy dating from around the year 1000, and most have reckoned that the poem itself was probably composed in the eighth century. Since the publication of the proceedings of the Toronto conference in 1981, however, it has become fashionable to suppose that the epic is a tenth-century work. I have, therefore, set out to reappraise the entire question of the origin of *Beowulf*.

I argue that there is no compelling linguistic evidence for the date of its composition, but that a number of independent orthographic, lexical and phonological indications suggest that it may have originated in an Anglian kingdom during the eighth century. I also attempt to show that comparative evidence, especially archaeology (which appears hardly to have been considered at all at the Toronto conference), provides some degree of corroboration for this suggestion. Taken together, what indications there are converge on the greater likelihood of composition before, rather than after, the establishment of Viking settlement in England during the latter part of the ninth century.

A curious characteristic of *Beowulf* is its ubiquitous Northern, especially Danish (Scylding), dynastic concerns. Following a hypothesis advanced by Klaeber, and utilising the insights afforded by recent work on the Old English royal pedigrees, I propose that these concerns probably derive from the genealogical traditions of an Old English royal family which claimed descent from the Scyldings. With this proposal in mind, I compare the eulogy for Offa of Angel in *Beowulf* with his listing in the late eighth-century Mercian royal genealogy, but conclude that it does not point exclusively to Mercia as the source of the poem's Northern concerns. I then examine the claim to Danish ancestry made in the late ninth-century version of the West Saxon dynastic pedigree, which lists names included in the upper part of the Scylding pedigree in *Beowulf*, but conclude that the poem was composed independently of any West Saxon genealogical influence.

I consider next the pedigree of Ælfwald, king of East Anglia during the first half of the eighth century, which lists the name *Hrōðmund* in its upper reaches, which is the same as that borne by a Danish prince in *Beowulf*. As *Hrōðmund* is alliteratively paired with *Hryp* in Ælfwald's

pedigree, I advance the view that the name may have been associated
with an early East Anglian dynastic foundation-legend. Turning to
Hroðmund in *Beowulf*, I seek to demonstrate that both he and his brother,
Hreðric, the sons of King Hroðgar, are central figures in a major episode
(ll.991–1250). I argue that the use of irony in this episode, so sharply
brought into focus by Hroðmund's mother, Queen Wealhþeow, reveals
within the Scylding dynasty a latent rivalry between cousins contesting
the question of King Hroðgar's successor. I conclude that, as Wealhþeow
herself seems to forebode in *Beowulf*, and as Northern comparative material also implies, Hreðric is destined to be killed by his cousin Hroþulf
in the course of a struggle for the Danish throne. As to the fate of
Hroðmund in all this, I reason that he could have escaped his brother's
fate by following the *wrecca*'s path into exile.

      I then reveal that there are independent indications that Hroðmund's
mother may have been regarded as an East Anglian dynastic ancestor. I
argue, on the basis of the probable etymology of the East Anglian dynastic eponym, *Wuffa*, that the Wuffings may have been regarded as descendants of the Wulfings of *Beowulf*. As Queen Wealhþeow appears to
have been a Wulfing princess prior to her marriage to King Hroðgar, and
thus a possible Wuffing forebear, her bridal function as *friþusibb folca*, 'the
kindred pledge of peace between peoples' (l.2017a), may have constituted an implicitly understood allegiance, realised through royal wedlock, between Scyldings and Wulfings. I contend that Wealhþeow may
represent an implicit genealogical link between the sixth-century Northern world of *Beowulf* and its Old English audience. The suggested genealogical importance of Wealhþeow's marriage in *Beowulf* would have been
only enhanced by her children, moreover, who would have been viewed
as the living proof of the kindred allegiance of their parents' two peoples.
I conclude that the listing of the name of one of her boys, *Hrōðmund*, in
the pedigree of a Wuffing king may signal an explicit East Anglian
dynastic claim to descent from the Scyldings.

      In the final chapter, I review my consideration of *Beowulf* and surviv-
ing Anglo-Saxon royal pedigrees and propose that East Anglia is the
kingdom most likely to have fostered the poem's Danish dynastic concerns. I then discuss the possibility that the epic could have been composed in East Anglia during King Ælfwald's reign (*ca* 713–749). I contend
that archaeology would complement such a possibility, insofar as, on the
present evidence, the detailed account of the Scylding ship-funeral in
Beowulf appears to reflect East Anglian dynastic conditions. I also note
that the depiction of the fen-dwelling monsters in *Vita Sancti Guthlaci*,
'The Life of St Guthlac', a work written in East Anglia during Ælfwald's
reign, is similar in some significant respects to the representation of the
monster Grendel in *Beowulf*. I argue that these similarities show that
early eighth-century East Anglians believed that their fens and marshes
were haunted by the same kind of Cain-descended monsters as we meet

in the poem, and that aspects of East Anglian folklore and place-name evidence reinforce this point.

I conclude that, although positive evidence is still wanting, there are grounds for regarding *Beowulf* as an eighth-century East Anglian composition.

Snape, Suffolk   *March, 1992*

THE GENEALOGIES OF THE DYNASTIES OF *BEOWULF*

1. THE DANISH *SCYLDINGAS*

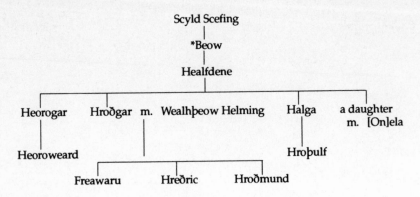

2. THE GEATISH *HREÐLINGAS*

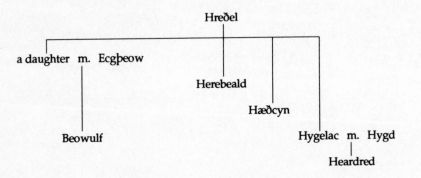

3. THE SWEDISH *SCYLFINGAS*

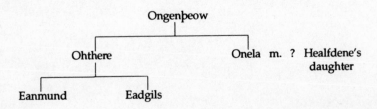

THE GENEALOGY OF THE KINGS OF EAST ANGLIA

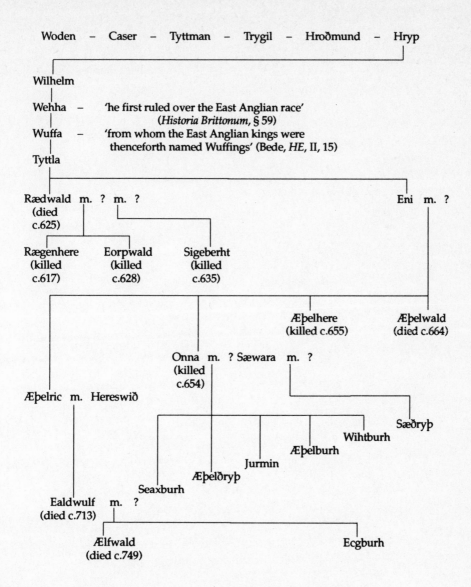

The Probable Sequence of Later East Anglian Kings

Beonna -> Æþelberht (killed 794) -> Eadwald -> Æþelstan -> Æþelweard
-> Eadmund (killed 869).

CHAPTER ONE

THE *BEOWULF* MANUSCRIPT

THE UNIQUE, hand-written text of *Beowulf* is contained in a composite book of early medieval manuscripts, now housed in the British Library, London, where it is catalogued as Cotton Vitellius A.XV. In its present form, this book was probably compiled by Sir Robert Cotton (1571–1631), from two previously separate volumes.[1] The first of these, folios 1^r–90^v, a group of texts from St Mary's Priory, Southwick, Hampshire, contains four items which are all written in what appears to be twelfth-century handwriting. The second, folios 91^r–206^v, is of unknown origin. It is usually referred to as the Nowell Codex, after one of its earliest known owners, Laurence Nowell (1529–1576), who has written his name on the top of the first folio of *Beowulf*.[2]

The Nowell Codex contains five items, the first three of which are in prose:

---

[1] For a detailed discussion of the assembly and subsequent history of Cotton Vitellius A.XV, see Kiernan, *Beowulf and the Beowulf Manuscript*, pp. 66–70; Gerritsen, "British Library MS Cotton Vitellius A.XV – A Supplementary Description"; and, also by Gerritsen, "Have with you to Lexington! The *Beowulf* Manuscript and *Beowulf*". The reader may find it easier to follow some of the arguments in this section with a copy of Zupitza's facsimile of the *Beowulf* manuscript.

[2] Following Kiernan (*Beowulf and the Beowulf Manuscript*, pp. 71–72, 81–85), I use here the eighteenth-century system of numbering the folios, in preference to the current one, which was introduced in 1884. The latter is correct for the ninety folios of the Southwick Codex, but in the Nowell Codex there were two whole quires and twelve folios out of order when the foliation was undertaken. The folio-numbering for the older system can be seen in the upper right-hand corner of each recto leaf in Zupitza's facsimile of the *Beowulf* manuscript. Its two disordered folios, folios 131 and 197, should be located after folios 146 and 188 respectively. They may be corrected by simply renumbering them with the misplaced location of the leaf in question set in brackets: thus the disordered folio 131 becomes folio 146A(131), while 197 becomes 188A(197). The differences between the foliations of the old and new systems as they relate to *Beowulf* may be tabulated as follows:

OLD [MS]	NEW [CURRENT]
129	132
130	133
132–146	134–148
146A(131)	149
147–188	150–191
188A(197)	192
189–196	193–200
198	201

(1) *The Passion of St Christopher*, folios 91(93)^r–95(97)r, the beginning of which is lost;

(2) *The Wonders of the East*, folios 95(97)^v–103^v, illustrated with coloured drawings;

(3) *The Letter of Alexander to Aristotle*, folios 104^r–128^v;

(4) *Beowulf*, folios 129^r–198^v; and

(5) *Judith*, folios 198^r–206^r, which is acephalous.

The handwriting shows that the Codex is the work of two scribes. The first, using an apparently early eleventh-century Anglo-Saxon Insular minuscule script, wrote out the three prose items and approximately the first two-thirds of *Beowulf*. At the beginning of the fourth line of folio 172^v (1.1939^b of the poem), the work of the first scribe ceases abruptly, both before the end of his sentence and before the completion of his last word, *[mo]ste*, the *e* of which appears to have been written by the second scribe. This second, perhaps older, scribe, using a Square minuscule script of seemingly later tenth-century date, has completed *Beowulf* (folios 172^v–198^v). He appears to have been also responsible for copying the next and last item of the codex, the fragmentary *Judith* (folios 199^r–206^v), and for making corrections to the work of the first scribe. Considered together, the handwriting styles of its two scribes imply that the Nowell Codex was probably produced between the last few years of the tenth and the end of the first decade of the eleventh centuries.[3]

Because the beginning of *Judith* is lost, it has been suggested that this poem might not have been part of the original compilation.[4] If not, despite the apparent continuity of the handwriting, the present Nowell Codex may not represent a single Old English compilation. If this is so, the implication of the continuity of the handwriting of the first scribe – that *Beowulf* and the three preceding prose texts represent a single unit – may also be mistaken. Unfortunately, the original quire assembly of the codex cannot be ascertained because each vellum leaf is now mounted separately in modern paper frames as a consequence of damage sustained when the Cottonian library was nearly destroyed by fire at Ashburnham House on 23 October 1731. Although the Cotton Vitellius A.XV survived, it was badly charred, and not rebound until 1845.[5]

Nevertheless, we may gain some indication of the original collation by a consideration of the way in which the hair- and flesh-sides of the leaves

---

[3] Ker, *Catalogue of Manuscripts Containing Anglo-Saxon*, p. 281. More recently, Dumville has argued for a narrower dating band of a few years either side of the year 1000 ("*Beowulf* come lately: Some Notes on the Palaeography of the Nowell Codex").

[4] See Sisam, *Studies in the History of Old English Literature*, pp. 67–68; Ker, *Catalogue*, p. 282; and Kiernan, *Beowulf Manuscript*, pp. 149–167. The poor condition of the verso side of the last folio of *Beowulf* (198) might also suggest that it was once the ultimate page of the volume, but see further below.

[5] Kiernan, *Beowulf Manuscript*, pp. 67–68.

are arranged relative to one another. Usually, a quire was formed from a gathering of four or five vellum sheets folded in such a way that the outer sheet had its hair-side facing outwards, while within the quire flesh-sides faced flesh and hair-sides faced hair.[6] The hair sides of the vellum of a manuscript can usually be distinguished as being smoother and yellower than the flesh sides, while the latter are generally whiter with a rougher surface texture. In the case of Cotton Vitellius A.XV, however, the hair sides tend towards brown and the flesh sides towards grey in appearance as a consequence of exposure to the heat from the Ashburnham House fire. Hair sides can also be distinguished by 'hair dots', which are a result of the shaving of the hide before use.

In the Nowell Codex, these considerations permit two possibilities: *Beowulf* either begins on the first leaf of a new quire or on the seventh folio of the fifth quire of the codex. Although he has acknowledged the latter, the former possibility has been advanced by Kiernan, who has contended that the poem once constituted a separate codex.[7] He has argued that the opening of *Beowulf* coincides with the first folio of the sixth quire of the codex and that this sixth quire consisted of four sheets and two singletons. For Kiernan, then, the codex was originally constructed as follows:[8]

QUIRE NUMBER	FOLIOS	NUMBER OF BIFOLIA PER QUIRE
1	91(93)–100(96)	5
2	101–106	3
3	107(115)–114(122)	3 (+2 singletons)
4	115(107)–122(114)	3 (+2 singletons)
5	123–128	3
6 (*Beowulf*)	129–139	4 (+2 singletons)
7	140–146A(131)	4
8	147–154	4
9	155–162	4
10	163–170	4
11	171–178	4
12	179–188	5
13	188A(197)–198	5
14	199–206	4

His interpretation depends on accepting the rather complicated notion that the fifth quire has only three sheets, and that the third and the fourth quires each consist of three sheets with two singletons attached, rather than the normal four sheets. The alternative interpretation – that *Beowulf*

---

[6] See Ker, *Catalogue*, pp. xxiii, xxv.
[7] Kiernan, *Beowulf Manuscript*, pp. 133–150; and "The Eleventh-Century Origin of *Beowulf* and the *Beowulf* Manuscript", pp. 11–12.
[8] Kiernan, *Beowulf Manuscript*, pp. 123–132.

begins on the seventh leaf of the fifth quire of the codex – is much less complicated.[9] By this reckoning, the first eleven quires of the codex, namely, all those bearing the handwriting of the first scribe, are normal four-sheet gatherings. The more likely interpretation of codex construction thus may be tabulated as follows:

Quire Number	Folios	Number of Bifolia per Quire
1	91(93)–98(100)	4
2	99(95)–106	4
3	107(115)–114(122)	4
4	115(107)–122(114)	4
5	123–128	4
(*Beowulf*)	129–130	
6	132–139	4
7	140–146A(131)	4
8	147–154	4
9	155–162	4
10	163–170	4
11	171–178	4
12	179–188	5
13	188A(197)–198	5
14	199–206	4

Accordingly, *Beowulf* appears to begin on the seventh folio of the fifth quire and thus seems likely to belong to the same compilation as the prose items which precede it.

Another method by which it can be possible to discern original quire assembly is through a consideration of the way in which the text-frame of each leaf has been ruled prior to writing. The normal procedure at the apparent time of writing (*ca* 1000) was to take the sheets of a quire and make prick-marks through them all together – four prick-marks along the two edges of the long sides, defining the vertical margins of the writing space for each individual leaf, and a row along the edges of the short sides to mark each of the horizontal lines of handwriting.[10] The text-frame of two or more sheets was then ruled by means of a pointed instrument between opposite pairs of prick-marks. In this way, any variations in the spaces between the rulings would be common to sheets prepared together so as to constitute a single gathering. Such patterns of rulings can, in theory, be relevant to the identification of individual quires. Just such a rule-pattern is discernible in the bottom line of folios 123–130. These can clearly be seen to have been ruled significantly lower than the bottom line on both preceding and ensuing folios. This suggests

---

9 This interpretation has been favoured by most scholars – see Ker, *Catalogue*, p. 281; and Gerritsen, "Have with you to Lexington!", pp. 15–16.
10 Ker, *Catalogue*, pp. xxiii–xxv.

that, although the original prick-marks have all been lost as a consequence of the Ashburnham House fire, these eight sheets were pricked
together for ruling as a discrete gathering. Folios 123–130, therefore, are
identifiable as a normal four-sheet quire (Quire 5), on the seventh leaf of
which *Beowulf* begins.[11]

The evidence of the rulings would thus seem to coincide with the more
likely interpretation of the relations between the hair and flesh sides of
the leaves noted above. That two types of codicological evidence
independently indicate the possibility that *Beowulf* begins on the seventh
leaf of the fifth quire corroborates the implication of the apparent continuity of the handwriting of the first scribe. It thus seems reasonable to
proceed on the assumption that the poem forms part of the same original
compilation as the preceding prose items. The question is, what kind of
compilation?

It is possible that an interest in the monstrous could have motivated
the compilation.[12] Indeed, four out of the five items in the Nowel Codex
can be said to be thematically unified by a common concern with supernatural entities, both good and bad. The exception is the fragmentary
Judith, unless one counts its eponymous heroine or her opponent
Holofernes as supernaturally gifted. Certainly *Beowulf* is centrally concerned with monsters.[13] *The Wonders of the East* is a catalogue of assorted
oriental monsters.[14] *The Letter of Alexander to Aristotle* is a fictional description of the various strange creatures encountered by Alexander the
Great during his Indian campaign.[15] The hero of the incomplete *Passion of
St Christopher* is represented as something of a wild giant, for he is said to
be *twelf fæðma lang*, 'twelve fathoms tall', as well as the *wyrresta wilddēor*,
'the worst of wild beasts'.[16]

The precise nature of St Christopher's bestiality can be ascertained
from the Old English *Passion of St Christopher*,[17] which states that *sē wæs
healf hundisces mancynnes*, 'he was of the race of mankind who are half
hound'. This canine trait appears to have been a distinctive characteristic
of the Anglo-Saxon view of the saint, for according to the Old English
Martyrology he was *of þǣre þēode þǣr men habbað hunda hēafod 7 of þǣre*

[11] As concluded by Boyle, "The Nowell Codex and the Poem of *Beowulf*", p. 23; Fulk,
"Dating *Beowulf* to the Viking Age", pp. 352–3; and Gerritsen, "Have with you to
Lexington!", pp. 15–16.
[12] As was first pointed out by Sisam, *Studies*, pp. 66–67.
[13] The centrality of the monsters to the narrative and thematic structure of *Beowulf* has
been widely accepted since Tolkien's classic paper, "*Beowulf*: The Monsters and the
Critics"; see also Niles, *Beowulf: the Poem and its Tradition*, pp. 3–30.
[14] Rypins (ed.), *Three Old English Prose Texts in MS Cotton Vitellius A.XV*, pp. 51–67.
[15] Rypins, *ibid.*, pp. 1–50.
[16] Rypins, *ibid.*, pp. 68–76; p. 68, l.19; p. 70, l.5.
[17] The OE *Passion of St Christopher* is preserved in the Cotton Otho MS B.X (Ker, *Catalogue*, pp. 224–9; 226).

eorðan on þære æton men hī selfe, 'from the nation where men have the head of a dog and from the country where men devour each other'. He himself is described therein as follows:

hē hæfde hundes hēafod, 7 his loccas wǣron ofer gemet sīde, 7 his ēagan scīnon swā lēohte swā morgenstēorra, 7 his tēð wǣron swā scearpe swa eofores tēxas;

'he had the head of a hound, and his locks were extremely long, and his eyes shone as bright as the morning star, and his teeth were as sharp as a boar's tusks'.[18]

St Christopher thus seems to have been a member of the race of the cannibalistic *Healfhundingas*, a race who are among the more notable monstrosities in two other items in the codex, *The Wonders of the East* and *The Letter of Alexander to Aristotle*.[19]

It is not impossible that the compilers of the Nowell Codex could have perceived a connection between St Christopher and the monster Grendel in *Beowulf*. Bearing in mind the description of St Christopher cited above, the parallels with Grendel are as follows:

(1) like St Christopher, Grendel is of giant humanoid form (ll.1351b–1353);
(2) he is also of man-eating stock;
(3) the horrific description of his devouring of the Geatish warrior Hondscioh implies that he too possessed very sharp teeth (ll.739–745a) and the reference to Beowulf holding his severed head by the hair (l.1647a) implies that Grendel had long hair;
(4) like the dog-headed saint, Grendel also has notably bright eyes: *him of ēagum stōd / ligge gelīcost lēoht unfæger*, 'from his eyes shone a baleful, fiery light' (ll.726b–727).

Although Grendel appears not to have any particularly canine characteristics, he does seem to be at least partly lupine in nature. This is implied by the use of the following terms to refer to Grendel and his mother: *werhðo* (l.589a); *heorowearh* (l.1267a); *brimwylf* (ll.1506a, 1599a); and *grundwyrgenne* (l.1518b).[20]

Moreover, another book of wonders written in England, the *Liber Monstrorum*, datable to *ca* 650 x 750, was similarly compiled using both *The Wonders of the East* and *The Letter of Alexander to Aristotle*.[21] The *Liber*

---

18 Kotzor (ed.), *Das altenglische Martyrologium*.
19 Rypins, *ibid.*, p. 33, ll.13–14; and p. 54, l.11).
20 For further discussion of the lupine significance of these terms, see Gerstein, "Germanic Warg: the Outlaw as Werwolf", pp. 141–142, 145–146.
21 *Liber Monstrorum*, ed. Porsia. Its likely English provenance and date have been discussed by Lapidge, "*Beowulf*, Aldhelm, the *Liber Monstrorum* and Wessex", pp. 162–167.

Monstrorum also mentions a prominent character from *Beowulf*, namely, the hero's uncle, Hygelac, king of the Geats, describing him as a giant.

> *Concerning Hyglac, king of the Geats.* And there are (monsters) of won-drous size, such as king Hyglac who ruled the Geats and was killed by the Franks. From the twelfth year of his life, no horse could carry him. His bones are preserved on an island in the Rhine, where it flows into the sea, and they are exhibited as a marvel to travellers coming from afar (I.2).

The mention of Hygelac here does not mean, however, that the author of the *Liber Monstrorum* knew the extant version *Beowulf*. He was appar-ently regarded as a giant because of the reputed size of his bones, which were preserved on an island in the Rhine estuary. The use of the present tense in the last sentence of the passage implies that these bones were still being exhibited at the time that the *Liber Monstorum* was being written.[22]

If then, as seems likely, the compilation of the Nowell Codex realises a late tenth-century Anglo-Saxon interest in supernatural wonders, it would appear that *Beowulf* was not necessarily included because of its quality as Old English heroic verse. Yet there is evidence that the two scribes valued the poem above the preceding prose items, for both ap-pear to have been interested enough in *Beowulf* to have re-read and corrected at least 180 errors. The second scribe appears also to have checked and corrected both his work and that of the first scribe.[23] Never-theless, over 300 errors remain unrectified. A significant quantity of these are typical copying-errors, such as dittography or haplography, and together they constitute clear evidence that the extant manuscript of *Beowulf* is a copy of an antecedent text now lost to us.[24]

Kiernan has suggested that the manuscript itself may be the autograph of *Beowulf*, contending that it was a separate codex dating from the reign of the Anglo-Danish King Knut (1016–1035).[25] His attempt to date the poem to after 1016 appears to have been motivated by the fundamental question of why *Beowulf* shows such ubiquitous and detailed Scandina-vian concerns, a question I shall address fully in subsequent chapters. Reviving the theory that the poem may be a composite work, Kiernan argued that it was made from two originally separate poems, with a third section, 'Beowulf's Homecoming' (ll.1888–2199), composed specifi-cally to unify the two.[26] Although *Beowulf* may perhaps ultimately be

---

[22] For further discussion of Hygelac, see Chapter Two below.
[23] As Kiernan observed, *Beowulf Manuscript*, p. 195.
[24] As Gerritsen has also concluded ("Have with you to Lexington!", pp. 20–24).
[25] Kiernan, *Beowulf Manuscript*, and "The Eleventh-Century Origin of *Beowulf*". His arguments for a date after 1016 are deployed in *Beowulf Manuscript*, pp. 18–23.
[26] Kiernan, *Beowulf Manuscript*, pp. 249–258, 271–272. The theory that *Beowulf* could be a

seen as a composite work in terms of the wide range of Old English
heroic and legendary material which it draws on, few scholars today
would regard the poem as we have it as a composite in the sense that
Kiernan has maintained. The classic cases for the unity of the narrative
and thematic structure of *Beowulf* have been advanced by Klaeber and
Tolkien,[27] and recent work has produced no compelling linguistic evidence against this position.[28]

The keystone of Kiernan's theory that *Beowulf* was contemporary with
its manuscript was his analysis of the severely defective state of folio
179[r], which is blotched and faded, as if affected by water. It also appears
as if a restoration of the text has been attempted before the vellum was
entirely dry. Kiernan asserted that the poor condition of folio 179[r] was
due to it being a palimpsest, partially reworked about ten or twenty
years later than the original by the second scribe;[29] and yet, despite
Kiernan's assertion that "there is no credible reason for the palimpsest
other than revision", this seems among the least likely of possibilities.[30]
All scholars agree that this folio is the first leaf of the twelfth quire of the
Nowell Codex; its opening lines introduce the final episode of the poem,
the hero's battle with the dragon. Both the twelfth and thirteenth quires
are the work of the second scribe; they each appear to have been made
up of five sheets, forming an individual unit within the codex. There are
indications that this unit was finished before the second scribe completed and corrected the work of the first scribe in the eleventh quire.[31] If
so, it may have been shelved separately for a while, which could have
led to some wear to its outward facing leaves, that is folio 179[r] and folio
198[v]; but that trained scribes would allow part of a work in progress to
sustain such damage, and then make so poor an attempt at restoration,
seems unlikely.[32] Of significance are the wormholes which penetrate the

---

composite poem was first proposed by Müllenhoff (*Beowulf* [1889]); see also Schücking,
Beowulfs Rückkehr; and two papers by Magoun, "*Beowulf A*: A Folk Variant" and
"*Beowulf B*: A Folk-Poem on Beowulf's Death".

[27] Klaeber, pp. cii–cvii; Tolkien, "*Beowulf*: the Monsters and the Critics".

[28] The handling of the temporal conjunction *siþþan* in the poem has been studied by
Bately, who concluded that it "provides no evidence against the theory that one man
was responsible for all three parts" ("Linguistic Evidence as a Guide to the Authorship
of Old English Verse: a Reappraisal, with Special Reference to *Beowulf*", p. 431). See also
Brodeur, "The Structure and Unity of *Beowulf*"; and Niles, *Beowulf: the Poem and its
Tradition*, pp. 152–162.

[29] Kiernan, *Beowulf Manuscript*, pp. 219–243, following the work of Westphalen (*Beowulf
3150–55: Textkritik und Editionsgeschichte*).

[30] Kiernan, *Beowulf Manuscript*, p. 11; see also Fulk, "Dating *Beowulf* to the Viking Age",
p. 349.

[31] Boyle, "The Nowell Codex", pp. 24–26.

[32] As Boyle pointed out "it is hard to imagine that Scribe B . . . had any hand in such a
spotty 'recovery' or touching up. A man as resourceful and as sensitive as he shows
himself to be in the eleventh quire, when he took over from Scribe A, would not have
made such a mess of his own handiwork" (*ibid.*, p. 32).

thirteenth quire from the back (folio 198^v), for one in particular extends through to the first leaf of the quire (folio 188A[197]^r), leaving no trace of a pupation chamber, but *not* into the last leaf of the twelfth quire (folio 188^v). The activities of this worm imply that the twelfth and thirteenth gatherings were unbound, separated and neglected for quite a while at some later point in the history of the codex.[33] This means that the worst of the damage to folios 179^r and 198^v may have been sustained then.

The present state of folio 179^r – which to me appears dimpled and blotted – raises the possibility that it could have been exposed to rainwater, with its opening leaf receiving the worst of the weather. Such an explanation could also account for the apparent damage to the top lines of folios 179^v, 180^r and 180^v, in that the weather could have caused the upper edge of folio 179 to curl up, exposing the top of not only its verso but also that of both sides of the following leaf.[34] But whatever the true explanation for the condition of folio 179^r, Kiernan's analysis of it – the keystone of his theory that the *Beowulf* manuscript may be its autograph – provides one of the least likely, thus rendering his theory untenable.

If the extant manuscript of *Beowulf* is a copy of an antecedent text now lost, the question is, whence comes the poem?

As already noted, the manuscript of *Beowulf* contains a number of dittographic and haplographic scribal errors which imply that it is a transcription of a text at least one stage earlier. Other cruces may suggest an even earlier stage: a significant number could be resolved by supposing scribal confusion in updating an exemplar which used *d* for *ð* or *þ*, an orthographic equivalence not current later than the eighth century.[35] If so, the poem may have existed in writing before the end of the eighth century. As the emendations on which this point is based have been individually identified on grounds independent of palaeographical considerations, it could constitute a positive indication for the date of the composition of *Beowulf*.[36] Yet as most of the cruces in question probably

---

[33] For a more detailed discussion of the worm, see especially Gerritsen, "British Library MS Cotton Vitellius A.XV", pp. 295–296; and "Have with you to Lexington!", pp. 25–31.
[34] As Boyle has suggested, "The Nowell Codex", pp. 31–32.
[35] As was first proposed by Wrenn, "The Value of Spelling as Evidence", p. 18. Before the eighth century, *d* seems to have been used as both voiced spirant and stop (Ker, *Catalogue*, p. xxxi). Those cruces which all editors and commentators, from 1950 onwards, agree on both the need to emend the manuscript reading and the proposed emendation, include ll.1331^b, 1362^b, 1741^a, 1837^a, 1991^a, 2055^a, 2093^b and 2959^b. Those which all agree on the need to emend, but not necessarily on the proposed emendation, include l.1278^b, a potential case of hypercorrection, and l.3119^a (on which see further below). Perhaps also of interest, though not all acknowledge the need to emend, are ll.985^a, 1107^a, 1375^b, 2964^a and 3152^b (see Kelly, "The Formative Stages of *Beowulf* Textual Scholarship", Parts I and II). Another possibility is l.414^a (Klaeber, p. 466). The consonant differences between the the proper name *Hreðel* (ll.374^b, 1847^b, 2191^b, 2358^a, 2430^b, 2474^b, 2992^a) and its variant *Hrædla* (ll.454^b, 1485^a) may also be relevant.
[36] As Dumville has noted, "*Beowulf* and the Celtic World", pp. 141–142.

result from simple mechanical errors, they do not necessarily imply an eighth-century exemplar.

There is one crux (l.1278ᵇ), however, which may be explained as resulting from an attempt at rectifying an earlier transcription error, involving the confusion between *d* and *ð*, by a scribe aware of the potential for this kind of mistake. All editors and commentators, from 1950 onwards, appear to agree that the manuscript reading *p̄eod* (l.1278ᵇ) is a result of scribal error at some stage, for as it stands, it does not quite make sense.[37] Moreover, all agree on the proposed emendation, but not on its exact form. There is a consensus for *dēoð*, though some prefer *dēað*.[38] In other words, what disagreement there is concerns the diphthong, not the consonants. There is a unanimous view among scholars that the latter are in the wrong order. As *p*, rather than *ð* is involved, simple mechanical error, such as the scribe forgetting to cross a *d*, is less likely to have produced the crux. It would thus appear to be more satisfactorily explained as a consequence of a mistaken attempt at rectifying a possible original **dēod* or **dēad*, the error arising through scribal confusion over *d* and *ð* or *p*. If this explanation is acceptable, it would imply the existence of an eighth-century text of *Beowulf*.

THE LANGUAGE OF *BEOWULF*

As might be expected of a manuscript written *ca* 1000, the language of *Beowulf* is largely Late West Saxon, but embedded within it are a variety of non-West Saxon, especially Anglian, dialectal features.[39] Although our knowledge of Old English dialects is, at best, general,[40] the language of the poem may thus indicate an ultimately Anglian origin, as Klaeber proposed.[41] The hypothesis is that the medley of spellings in the extant manuscript may be explained as a consequence of the copying and recopying of a putative archetype written in an Anglian dialect.[42] Certain forms would have been updated in this process, while others may have

[37] As Andrew pointed out, *Postscript on Beowulf*, § 181.
[38] See Kelly, "*Beowulf* Textual Scholarship", Part I, p. 266, and Part II, p. 245.
[39] The different categories of dialectal forms are listed by Klaeber (pp. lxxi–lxxxviii); see also Thomas, "Notes on the Language of *Beowulf*"; Cameron, *et al.*, "A Reconsideration of the Language of *Beowulf*", pp. 73–75; and Tuso, "*Beowulf*'s Dialectal Vocabulary and the Kiernan Theory", pp. 4–9.
[40] See A. Campbell, *Old English Grammar*, §§ 5–22, and references there cited; and also Crowley, "The Study of Old English Dialects". A useful discussion of the sources of early OE dialectology is included in Toon's *The Politics of Early Old English Sound Change*, pp. 66–87.
[41] Klaeber, pp. lxxxviii–xcv.
[42] As Kiernan observed, this is "a reasonable deduction and, at first sight, the only possible one. Many of the spellings in *Beowulf* simply could not have developed from standard Early West Saxon phonological forms, while they could have developed from standard Northumbrian, or Mercian, or in some cases, Kentish forms. So it was natural

been simply overlooked. Some may have been resistant to phonological modernisation, however, because they were metrically bound as part of a traditional poetic phrase, which could account for the survival of older dialectal features. Klaeber's theory thus points to the possibility of early Anglian composition.

Yet there is an alternative explanation for the language of *Beowulf*, for Old English verse-makers appear to have used a poetic register which was conservative and supra-dialectal in character.[43] That Old English poets composed in such a register is suggested by the fact that all the surviving copies of two tenth-century poems, each of indisputably West Saxon orientation, *The Battle of Brunanburh* and *The Capture of the Five Boroughs*, are rich in non-West Saxon forms.[44] The use of a special poetic register in Old English verse could then account for the presence of some of the older forms in the language of *Beowulf* without necessarily pointing to early composition, as Kiernan argued.[45] This point certainly makes the positive identification of the poem's textual history problematic, for potentially relevant dialectic forms may not be distinguished from those preserved in the lexicon of a conservative poetic register. Klaeber himself acknowledged the use of poetic diction, but still deemed it possible to discern the outlines of a textual history.[46] We are not, therefore, compelled to reject Klaeber's theory of a possible early Anglian origin. Even so, Kiernan's counter-arguments are forceful and do provide an alternative explanation for the language the poem which is plausible. As such,

---

to assume that the mixture of forms was brought about in the course of a long and very complicated transmission . . ." (*Beowulf Manuscript*, p. 28).

[43] This point was first noted by Jesperson, *Growth and Structure of the English Language*, § 53; later advanced by Sisam, *Studies*, pp. 119–139, especially p. 138; see also Kiernan, *Beowulf Manuscript*, pp. 43–46.

[44] Both poems are preserved in the *Anglo-Saxon Chronicle*, MS A, under the years 937 and 942 respectively (ed. Bately). *Brunanburh* is also edited separately by A. Campbell; see also A. Campbell, *Old English Grammar*, § 18.

[45] Kiernan wrote that "a close examination of the amorphous mass of linguistic data assembled by Klaeber shows that the forms are actually indigenous to the Late West Saxon literary dialect or to the archaic poetic word-hoard . . ." (*Beowulf Manuscript*, p. 50). Tuso has recently concluded that "what we know about *Beowulf*'s dialectal vocabulary tends to support Kiernan's view that the poem is written in general OE poetic dialect . . ." ("*Beowulf*'s Dialectal Vocabulary and the Kiernan Theory", p. 3). See also Bately, "Linguistic Evidence as a Guide to the Authorship of Old English Verse", p. 411, note 11; and Cameron *et al.*, "A Reconsideration of the Language of *Beowulf*", p. 37.

[46] As he put it, ". . . the significant coexistence in the manuscript of different forms of one and the same word, without any inherent principle of distribution being recognizable, points plainly to a checkered history of the written text as the chief factor in bringing about the unnatural medley of spellings. . . . It is perfectly safe to assert that the text was copied a number of times, and that scribes of heterogeneous dialectal habits and different individual peculiarities had a share in that work. Although the exact history of the various linguistic and orthographic strata cannot be recovered, the principal landmarks are still plainly discernible" (pp. lxxxviii–lxxxix).

the precise significance of the mixture of forms in *Beowulf* remains uncertain.

The suggested use of a conservative poetic register in Old English verse renders other attempts to date and locate *Beowulf* by linguistic means similarly equivocal. For example, because of this point we cannot be confident as to the significance of Schabram's study of the Old English words for 'pride', which might otherwise suggest independently that the poem may have originated in an Anglian kingdom.[47] It has also been argued that the alliteration of palatal and velar *g* in *Beowulf* could be indicative of composition before the tenth century.[48] Yet this point hardly constitutes positive evidence for the date of the composition of the poem, for we cannot rule out the possibility that a tenth-century poet might work in an earlier style, especially if he drew on Old English poetic tradition.[49] It has been observed, moreover, that *Beowulf* stands apart from other Old English poetry in its use of compounds, especially the number of those in which the second element is a noun, which could suggest an early date of composition.[50] Again, however, the point is not necessarily of chronological significance, for such compounds may reflect individual artistic competence in the traditional language of poetry.[51] For the same reason, the characteristically prominent use of apposition cannot be used in itself as linguistic evidence for the date of the composition of *Beowulf*.[52]

Another possible dating criterion depends purely on a feature of the poem's syntax. There is an apparent tendency in *Beowulf* not to use the definite article *se*, such as appears with increasing frequency in combination with nouns and weak adjectives as the Old English period progresses. There does seem to be a greater proportion of usages of combinations of nouns and weak adjectival forms without the definite article in *Beowulf* than in any other Old English poem.[53] In other words, *Beowulf* appears different from the rest of the poetic corpus in that, in this

---

[47] Schabram, *Superbia: Studien zum Altenglische Wortschatz* (1965).

[48] Amos, *Linguistic Means*, pp. 94, 100–2, 168.

[49] As Amos concluded, a "poet's metrical practice with respect to the alliteration of palatal and velar *g* is probably a valid chronological criterion, as long as it is recognized that metrical practice is in part a function of personal poetic style, and that there is no *a priori* reason that a late poet might not adopt an earlier, traditional style" (*Linguistic Means*, p. 102).

[50] Girvan, *Beowulf and the Seventh Century*, pp. 4–7; Amos, *Linguistic Means*, p. 158; and Niles, *Beowulf*, pp. 138–151.

[51] As Amos noted, *Linguistic Means*, pp. 159, 161, 164. Niles argued that "the high incidence of compounding in the poem . . . might indicate not only that the author . . . was familiar with the old oral tradition, but that he was a living part of it" (*Beowulf*, p. 146).

[52] On the the use of apposition, see Robinson, *Beowulf and the Appositive Style* (Knoxville, 1985).

[53] On this, the 'Lichtenheld' test, see Chambers, *Introduction*, pp. 106–107; Mitchell, *Old English Syntax*, 1985), §§ 114, 336; and Amos, *Linguistic Means*, pp. 110–112.

syntactic matter, it seems to be nearer to the earlier Old English position. One way to explain this difference could be to assume that *Beowulf* is closer to the prehistoric usage of *se* because of its possible early composition. On its own, however, this point cannot constitute compelling evidence for early composition, for the observable difference may not necessarily be chronologically determined; again, it may be a consequence of individual artistic style working within the conservative language of verse.[54]

It has been deemed possible to infer the presence of archaic forms in the text on the basis of metrical considerations, in that certain lines appear not to scan unless they are assumed to have contained older, uncontracted spellings.[55] Theoretically, for example, if the poem was composed before loss of intervocalic *h* in Old English, a sound-change datable to around the end of the seventh century,[56] the diphthongs produced by the resulting contractions of the affected forms in the course of transmission would require disyllabic scansion. Such disyllabic diphthongs would thus not necessarily be explained by the use of the diction of Old English poetic tradition. As there does appear to be a higher proportion of such disyllabic diphthongs in *Beowulf* than in other Old English verse,[57] we might have a hint of evidence pointing to early composition, perhaps even within a generation or two of the end of the seventh century.[58]

Yet if so, composition is unlikely to have been much earlier, as is implied by the presence of Latin loan-words in the text. *Beowulf* contains two categories of Latin loan-words: those which appear to have undergone early Old English sound-changes and so may have been borrowed in the prehistoric period; and those which appear not to have undergone such sound-changes and so may have been borrowed after the coming of Christianity to England.[59] Of these, the presence of three instances of a

---

[54] Amos, *Linguistic Means*, p. 124; and Dumville, *"Beowulf* and the Celtic World", p. 129; the same factors make all other possible tests of dating by syntax similarly equivocal (Amos, *ibid.*, pp. 125–140).

[55] As was first proposed by Sievers, "Die Metrik des *Beowulf"* (1885). Klaeber prints a list of possible examples (pp. 274–275). For a recent discussion of this test, see Fulk, "West Germanic Parasiting, Sievers' Law, and the Dating of Old English Verse".

[56] See A. Campbell, *Old English Grammar*, §§ 234–239, 461; and Amos, *Linguistic Means*, pp. 40–44.

[57] See Amos, *Linguistic Means*, pp. 45–47, and Chart 2, p. 50.

[58] As Cable argued, it may "count for something in placing *Beowulf* earlier than most other poems" ("Metrical Style as Evidence for the Date of *Beowulf*", p. 82). See also Fulk, "West Germanic Parasiting, Sievers' Law, and the Dating of Old English Verse".

[59] On the two categories of Latin loan-words in OE, see A. Campbell, *Old English Grammar*, §§ 493–564. In *Beowulf*, words of the first category include *candel*, 'candle' (ll.1572ᵃ, 1965ᵇ; A. Campbell, *ibid.*, §§ 495, 511, 521), and *draca*, 'dragon' (ll.892ᵇ, 2088ᵇ, 2211ᵇ, 2290ᵇ, 2402ᵇ, 2549ᵇ, 3131ᵇ; A. Campbell, *ibid.*, §§ 164, 495, 526, 530). A good example of the second category in the poem is *gīgant*, 'giant' (ll.113ᵃ, 1562ᵇ, 1690ᵇ; A. Campbell, *ibid.*, § 548).

good example of the second category in the poem, $g\bar{\imath}gant$, 'giant' (ll.113[a], 1562[b], 1690[b]), may imply that composition is unlikely to have been much before the middle of the seventh century.[60]

Concomitantly, the absence of demonstrable Scandinavian loan-words in *Beowulf* may also have chronological implications.[61] Old Norse loan-words do appear in some of the Old English poetry which is datable to the tenth century, that is, after the establishment of Scandinavian settlement in England in the last quarter of the ninth century, implying, as we might expect, interaction between Old English and Old Norse tongues. *The Battle of Brunanburh*, which cannot have been composed before 937, includes the word *cnearr*, 'ship' (l.35[a]), derived from the early ON **knarru*.[62] Moreover, the fact that this word is also used in a compound (l.53[b]) suggests assimilation. *The Battle of Maldon* also contains several probable Scandinavian lexical items, such as *dreng*, 'warrior' (l.149[a]); or *grið*, 'truce' (l.35[b]).[63] The apparent absence of Old Norse loan-words seems especially curious in *Beowulf*, a poem so intimately concerned with Northern kings and their families.[64] The lack of borrowed Scandinavian lexical items in *Beowulf* may therefore imply that the material which informs the poem was not derived from sources later than the Viking Age.

This lexical point is corroborated by the forms of the names of some of the Scandinavian dynastic figures involved. For example, the consonant ð in the Danish royal name *Hröðgār* appears to have been lost in Norse as early as the ninth century.[65] Runic inscriptions indicate that the middle consonants of another Danish royal name, *Hröþulf*, were similarly lost by the ninth century. The stone-carved runic forms of the name in question are *rulufR* (Orevad, Ostergötland, Sweden) and *rhuulfR* (Helnæs, Fyn, Denmark), both of which are probably early ninth century in date.[66] Furthermore, Fulk has drawn our attention to the Vatn stone in Norway, which bears a possibly early eighth-century inscription containing the

---

[60] As also noted by Amos, *Linguistic Means*, pp. 142–3; Girvan, *Beowulf and the Seventh Century*, pp. 24–25; and Whitelock, *The Audience of Beowulf*, pp. 5–6, 10–11. Bede notes the establishment of a school of literacy in East Anglia as early as the 630s (*HE*, III, 18). See further P. Jones, "The Gregorian Mission and English Education". The relation of *Beowulf* and the Anglo-Saxon church is discussed in Chapter Two.

[61] The absence of identifiable Scandinavian loan-words has been noted by Klaeber (p. cxvii); and by Frank, "Skaldic Verse and the Date of *Beowulf*", p. 123.

[62] A. Campbell (ed.), *The Battle of Brunanburh*; Wrenn, *A Study of Old English Literature*, p. 184.

[63] Scragg (ed.), *The Battle of Maldon*; see also Amos, *Linguistic Means*, p. 144; Frank, "Skaldic Verse and the Date of Beowulf", p. 124; and Fell, "Old English *Wiking*: a Question of Semantics", pp. 309–310.

[64] On the poem's Northern dynastic horizon, see further in Chapter Two.

[65] De Vries, *Altnordisches etymologisches Wörterbuch*, s.v. *Hróarr*, and references there cited.

[66] De Vries, *Altnordisches etymologisches Wörterbuch*, s.v. *Hrólfr*; see also Moltke, *Runes and their Origin: Denmark and Elsewhere*, pp. 154, 156.

name *rholtR*. The latter form would appear to derive from **HrōpuwaldaR*, which would itself give rise to the attested Old English name *Hrōðweald*. If so, as Fulk has pointed out, this would suggest that **HrōpuwulfaR* was developing into *Hrólfr* before the ninth century.[67] Comparable examples in the poem include the Danish royal names *Hrēðrīc* and *Hrōðmund*. Russian sources, unlikely to be later than the tenth century, contain a version of the former which lacks the consonant *ð*. Irish sources of simi- lar antiquity contain a form of the latter which has lost the same conso- nant.[68] The forms of these loans imply that the consonant *ð* was lost in Old Norse before borrowing took place, that is, probably before the tenth century. The related names of the Danish kingdom, *Scedeland* (1.19[b]) and *Scedenīg* (1.1686[a]) seem similarly unlikely to be transpositions from Old Norse.[69] As they stand in *Beowulf*, although etymologically related to their later Northern equivalents, none of these names show any evidence for any Scandinavian sound changes. As such, it seems unlikely that they are transpositions from Viking Age Old Norse.

Special pleading, however, has been sought against this point by some scholars. Stanley, for example, has argued that these names could have been transposed by someone "who was unusually good at comparative Germanic philology".[70] Yet, as Chambers noted, the way in which Scan- dinavian aristocratic names are transposed in the *Anglo-Saxon Chronicle* reveals a clear Old English tendency to misconstrue Northern names in the Viking Age.[71] For example, the name of the Danish king defeated by Ælfred of Wessex in 878 is spelt *Godrum* in the A version of the *Chronicle* (*s.a.* 875, 878, and 890), in a part of the manuscript which appears to have been written around the end of the ninth century.[72] If *Godrum* represents a Viking Age Anglo-Saxon attempt at transposing the Scandinavian per- sonal name *Guðormr* into Old English, the attempt has not been a success. The second element appears to have been completely misunderstood: metathesis of *r* has occurred, and the element *-rum* in this context is meaningless in Old English.[73]

The contrasting accuracy of the forms of the names in *Beowulf* suggests that they did not arrive in England by the same route. Rather, they are

---

[67] Fulk, "Dating *Beowulf* to the Viking Age", p. 344.
[68] De Vries, *Altnordisches etymologisches Wörterbuch*, *s.v.* Hroerekr and Hrómundr.
[69] Norreen, *Altisländische und Altnorwegische Grammatik*, § 292; Svennung, *Scadinavia und Scandia*, pp. 36–51; de Vries, *Altnordisches etymologisches Wörterbuch*, *s.v.* Skáney; and Fulk, "Dating *Beowulf* to the Viking Age", pp. 343–344.
[70] Stanley, "The Date of *Beowulf*: some Doubts and no Conclusions", p. 207. The unten- able nature of this view has been demonstrated by Fulk ("Dating *Beowulf* to the Viking Age", pp. 344–345).
[71] Chambers, *Introduction*, p. 323.
[72] Bately (ed.), *The Anglo-Saxon Chronicle: MS A*, pp. xxiv–xxv.
[73] De Vries, *Altnordisches etymologisches Wörterbuch*, *s.v.* Guðormr.

more readily explicable if they stem from an ancestral Old English root.[74]
Although the spellings of these names cannot in themselves be used as
linguistic evidence for an early date of composition,[75] their forms do
suggest that they were committed to writing at an early stage. As such,
whatever the date of the composition of *Beowulf*, the implication is that
the Northern dynastic traditions woven into the poem were of early
English derivation. This point, along with the noted absence of Scandinavian loan-words, may suggest the possibility of pre-Viking composition.

It would thus appear that the evidence of the language of *Beowulf* does
not warrant any clear conclusions as to the date and location of its
composition.[76] Nevertheless, as we have seen, there are a number of
independent indications pointing towards an early origin. Metrical considerations suggest that composition may have been within a generation
or two of the end of the seventh century, while the presence of certain
Latin loan-words in the poem implies that the earliest possible date of
composition is unlikely to have been much before the middle of the
seventh century. The apparent absence of borrowed Norse loan-words,
moreover, along with the phonologies of certain personal names, points
to the use of Old English traditions of the Northlands which were pre-
Viking English in origin. These indications suggest that composition may
have been before the latter part of the ninth century, if not earlier.
Although there is nothing compelling enough to rule out a possible
tenth-century date, it would seem curious that the poem, almost exclusively concerned as it is with Northern dynastic affairs, appears not to
have derived its material from Viking sources. Indeed, if the composition
of *Beowulf* could be dated to the tenth century, as some scholars have
recently attempted,[77] then surely special pleading would be required to

---

74 As Chambers pointed out, the forms in question are "so correctly transliterated as to
necessitate the assumption that they were brought across early, at the time of the
settlement of Britain or very shortly after, and underwent phonetic development side
by side with other words in the English language. Had they been brought across from
Scandinavia at a later date, much confusion must have ensued in the forms" (*Introduction*, p. 103).
75 As A. Campbell noted, "in using names for linguistic purposes it should always be
remembered that in them archaic and dialectal forms tend to be crystallized, so that
they do not reflect the dialect of the writers of the texts in which they are preserved"
(*Old English Grammar*, § 7).
76 On the subject of linguistic tests, Sisam's somewhat sceptical observations appear to
remain generally true: "because these tests leave out of account differences of authorship, of locality, of subject, and of textual tradition, the detailed results, whether of
relative order or absolute date, are little better than guess-work hampered by statistics"
(*Studies*, p. 6).
77 See for example, the arguments of Jacobs, "Anglo-Danish Relations, Poetic Archaism
and the Date of *Beowulf*; Poussa, "The Date of *Beowulf* Reconsidered: the Tenth Century?"; and Murray, "*Beowulf*, the Danish Invasions, and Royal Genealogy".

account for *both* the absence of Scandinavian loan-words and the accuracy of its Northern personal name-forms.

What linguistic indications there are, then, suggest that *Beowulf* was composed perhaps between the late seventh and early ninth centuries, perhaps in an Anglian kingdom, a point consistent with the possible orthographic evidence (discussed above) that the poem may have existed in writing before the end of the eighth century. Taken together, independent linguistic and orthographic considerations permit the hypothesis that *Beowulf* may have been composed during the eighth century. Let us now explore the implications of this hypothesis.

CHAPTER TWO

THE QUESTION OF THE POEM'S ORIGIN

I HAVE ARGUED in the preceding chapter that purely palaeographic and linguistic considerations provide no clear evidence for the origin of *Beowulf*. Independent orthographic, lexical, and phonological indications, however, permit the hypothesis that it may have been composed during the eighth century, perhaps in an Anglian kingdom. These indications provide a basis for further discussion of the question of its origin.

In my consideration of the poem's vocabulary, I suggested that several instances of the Latin loan-word *gīgant* imply that *Beowulf* is unlikely to have been composed before the second half of the seventh century. Concomitantly, the poem's two allusions to the Old Testament legend of Cain and Abel (ll.106–110, 1261b–1265a), along with the similarities between its Creation song (ll.90b–98) and that in the Old English *Genesis*, indicate that its audience had been influenced by Christianity, at least indirectly.[1] Such an influence may also be inferred from the status of the poem as an epic, insofar as its lengthy narrative form may be regarded as a consequence of the interaction of monastic and Classical literacy with vernacular Germanic poetry.[2] Like other epics of the world, such as *Gilgamesh* or the *Odyssey*, *Beowulf* confronts the perennial question of the purpose of mortal life. Although he queried the accuracy of the term 'epic',[3] Tolkien referred to this essential question when he wrote that *Beowulf* is "concerned primarily with *man on earth*, rehandling in a new perspective an ancient theme: that man, each man and all men, and all their works shall die".[4] Drawing an analogy with the basic unit of Old English verse, the alliterative line, he described the narrative structure of the poem as

> essentially a balance, an opposition of ends and beginnings. In its simplest terms it is a contrasted description of two moments in a great life,

---

[1] For a recent consideration of this matter, see Niles, *Beowulf: The Poem and Its Tradition*, pp. 66–95.

[2] As A. Campbell argued, "The Old English Epic Style"; see also J. Opland, *Anglo-Saxon Oral Poetry: A Study of Traditions*, pp. 136–137; and "From Horseback to Monastic Cell: The Impact on English Literature of the Introduction of Writing"; as well as the interesting, though not convincing, objections to this view advanced by Niles, *Beowulf: The Poem and Its Tradition*, pp. 55–63.

[3] Tolkien, "*Beowulf*: the Monsters and the Critics", p. 275.

[4] Tolkien, *ibid.*, p. 265.

rising and setting; an elaboration of the ancient and intensely moving contrast between youth and age, first achievement and final death.[5]

Although this theme is not at all incompatible with Christianity, it is articulated in *Beowulf* through a tale of erstwhile nobility, heroism and tragedy which is set in the pre-Christian Northlands. That a poem of this style was somehow preserved in writing at a time when the technology of literacy was the monopoly of the Church certainly seems curious.[6] The oft-cited evidence of Alcuin's letter to Bishop Hygebald of Lindisfarne, written around the year 797,[7] demonstrates the uncompromising opposition of the ecclesiastical establishment to the recital of Old English heroic verse within its jurisdiction:

> let the word of God be read at the priestly repast. There should the reader be heard, not the harpist; the sermons of the Fathers, not the songs of the pagans. What has Ingeld to do with Christ? (*Quid Hinieldus cum Christo?*) The House is narrow, it cannot hold both. The King of Heaven wished to have no fellowship with so-called kings who are pagan and lost; for the eternal King reigns in Heaven, the lost pagan laments in Hell. Hear the voices of readers in your houses, not the crowd of revellers in the streets.

Yet the same evidence also reveals that Old English heroic poetry must have been current in monastic circles in the first place. The hero Ingeld to whom Alcuin referred is a formerly famous and tragic figure whose story must have been well known in Anglo-Saxon England, for it is alluded to in both *Beowulf* (ll.2020–2069[a]) and *Widsith* (ll.45–49).[8]

Other surviving episcopal correspondence suggests that Lindisfarne was not an isolated case. English bishops meeting at *Clofesho* (in 746 or 747), for example, had cause to forbid not only the patronage of poets in monasteries, but also excessive drinking therein.[9] This situation appears to be indicative of the fundamentally aristocratic character of early English Christianity, as the historian Patrick Wormald has shown in his seminal study of the subject.[10] Demonstrating the importance of the family-monastery or *minster* in early Anglo-Saxon England, an institution founded by, or closely associated with, an aristocracy,[11] Wormald concluded that the early English Church

---

[5] Tolkien, *ibid.*, p. 271.
[6] A matter which has been discussed by John, *"Beowulf* and the Margins of Literacy"; and Wormald "The Uses of Literacy in Anglo-Saxon England and Its Neighbours".
[7] Dümmler (ed.), *Alcuini Epistolae*, p. 183.
[8] On the story of Ingeld, see further below.
[9] Haddan and Stubbs (ed.), *Councils and Ecclesiastical Documents Relating to Great Britain and Ireland*, pp. 363–376.
[10] Wormald, "Bede, *Beowulf* and the Conversion of the Anglo-Saxon Aristocracy", especially pp. 42–57.
[11] Wormald, *ibid.*, pp. 52–54.

had been successfully assimilated by a warrior nobility, which had no intention of abandoning its culture, . . . and whose persisting 'secularity' was an important condition of the richness of early English Christian civilisation. Quite simply, the Anglo-Saxon Church became part of the Establishment.[12]

In such circumstances, the clerical preservation, and even composition, of *Beowulf* does not seem so curious. As Wormald put it,

does the composition . . . of a great secular poem about pagan kings of the past still seem anomalous in a society where monasteries function partly as the royal court, and partly as royal family property . . .? Is *Beowulf* an unthinkable product for a monastic scriptorium, when not only Alcuin, but also councils of the Church talk of drunkenness, banquets and the patronage of harpists in clerical environments . . .?[13]

Although Wormald's work has enabled a clearer historical understanding of the kind of religious and political context which the poem itself implies,[14] it does not permit us to specify the place or date of its composition.[15] As there are no compelling arguments why the integrated aristocratic and monastic setting which he has described cannot be located in the tenth century,[16] the problem of when and where *Beowulf* originated remains open.

BEOWULF AND THE HEROIC AGE OF THE NORTH

Let us return, therefore, to another of the textual indications emerging from the foregoing chapter. As I argued there, the archaic forms of several of the proper names in the poem imply that it drew on an

---

[12] Wormald, *ibid.*, p. 57.

[13] Wormald, *ibid.*, p. 58.

[14] Klaeber once wrote of the problem "of finding a formula which satisfactorily explains the peculiar spiritual atmosphere of the poem" (p. cxxi, note 2). Wormald's historical approach has contributed greatly to resolving this problem. Recent literary research, moreover, has tended to reinforce the strength of his approach. Robinson, for example, in his book, *Beowulf and the Appositive Style*, has elucidated the use of apposition – operating at both the level of syntax and of narrative structure – as a vital literary device through which to reconcile the Christian present and the pre-Christian past.

[15] Wormald "would defend dating limits of 675–875, but would wish to make no further commitment on historical grounds" ("Bede, *Beowulf* and the Conversion", p. 95).

[16] This point is well made by Dumville, "*Beowulf* and the Celtic World: the Uses of Evidence", pp. 156–159; and as Whitelock observed, "it is not enough to show, however convincingly, that the poem fits into a certain historical context, unless one can also show that no other historical context exists into which it could equally well be fitted; and, as our evidence is fragmentary and unequally distributed, there may well have been contexts about which we know little or nothing which would have suited our requirements very well" (*The Audience of Beowulf*, p. 28).

inherited verse-tradition with roots in the pre-Christian period. Because these names appear to contain no evidence of any Old Norse sound-changes, they are more likely to have been of ancestral Old English origin than transpositions of Viking Age Norse names, an implication consistent with the apparent absence of any identifiable Old Norse loan-words in *Beowulf*. Prominent among the proper names in question are those borne by the leading members of the Danish royal family (OE *Scyldingas*, ON *Skjǫldungar*), such as Hrōðgār, Hrōþulf, Hrēðrīc and Hrōðmund, as well as those used to refer to the Danish kingdom, *Scede-land* and *Scedenīg*.[17]

If the forms of these names are of pre-Viking English origin, then the source of the tales of their bearers' deeds might be of a similar antiquity. This point emerges independently if we compare the depiction of the *Scyldingas* in *Beowulf* with surviving Northern sources concerned with the *Skjǫldungar*, all of which date from the Viking Age, or later. These are

(1) Arngrímur Jónsson's late sixteenth-century abstract of the lost, probably twelfth-century, *Skjǫldunga saga* (chs 11–13);[18]
(2) the probably fourteenth-century *Hrólfs saga kraka*;[19] and
(3) the early thirteenth-century *Gesta Danorum* by Saxo Grammaticus,[20] containing its author's Latin version of the *Bjarkamál* (Book 2), an Old Danish poem which is thought to have originated in the tenth century or earlier. According to the thirteenth-century Icelandic historian Snorri Sturluson, *Bjarkamál* was already old and widely known when it was recited to the men of King Óláfr Haraldsson before the Battle of Stiklastaðir in 1030.[21]

In *Beowulf*, the prominence of the Danish royal family is apparent from the opening lines:

> Hwæt, wē Gār-Dena   in gēardagum,
> þēodcyninga   þrym gefrūnon,
> hū ðā æþelingas   ellen fremedon.

'*Hwæt*, we have heard of the renown of the spear-Danes' folk-kings in days of yore – and of how those nobles achieved deeds of courage' (ll.1–3).

---

[17] See the references given for these points in the previous chapter, notes 65–69.
[18] Benediktsson (ed.), *Arngrimi Jonae*, vol. 9.
[19] Slay (ed.), *Hrólfs saga kraka*.
[20] Olrik and Raeder (ed.), *Saxonis Gesta Danorum*.
[21] Aðalbjarnarson (ed.), *Heimskringla*, ch. 208. Snorri also quotes the opening of this poem in his account of the life of this Norse royal saint in *Heimskringla*. Olrik has attempted a detailed reconstruction of the *Bjarkamál* (*Heroic Legends of Denmark*, pp. 85–136).

We may ourselves infer from these lines that the intended audience of the poem was already acquainted with the heroic deeds of the Danish *þēodcyningas*, most probably through the medium of orally maintained verse, as the use of the narrative formula *wē . . . gefrūnon* may imply.[22] Tolkien's view on the existence of such a background of verse traditions is worth citing:

> This must be admitted to be practically certain: it was the existence of such connected legends – connected in the mind, not necessarily dealt with in chronicle fashion . . . – that permitted the peculiar use of them in *Beowulf*. This poem cannot be criticized or comprehended, if its original audience is imagined in like case to ourselves, possessing only *Beowulf* in splendid isolation.[23]

We have already noted a good example of the use of such "connected legends" in the poem, namely, the story of Ingeld. This is alluded to in both *Beowulf* (ll.2024b–2069a) and *Widsið* (ll.45–49), as well as in Alcuin's famous letter to Bishop Hygebald of Lindisfarne, *ca* 797, cited above. Hunter has argued similarly that the reference to Ingeld in *Beowulf* is

> one of the many allusive accounts of events and personalities in the heroic past which were thrown off without explanation to an audience who could be assumed to understand them.[24]

The picture of the *Scyldingas* in the poem is dominated by the lord of Heorot, King Hroðgar. We are told unequivocally that he is

> ... woroldcyninga
> ðǣm sēlestan   be sǣm twēonum
> ðāra þe on Scedenigge   sceattas dǣlde

'the finest of the world-kings between the seas who dealt out treasures in the Danish realm' (ll.1684b–1686).

The formulaic eulogy *þæt wæs gōd cyning*, 'that was a good king', is also used to describe him (l.863b). This phrase is used on only two other occasions in *Beowulf* (ll.11b, 2390b), and it suggests that Hroðgar was intended to represent an exemplary ideal of kingship. In keeping with this ideal, he enjoys divine blessings, as for example, when we are told that *wæs Hrōðgāre / herespēd gyfen*, 'luck in war was given to Hroðgar' (ll.64–65a). As this clause is in the passive voice, the unstated proposition

---

[22] Parks, "The Traditional Narrator and the 'I heard' Formulas in Old English Poetry".
[23] Tolkien, "*Beowulf*: the Monsters and the Critics", pp. 274–275.
[24] Hunter, "Germanic and Roman Antiquity and the Sense of the Past in Anglo-Saxon England", p. 32. For a detailed study of Ingeld, see Malone, "The Tale of Ingeld".

is that Hroðgar is given herespēd, 'luck in war', in the sense that it is "granted" to him by an unspecified divine agency.[25] He has, furthermore, a reputation for great wisdom – he is described by the hero as "gomela Scilding, / felafricgende", ' "the old and very learnéd Scylding" ' (ll.2105b–2106a), and as "wintrum frōd", ' "wise in winters" ' (l.2114a).[26] The depiction of his queen, Wealhþeow, one of the two most prominent females in the poem, only complements the eulogistic picture of old King Hroðgar.[27] Indeed, the implication is that the memory of Hroðgar was held in high honour in the Old English traditions of the Scyldings with which the audience of Beowulf were familiar.

In surviving Scandinavian sources concerned with the Skjǫldungar, however, Hroðgar (ON Hróarr) and his gracious queen are much less prominent.[28] Nowhere in the North is Hróarr depicted as the venerable lord of Heorot whom we meet in Beowulf.[29] The one possible exception is contained in the twelfth-century Chronicon Lethrense (ch. 3), which states that Hróarr 'enriched [Lejre] with many treasures', a reference which might just echo Hroðgar's building of Heorot in Beowulf (ll.67b–82a).[30] If we accept that the legendary hall of Heorot was located in the vicinity of Gammel Lejre, near Roskilde on the island of Sjælland, then this reference could be explained as a result of the Lejre Chronicler's locally-derived knowledge. Today, the little village of Gammel Lejre is surrounded by the remains of an impressive ritual landscape, including a large stone ship-setting and many burial-mounds. Although its association with the Skjǫldungar could have been inspired retrospectively, the site of a large boat-shaped hall, dating from around the year 800, has been recently excavated by Tom Christensen, and there are indications that similar halls stood here even earlier.[31] We must await, however, the

25 Smithers, "Destiny and the Heroic Warrior in Beowulf", p. 70.
26 As may be obvious from the foregoing, I do not share the view that Beowulf is implicitly critical of Hroðgar, a view recently been furthered by Niles (Beowulf, pp. 107–111). Niles has written that Hroðgar "appears as only the shell of a good king" (ibid., p. 110). In disagreeing with Niles, I follow A.P. Campbell and the majority of Beowulf scholars in lamenting the rise of this view and urging a "return to the poem itself, in which old Hroðgar has a noble and honourable place" ("The Decline and Fall of Hrothgar and His Danes", p. 429); see similarly Tripp, "The Exemplary Role of Hrothgar and Heorot".
27 Wealhþeow's status in Beowulf is the subject of close scrutiny later in Chapters Four and Five of this study.
28 Hróarr's marriage to the daughter of an English king is mentioned in passing in Hrólfs saga kraka, ch. 5, and in Skjǫldunga saga, ch. 11. These references are discussed further in Chapter Four.
29 See Beowulf and Its Analogues, ed. Garmonsway and Simpson, pp. 127–141, for a convenient presentation of translated Northern references to Hroðgar.
30 As pointed out by Olrik, The Heroic Legends of Denmark, p. 338; and by Chambers, Introduction, pp. 17, 365; for the reference itself, see Garmonsway, Beowulf and Its Analogues, p. 128.
31 For reports on Tom Christensen's recent excavations at Gammel Lejre, see The Times for 6 April 1988, and for 14 February 1992.

results of continuing work before accepting that Gammel Lejre was the seat of the Scylding kings during Denmark's late Iron Age, for the possibility that it was located at another site dating from this period, such as on the Stevns promontory, Sjælland, or near Gudme on the island of Fyn, cannot yet be ruled out.[32]

More prominent than Hroðgar in Scandinavian sources of the *Skjǫldungar* is his younger brother, Halga (ON *Helgi*), who is mentioned but once in passing in *Beowulf* (1.61^b) in contrast to the references to him in Saxo's *Gesta Danorum*, in *Hrólfs saga kraka* and in *Skjǫldunga saga*. Most prominent of all, however, is Hroðgar's nephew, Halga's son, Hroþulf (ON *Hrólfr*), the most renowned of all the *Skjǫldungar* in Northern heroic legend. It is he, and not his uncle Hróarr, who receives the support of Beowulf's own Northern counterpart, Boðvarr Bjarki, hero of the *Bjarkamál*. An entire saga is devoted to Hroþulf, namely, *Hrólfs saga kraka*. The following quotation from Arngrimur Jónsson's abstract of *Skjǫldunga saga*, ch. 12, exemplifies his reputation in the Northlands:

> Hrólfr Kraki, most famous among the kings of this line, was outstanding for many qualities: wisdom, power, wealth, courage, moderation, amazing generosity, and his tall and thin stature (ch. 12).

Beowulf, however, presents Hroþulf as a curiously silent figure. Named only twice in the poem (ll.1017, 1181),[33] he is overshadowed there by his venerable uncle Hroðgar.

A similar contrast between *Beowulf* and Scandinavian sources is apparent in the presentation of another branch of the family, that of Hroðgar's elder brother, Heorogar, who is mentioned in 1.61^a, and again in ll.467^b–469 and 2158–2159. His quality is praised unequivocally by Hroðgar: "*sē wæs betera ðonne ic*", ' "he was better than I" ' (1.469^b). In the North, however, the respected Heorogar does not appear at all. His son in *Beowulf*, Heoroweard, although only referred to once (ll.2160–2162^b), is also a reputable figure in the poem's view of the Danes, described as *hwæt*, 'valiant' (1.2161^a), and *hold*, 'loyal' (1.2161^b). Heoroweard (ON *Hjǫrvarðr*) is plausibly identifiable in several Scandinavian sources,[34] but nowhere is he included as a respected member of the Danish royal family as we find him in *Beowulf*. Rather, he is presented as the villain who was

---

[32] The Stevns possibility was suggested to me by Lotte Hedeager; the point was also made by Gad Rausing, "*Beowulf, Ynglingatal* and the *Ynglinga saga*, p. 175. Gudme was suggested to me by Ulf Näsman; on its archaeology, see Thrane, "Das Gudme-Problem und die Gudme-Untersuchung".

[33] Both of these instances are in the same episode, in which he plays a silent but crucial part, as is demonstrated in Chapter Four.

[34] Heoroweard is identifiable as the *Hiarwardus* of the *Chronicon Lethrense*, the *Hiǫrvardus* of *Skjǫldunga saga*, the *Hiartwarus* of Saxo's *Gesta Danorum*, and the *Hjǫrvarðr* of *Hrólfs saga kraka*: see Lind, *Norsk-isländska dopnamn och fingerade namn från meideltiden, s.v. Hjǫrvarðr*.

held responsible for the downfall of the renowned Hrólfr, despite the valiant last stand of the latter's followers, one of the most celebrated battles of the Northlands.

Beowulf and the surviving Scandinavian sources in question thus appear to eulogise separate branches of the dynasty. It seems then that the Danish material in *Beowulf* is not derived from, nor influenced by, any known Northern tradition of the *Skjǫldungar*, not even that evident in the earliest traceable source, the Old Danish *Bjarkamál*. For as Malone put it, if the poem was derived from Viking Age material, then

> Hroþulf, not Hroðgar, would have been the Danish king served by the hero, and the historical allusions would have been more in keeping with the Scandinavian tradition as we know it in Saxo and the Icelandic monuments.[35]

Similarly, although a version of the *Beowulf* tale appears to have been known later in Iceland,[36] it does not seem to have influenced the depiction of the *Skjǫldungar* in Icelandic sources. The suggestion is, therefore, that the audience of *Beowulf* were acquainted with Old English traditions of the Scyldings which were current in England before the period of Viking settlement in the latter part of the ninth century.

The poem's presentation of the Swedish dynasty, the *Scylfingas* (ll.2379ᵇ–2396, 2472–2489 and 2922–2998), is also in contrast to the picture provided by surviving Scandinavian sources concerned with this family. The principal Northern source concerned with the dynasty is the thirteenth-century *Ynglinga saga*, which forms the beginning of the Snorri Sturluson's great saga of the kings of Norway, *Heimskringla*.[37] *Ynglinga saga* itself is based on much earlier genealogical verse, especially the *Ynglingatal*, 'The Tally of the Ynglings', attributed by Snorri to the ninth-century poet Þjóðólfr of Hvin.[38] Of prominence in the picture of this family in *Beowulf* is King Onela, who is praised as

> þone sēlestan   sǣcyninga
> þāra ðe in Swīorīce   sinc brytnade,
> mǣrne þēoden,

> 'the famous folk-chieftain, the best of the sea-kings who distributed treasure in Sweden' (ll.2382–2384ᵃ).

The same kind of formulaic eulogy is used in the poem to describe Hroðgar the Scylding, as in ll.1684ᵇ–1686 (cited above). Again, as with

---

35 Malone, untitled review (1931), pp. 149–150. A similar point was also made by M.Clarke, *Sidelights on Teutonic History*, pp. 91–93.
36 Fox and Pálsson (ed. and tr.), *Grettir's Saga*.
37 Aðalbjarnarson (ed.), *Heimskringla*.
38 This poem and its genre is discussed in the next chapter.

Hroðgar (1.803[b], also cited above), the phrase *þæt wæs gōd cyning* (1.2390[b])
also appears to refer to Onela.[39] This apparently unequivocal praise for
Onela (ON *Áli*) in *Beowulf* is in sharp contrast to the way that he is
depicted in Northern sources. There, his status as a member of the Scylfing dynasty is obscured, for he is named as a king of Uppland, Norway,
rather than of Uppland, Sweden,[40] and the focus of interest is directed
much more towards his nephew, Eadgils (ON *Aðils*). *Beowulf*, however,
describes Eadgils and his brother, Eanmund, as *wræcmæcgas*, 'exiles'
(1.2379[b]), who had *forhealden helm Scylfinga*, 'rebelled against the Scylfing
chief [Onela]' (1.2381). The struggle between Onela and Eadgils is
referred to as taking place *ofer sæ sīde*, 'over the broad waters' (1.2394[a]),
involving *cealdum cear-sīðum*, 'cold and sorrowful forays' (1.2396[a]) in
which Onela is killed (1.2396[b]). In Scandinavian sources, this dynastic
power-struggle is also alluded to when it is said that Aðils killed Áli in a
winter-battle on the frozen surface of Lake Vänern, one of the great lakes
of what is now central south-western Sweden.[41]

There are also significant differences between the version of the legend
of the *Wælsingas* alluded to in *Beowulf* (ll.874[b]–897) and that known later
in the North.[42] In *Beowulf*, the central dragon-slaying deed of this legend
is attributed to Sigemund (ON *Sigmundr*), and not to his son (ON
Sigurðr) as we find in later Scandinavian sources. Again, the difference
seems best explained as a consequence of the earliness of the formation
of the tradition which was familiar to the audience of *Beowulf*.[43] Certainly,
the personal name which forms the base of the Norfolk place-name
Walsingham suggests that the *Wælsingas* were not unknown in early
England.[44]

Besides these differences of emphasis between *Beowulf* and its Northern analogues, there are also considerable differences in style. The point
has been well made by T. Andersson:

[39] As Farrell pointed out (*Beowulf, Swedes and Geats*, p. 7).
[40] See Klaeber, pp. xlii–xlv; Chambers, *Introduction*, pp. 4–7; G. Turville-Petre, *The Heroic Age of Scandinavia*, pp. 38–43; G. Jones, *A History of the Vikings*, pp. 35–39; and Gad Rausing, "*Beowulf, Ynglingatal* and the *Ynglinga Saga*".
[41] See Garmonsway and Simpson (ed.), *Beowulf and Its Analogues*, pp. 216–221. This conflict is discussed further in Chapter Four.
[42] The principal source is the thirteenth-century *Vǫlsunga saga* (ed. B.M. Olsen), itself a prose paraphrase of earlier heroic verse of the kind preserved in the *Poetic Edda* (ed. Dronke).
[43] Farrell has made the same point in "*Beowulf* and the Northern Heroic Age", pp. 188–190. See also H.M. Chadwick, *The Heroic Age*, pp. 122–123, 139–142; Neckel, "Sigmunds Drachenkampf"; and Klaeber, pp. 160–161.
[44] The place is called *Walsingaham* in the will of Bishop Ælfric of 1035 x 1040 (Sawyer no.1489) and *Wælsingaham* in the will the Lady Wulfgyth of *ca* 1046 (Sawyer no.1535); see F. Moorman, "English Place-Names and Teutonic Sagas", pp. 89–92, for some pro-
vocative assertions in this area.

it is a question of judging whether the underlying tale grew organically in the poet's own culture, or whether it was taken over by deliberate design from another culture. . . . It seem more likely that *Beowulf* is . . . a peculiarly English expression of the Germanic tradition, aged in vessels, not tapped at the last moment from Odin's vat. If *Beowulf* were taken over from Viking lore in the ninth or tenth century, would it not have some of the harsher and chillier ring of Viking verse?[45]

It is, of course, not only during the Viking period that England had contact with the Northlands, for archaeology reveals that pre-Viking Anglian England had its own close cultural connections with the Baltic, especially during the fifth and sixth centuries.[46] Evidence for links with Scandinavia becomes rarer after the end of the sixth century, although there are indications that Anglo-Scandinavian trade in glass claw-beakers may have continued at least until the mid-seventh century.[47] Such connections across the North Sea provide a context for transmission, long before the Viking Period, of Danish dynastic traditions to England.

THE HISTORICAL HORIZON OF *BEOWULF*

The suggested earliness of the formation and transmission of the poem's Northern heroic material appears to be consistent with its historical horizon. This horizon is to be inferred principally from the five references to the fall of Beowulf's uncle, the Geatish king, Hygelac, during his foray against Frankish territories around the lower Rhine (ll.1202–1214^a, 2201^b, 2354^b–2366, 2493^b–2508^a and 2910^b–2921). If we are correct in identifying the same event in the sixth-century *Historia Francorum* of Gregory of Tours, Hygelac's death in battle in the area can be estimated to have occurred around the year 523.[48] The five references to this apparently major international event in *Beowulf* may then be verified with sufficient certainty to enable each of them to be regarded as likely instances of the preservation of early sixth-century historical fact.[49] Of course, we do not expect *Beowulf* to be primarily concerned with recording the kind of historical fact and chronological precision required by modern historiography. As Tolkien pointed out,

---

[45] T. Andersson, "The Dating of *Beowulf*", p. 300.
[46] Hines, *The Scandinavian Character of Anglian England in the pre-Viking Period*; and Carver, "Pre-Viking Traffic in the North Sea".
[47] Evison, "Anglo-Saxon Glass Claw-Beakers"; and Näsman, "Vendel Period Glass".
[48] Gregory of Tours, *Historia Francorum*, III.3 (ed. Krusch and Levison, p. 99); for a seminal discussion, see Chambers, *Introduction*, pp. 381–387; Klaeber, p. xxxix.
[49] On the historical significance of this event, see Magoun, "The Geography of Hygelac's Raid on the Lands of the West Frisians and the Hætt-ware, *ca* 530 A.D."; "Beowulf and King Hygelac in the Netherlands"; and Storms, "The Significance of Hygelac's Raid".

> *Beowulf* was not designed to tell the tale of Hygelac's fall, . . . still less to write a history of the Geatish kingdom and its downfall. But it used knowledge of these things for its own purpose – to give that sense of perspective, of antiquity with a greater and yet darker antiquity behind.[50]

Yet the references to this event show that the poem's view of the past is not based on fantasy. We may, therefore, also consider the possibility that other peoples and events in *Beowulf* may have a similar basis in sixth-century history.

The prominence of the Danish Scyldings in the poem has already been noted. I have argued that the differences between the Old English traditions of the *Scyldingas* used in *Beowulf* and those of the *Skjǫldungar* in Scandinavian sources imply that independent traditions of the Danish royal family developed on either side of the North Sea. These differences, however, should not obscure the fact of a significant degree of essential agreement between the two traditions. They have, for instance, remained consistent enough to be recognisably concerned with the same royal family. Such consistency between putatively independent traditions is a possible indication of their basis in history, in that the degree of agreement can be explained if both are understood as ultimately deriving from the same historical context.[51]

The same argument is applicable to the presentation of the Swedish royal family in *Beowulf*, the *Scylfingas*. Again, the fact of some degree of essential agreement between *Beowulf* and Northern sources, despite the difference of emphasis noted above, points to the possibility that the traditions of the Swedish dynasty have some basis in history. Moreover, the burial mound of at least one of the Scylfing kings mentioned in the poem, Ohthere (ll.2380[b], 2394[b], 2612[a], 2928[b] and 2932[b]), who appears to be identifiable as the *Óttarr Vendilkráka* of *Ynglinga saga* (ch. 27),[52] may have survived through to the present day, still bearing the name of its alleged occupant. The mound in question is sited at Husby in the parish of Vendel in Uppland and was known as *Ottarshögen* as early as 1675.[53] Archaeologically, this mound is a high-status cremation burial datable to around the beginning or early part of the sixth century.[54] Now, if Ohthere's death were to be dated solely in terms of the consistency with

---

[50] Tolkien, "*Beowulf*: the Monsters and the Critics", p. 275.

[51] Consistency between independent traditions is one of the indicators for the presence of historical elements in heroic poetry formulated by H.M. Chadwick and N.K. Chadwick, *The Growth of Literature*, vol. 1, pp. 133–136, especially points (c) and (e).

[52] See Stjerna, *Essays on Questions Connected with the Old English Poem of Beowulf*, pp. 50–62; and Chambers, *Introduction*, pp. 343–345, 408–411.

[53] See Lindqvist, *Uppsala Högar och Ottarshögen*, pp. 329–330; and Chambers, *Introduction*, pp. 410–411.

[54] Several finds, including a fifth-century gold coin from Byzantium, have enabled the

which the peoples and events in *Beowulf* are presented – with the exter-
nally verifiable dating of Hygelac's fall (*ca* 523, as noted above) as the
basis for an approximate chronology – then it can be said to have occurred around the year 525.[55] Although chronological accuracy is of
course impossible, the near-agreement of this date with that which is
independently deduced by archaeological evidence is impressive, and
may provide grounds for regarding Ottarshögen as the last resting place
of King Ohthere. The possibility that the traditions of the Swedish
dynasty which inform *Beowulf* are based in history is, therefore, strengthened.

There seems, furthermore, to be a close archaeological relationship
between Ottarshögen and one of the three great mounds not far away at
Gamla Uppsala. The easternmost of these was built using very similar
methods and, although none of its high-status contents could be individually dated with such confidence as the finds from Ottarshögen, it appears to be of approximately the same period.[56] Insofar as this mound is
potentially identifiable as that of Ohthere's father, Ongenþeow, another
king whose last battle is alluded to more than once in the poem (ll.2472–
2489, 2922–2988),[57] it can be said to contain further archaeological corroboration of the basis in history of the Old English traditions of the
Scylfingas used in *Beowulf*.

Although the historicity of no other event can be fixed with as much
confidence as the fall of King Hygelac, none of the other potentially
historical elements in the world of the poem need to be dated more than
a generation later. The latest potentially historical event in *Beowulf* is
probably the fall of King Onela of Sweden (ll.2391–2396), which Klaeber
dated to approximately the year 535.[58] The historical horizon of *Beowulf*
thus can be said to extend no later than the middle of the sixth century. If
so, then the Northern dynastic traditions in *Beowulf* would appear to
have undergone at least a century, or more, of transmission before the
earliest likely date of composition indicated by the linguistic considerations discussed in the foregoing chapter, that is, around the middle of
the seventh century. Given the potential for distortion and embellish-
ment which can arise in the course of transmission, as, for example, can
be seen in the traditions of King Eormanric of the Goths,[59] the apparent
degree of historical veracity in *Beowulf* implies that the traditions it has

mound to be dated with some confidence to around the year 500 or slightly later
(Lindqvist, *Uppsala Högar*, pp. 330–331, 344).
[55] See similarly Chambers, *Introduction*, p. 412; and also Nerman, *Det Svenska Rikets
Uppkomst*, p. 137.
[56] Lindqvist, *Uppsala Högar*, p. 344.
[57] Lindqvist, *ibid.*, p. 353; Chambers, *Introduction*, pp. 411–419; but note the cautionery
words of Farrell, *Beowulf, Swedes and Geats*, pp. 55–58.
[58] Klaeber, p. xxxviii.
[59] See Brady, *The Legends of Ermanaric*.

incorporated were formed at a date near in time to the events to which they seem to refer.

This point does not, of course, constitute a compelling argument that the poem itself is an early composition, and the possibility that *Beowulf* utilised pre-Viking traditions which were preserved in writing cannot be ruled out. It has been argued that this was the case with the references to the one datable event in the poem, the fall of King Hygelac.[60] The tragic last stand of a great battle-leader, however, is just the kind of event likely to inspire heroic verse, as we find in the case of Hrólfr in *Bjarkamál*, or of Byrhtnoð in *The Battle of Maldon*. The audience of *Beowulf*, moreover, appear to have shared knowledge of heroic legend which is difficult to account for in exclusively literary terms. Although some could have been literate, it seems less likely that the majority would have been. As such, the historical horizon of *Beowulf* can be said to point to the probable earliness of the formation of its Northern dynastic traditions.

THE ARCHAEOLOGICAL HORIZON OF *BEOWULF*

Archaeological evidence also suggests that the traditions which inform the poem were of early formation. The importance of archaeology to our understanding of the aristocratic world of *Beowulf* is a subject which has been addressed previously in a number of studies.[61] In 1957, Professor Cramp pointed out that "no critic of the poem can afford to neglect the new material evidence that is constantly being produced", but concluded that "what archaeology brings to the poem is not yet a solution to its date; there is not a sufficient body of relevant evidence to do this".[62] This conclusion was cited again in the 1981 Toronto study of the dating of *Beowulf* as though there had been no developments in archaeology since 1957.[63] Yet the amount of evidence available for study has increased enormously and is still expanding.

Of particular value for *Beowulf* scholars has been Brian Hope-Taylor's account of his excavations at the Bernician royal palace site at Yeavering, Northumberland, which has provided convincing verification of the basis in early Anglo-Saxon reality of great royal hall complexes and

---

[60] Goffart, "*Hetware* and *Hugas*: Datable Anachronisms in *Beowulf*".

[61] Stjerna, *Essays on Questions Connected with the Old English Poem of "Beowulf"*; Cramp, "*Beowulf* and Archaeology"; Chambers, "*Beowulf* and the Archaeologists", *Introduction*, pp. 345–365; Wrenn, "Sutton Hoo and *Beowulf*"; Whitbread, "*Beowulf* and Archaeology: Two Footnotes"; Bruce-Mitford, "Sutton Hoo and the Background of the Poem"; Farrell, *Beowulf, Swedes and Geats*; Ellis Davidson, "Archaeology and *Beowulf*; and Hines *The Scandinavian Character of Anglian England in the pre-Viking Period*, pp. 295–300.

[62] "*Beowulf* and Archaeology", pp. 57, 77.

[63] Murray, "*Beowulf*, the Danish Invasions, and Royal Genealogy", p. 102, note 5.

folk-centres like King Hroðgar's Heorot (ll.67b–85, 920b–927a).[64] Another outstanding contribution has been Rupert Bruce-Mitford's definitive reports of the excavations of the East Anglian royal ship-burial from Mound One at Sutton Hoo in Suffolk.[65] There appears to be a curiously close relationship between the events entailed by this ship-burial and the account of the royal ship-funeral in *Beowulf* (ll.26–52), a relationship which I shall examine in my consideration of the poem's descriptions of pre-Christian burial-rites later in this chapter. Many of the excavated contents of Mound One at Sutton Hoo also appear to verify passages from the poem. For example, the high-antlered bronze stag from the great whetstone shows that the hart, after which King Hroðgar names his royal mead-hall (l.78b), was a genuine emblem of kingship in early England (Fig. 1).[66] Moreover, the fact that the remains of a stringed musical instrument were discovered in Mound One (Fig. 2),[67] and which may thus have been royal personal property, gives credence to Beowulf's report of King Hroðgar himself playing one:

> ". . . gomela Scilding,
> felafricgende   feorran rehte;
> hwīlum hildedēor   hearpan wynne,
> gomenwudu grētte,   hwīlum gyd āwræc
> sōð 7 sārlīc,   hwīlum syllīc spell
> rehte æfter rihte   rūmheort cyning . . ."

' "The old Scylding, steeped in learning, related tales from far-off times; sometimes this battle-bold one played the harp in delight, the joy-wood, sometimes he recited a true and tragic song, and sometimes that roomy-hearted king told tales of wonder" ' (ll.2105b–2110).

Some of the war-gear from Mound One also seems to resemble the often detailed descriptions of aristocratic war-gear in the poem. The splendid sword, for example, which has a pattern-welded blade and a hilt and harness adorned with the most exquisite gold-cloisonné jewellery (Fig. 3),[68] may be very accurately described, like the weapon presented to

---

[64] Hope-Taylor, *Yeavering: An Anglo-British Centre of Early Northumbria*; as has been shown by Cramp, "*Beowulf* and Archaeology", pp. 68–77; and Ellis Davidson, "Archaeology and *Beowulf*", pp. 353–4.

[65] Bruce-Mitford, *The Sutton Hoo Ship-Burial*, (henceforth *SHSB*). On the East Anglian royal status of this burial, see Bruce Mitford, *ibid.*, vol.1, pp. 685–688, who also argued that it was a Wuffing burial, perhaps that of King Rædwald (*ibid.*, pp. 690–713). The recent claim that it may have been a cenotaph to King Sæberht of Essex (Parker Pearson *et al.*, "Three Men and a Boat") seems interesting but unlikely.

[66] Bruce-Mitford, *SHSB*, vol. 2, pp. 311–393, especially pp. 346, 376, and 382; for a general discussion, see Nicholson, "*Beowulf* and the Pagan Cult of the Stag".

[67] Bruce-Mitford, *Aspects of Anglo-Saxon Archaeology*, pp. 188–197; and *SHSB*, vol. 3, pp. 611–731.

[68] Bruce-Mitford, *SHSB*, vol. 2, pp. 273–309, 456–481, 564–581.

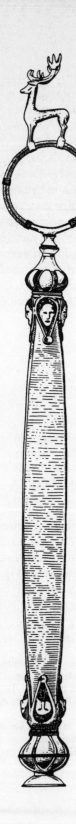

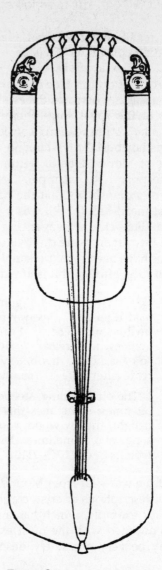

Figure 2

The reconstructed lyre from Mound 1
at Sutton Hoo (Scale 1 to 5)

Figure 1

The reconstructed ceremonial
whetstone from Mound 1 at
Sutton Hoo (Scale 1 to 6)

Beowulf by King Hroðgar, as a *māðþumsweord*, 'treasure-sword' (1.1023ᵃ); or, like the sword given later to the hero by King Hygelac, as a *sincmāðþum*, 'bejewelled treasure' (1.2193ᵃ). The first element of the latter compound, *sinc*, may refer specifically to the lapidary technique of 'sinking' precious cut garnet or millefiori glass into gold-cloisonné settings.[69] If so, *sincmāðþum* would an especially apt compound to use to describe the Sutton Hoo sword. Similarly, the knee-length mailcoat from Mound One, unique in Anglo-Saxon archaeology, was clearly an example of the highest quality smithy-work.[70] Such a standard of craftsmanship could have inspired the choice of some of the phrases which emphasise the quality of Beowulf's own fine byrnie of chain-mail. For example, it is described as *searonet seowed smiþes orþancum*, 'the byrnie-net woven by the skills of the smith' (1.406). The hero himself refers to it as

> "beaduscrūda betst,   þæt mīne brēost wereð,
> hrægla sēlest;   þæt is Hrǣdlan lāf,
> Wēlandes geweorc."

> ' "the best of battle-dress, that protects my breast, the finest of gear; it is Hreðel's heirloom, the work of Weland' "(ll.453–455ᵃ).

That it is said also to be *locen*, 'locked' (1.1505ᵃ), recalls the alternating use of welding and copper riveting to 'lock' the rows of interlinked rings in the Sutton Hoo mailcoat.[71]

There are also some remarkably close parallels between features of the Sutton Hoo helmet (Fig. 4) and the descriptions of helmets in *Beowulf* (ll.303ᵇ–306ᵃ; 1030–1033ᵃ; 1448–1454).[72] Uniquely among surviving Germanic helms, the Mound One example has a fully protecting face-plate, and so would be described aptly by such *Beowulf* compounds as *beadugrīma*, 'battle-mask' (1.2257ᵃ), *heregrīma*, 'war-mask' (ll.396ᵃ, 2049ᵃ, 2605ᵃ), *grīmhelm*, 'mask-helm' (1.334ᵇ), and *wīgheafola*, 'war-head' (1.2661ᵇ). The last compound is especially appropriate for the Sutton Hoo helmet, as it would have provided complete protection for its wearer's head in battle.[73] The Mound One example has also enabled the full understanding of the description of a certain detail of the helm presented to Beowulf by King Hroðgar:

---

[69] As suggested by Storms, "The Sutton Hoo Ship Burial: An Interpretation", p. 310; and by P. B. Taylor, "The Traditional Language of Treasure in *Beowulf*", p. 196.

[70] Bruce-Mitford, *SHSB*, vol.2, pp. 232–240.

[71] See the penetrating study of the words used to describe chain-mail in the poem by Brady, " 'Weapons' in *Beowulf*" pp. 110–121.

[72] For the full report on the example from Sutton Hoo, see Bruce-Mitford, *SHSB*, vol.2, pp. 138–231. The parallels have been discussed by Cramp, "*Beowulf* and Archaeology", pp. 61–63; Bruce-Mitford, "Sutton Hoo and the Background to the Poem", pp. 95–96; and Ellis Davidson, "Archaeology and *Beowulf*, p. 356.

[73] As Brady pointed out, " 'Weapons' in *Beowulf*", pp. 86–90.

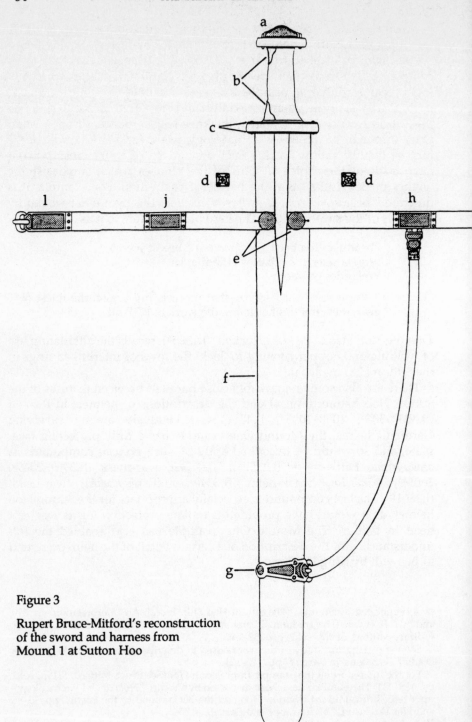

Figure 3

Rupert Bruce-Mitford's reconstruction
of the sword and harness from
Mound 1 at Sutton Hoo

(a)   gold and garnet cloisonné pommel
(b)   gold filigree clips on grip
(c)   gold and gold filigree crossguard fittings
(d)   a pair of gold, garnet, millefiori, and blue glass cloisonné mounts
       (part of sword-knot)
(e)   a pair of gold and garnet cloisonné scabbard-bosses
(f)   fur-lined scabbard of wood, leather, and textile, enclosing
       pattern-welded blade
(g)   gold and garnet cloisonné curved scabbard-buckle
(h)   gold and garnet cloisonné strap-distributor
(i, j) two pairs of gold and garnet cloisonné strap-mounts
(k)   gold and garnet cloisonné counter-plate
(l)   gold and garnet cloisonné belt-buckle

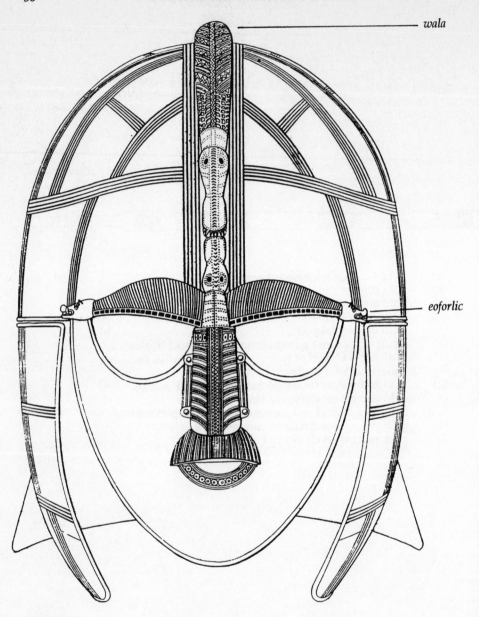

wala

eoforlic

Figure 4

The reconstructed *grimhelm* from Mound 1 at Sutton Hoo (scale 1 to 3)

> Ymb þæs helmes hrōf   hēafodbeorge
> wīrum bewunden   walā ūtan hēold,
> ðæt him fela lāf   frēcne ne meahte
> scūrheard sceþðan . . .

'Around the outside of that head-guarding helm's top was set a wire-bound *wala*, so that the quench-hardened, filed blade might not scathe it severely' (ll.1030–1033ª).

The precise significance of the noun *wala* (1.1031ᵇ) was uncertain until Bruce-Mitford demonstrated that it referred to the reinforcing iron crest running from the front to the back of the outside of the helmet, as on the Sutton Hoo helm.[74] This outer crest is made out of a single piece of D-sectioned tubing and is inlaid with silver wires, and would appear thus to parallel precisely the description of the *wala* in *Beowulf* as being *wīrum bewunden*, 'wire-bound' (1.1031ª). Another close parallel is contained in the description of the helmets of Beowulf's warband as they disembark on their way to Heorot: *eoforlīc scionon / ofer hlēorber[g]an gehroden golde*, 'the boar-figures, adorned in gold, shone over the cheek-guards' (ll.303ᵇ–306ª). The *eoforlīc*, 'boar-figures' (1.303ᵇ), are depicted as being positioned *ofer hlēorber[g]an*, 'over the cheek- [or face-] guards' (1.304ª), which is *exactly* where they are located on the Sutton Hoo helmet.[75] Its two gilt-bronze boars' heads form the terminals to the eyebrow-pieces – which themselves form the figures of the boars' bodies – on the face of the *wīgheafola*. They cover the precise point where the upper corners of the *hlēorberge* join the helmet proper.

The irrefutably substantial evidence of archaeology thus shows that the picture of a world of aristocratic warriorship which we see in *Beowulf* is not based on fantasy. Yet the value of archaeology to the matter of the poem's origin, however, remains uncertain. The present evidence suggests that, in an Anglo-Saxon context, the archaeological horizon of *Beowulf* can be seen to extend no later than around the end of the seventh century.[76] This horizon may be inferred, for example, from the archaeology of boar-helms, which are certainly viewed as important items in the poem's world. The latest known example, which has a single boar-figure mounted on its crown, was found in what appears to have been a mid-seventh-century burial at Benty Grange in Derbyshire.[77] The apparent

---

[74] Bruce-Mitford, *Aspects of Anglo-Saxon Archaeology*, pp. 210–213; *SHSB*, vol. 2, p. 158), following a suggestion originally made by Knut Stjerna (*Essays on Questions Connected with the Old English Poem of Beowulf*, p. 14). The prior uncertainty concerning the significance of *wala* is shown by Klaeber's note on line 1031, p. 169.
[75] As Cramp pointed out, "*Beowulf* and Archaeology", p. 62–63; the boar-images on the helmet from grave 14 at Vendel in Sweden are similarly located.
[76] Hines has argued for a similar archaeological horizon, *The Scandinavian Character of Anglian England in the pre-Viking Period*, pp. 296–298.
[77] Bruce-Mitford, *Aspects of Anglo-Saxon Archaeology*, pp. 223–42.

reference to the use of angons in *Beowulf* (ll.1437–1438) may also point to an early archaeological horizon.[78] The combination of sword and *seax* (ll.2703^b–2704), as used by the hero in his fight with the dragon, may be among the most modern objects described in the poem relative to an Anglo-Saxon archaeological context. Dating evidence for this combination is difficult,[79] but it does not seem to appear in England as an aristocratic weapon-set until the seventh century, while the early type of *seax* (type I) used in the combination may have been out of fashion by the ninth century.[80] However, too much weight should not be placed on the implications of this weapon-set in *Beowulf*; like the hero's specially made iron shield (ll.2337–2341^a), it is only used to fight the dragon, and so may not necessarily reflect normal usage.

Either way, the poem's suggested seventh-century archaeological horizon is at best provisional. As it is deduced largely on the basis of typologies, it will always be susceptible to change as a consequence of new discoveries. Another point which must be borne in mind is that early Christian Anglo-Saxon England seems almost archaeologically invisible in comparison to the pre-Christian period, for one of the changes which the new religion brought about was a different attitude to the afterlife. From the viewpoint of archaeology, this difference of attitude is realised through the change of burial practices. Burials containing grave goods, the major source of material evidence in the pre-Christian period, thus appear to become increasingly scarce after the seventh century.[81] The greatest caution is therefore necessary when applying archaeologically-based dating criteria to other contexts.

It is also difficult to distinguish, with any degree of certainty, passages in *Beowulf* which might have been based on contemporary conditions from those based on inherited verse traditions. Even the most apparently authentic descriptive passages in *Beowulf* might have been be based on inherited accounts originating much earlier in time, as seems to have been the case with the group of Old Irish heroic tales known collectively as the 'Ulster Cycle', the most famous of which is the *Táin Bó Cúailnge*, 'The Cattle-Raid of Cooley'.[82] The earliest detectable written forms of the Ulster Cycle date from the eighth or ninth centuries, yet appear to contain details of Celtic Iron Age culture not later than the fourth or early

78 Hines, *The Scandinavian Character of Anglian England*, p. 297.
79 Personal communication, H. Härke.
80 See the discussion by M. Biddle and B. Kjølbye-Biddle, "The Repton Stone", pp. 269–271, 281–282.
81 As Whitelock pointed out, "Anglo-Saxon Poetry and the Historian", p. 86. A few burials with grave-goods dating from the eighth-century have come to light in recent excavations by the Suffolk Archaeological Unit, such as Grave 93 at the Boss Hall cemetery site near Ipswich (J. Newman, "The Boss Hall Anglo-Saxon Cemetery, Ipswich").
82 Kinsella (ed.), *Táin Bó Cúailnge*.

fifth centuries.[83] Similarly, Homer's *Odyssey* and *Iliad*, although probably written in the Aegean Iron Age during the second half of the eighth century B.C., preserve a wealth of information on Mycenaean Bronze Age culture from around the eleventh century B.C.[84]

Even so, the use of inherited accounts need not necessarily have determined the way that all material culture is presented in *Beowulf*.[85] Homer, for example, referred to weapons made of iron, the norm in his day, where bronze was used in Mycenaean culture.[86] It is, therefore worth reconsidering the possibility that the poem might reflect at least something of contemporary English realities from the time of its composition.

Let us return first to the vivid description of the boar-helms of Beowulf's warband as they disembark on their way to Heorot, one detail of which – the position of the *hlēorberge* – was mentioned above.

> Gewiton him þā fēran; flota stille bād
> seomode on sāle sīdfæþmed scip,
> on ancre fæst. Eoforlīc scionon
> ofer hlēorber[g]an gehroden golde,
> fāh 7 fȳrheard; ferhwearde hēold
> gūþmōd grimmon. Guman ōnetton,
> sigon ætsomme, oþ þæt hȳ [s]æl timbred
> geatolīc 7 goldfāh ongyton mihton;

> 'Faring then they went; the still boat awaited, hovering on its mooring, the wide-fathomed ship fast at anchor. The fierce and fire-hardened boar-figures, adorned in gold, shone over the face-guards; the war-spirit guarded the lives of the stern ones. The men hastened, marched together, until they were able to see the splendid and gold-bright betimbered hall' (ll.301–308).

The overall interpretation of this passage, and therefore its translation,[87] does not depend on the emendations in ll.304[a] and 306[a],[88] so much as the question of the subject of the clause *ferhwearde hēold* (l.305[b]). Klaeber's proposal that the subject is *gūþmōd* seems satisfactory because it essentially follows the manuscript reading. The suggestion is that *gūþmōd*

---

[83] Jackson, *The Oldest Irish Tradition: A Window on the Iron Age*. In the Ulster Cycle, we appear to have, as Dumville has pointed out, an accurate "transmission of the ethos and details of material culture of a society distant in time (and perhaps place) from the eighth- or ninth-century Irish author" ("*Beowulf* and the Celtic World ...", p. 134).

[84] Luce, *Homer and the Heroic Age*, pp. 116–117, for example.

[85] As Whitelock suggested, "Anglo-Saxon Poetry and the Historian", p. 87.

[86] Luce, *Homer and the Heroic Age*, pp. 58–61.

[87] Apart from minor differences in punctuation, I follow Klaeber's reconstruction of this passage.

[88] All scholars accept the need to emend here and a majority agree on the forms which are required – see Kelly, "The Formative Stages of *Beowulf* Textual Scholarship: part II", p. 242.

refers appositively to the personification of *eoforlīc*. The change of number – as the verb-forms indicate, *eoforlīc* is in the plural while *gūþmōd* is in the singular does not place the sense of the passage in jeopardy. Having had our attention drawn to the boar-figures on the warriors' helmets, we then hear about the protective power of the sign of the boar. The use of apposition, moreover, with *gūðmōd* referring appositively to the personification of *eoforlīc*, is a characteristic feature of the poem's style.[89] There is a parallel usage of personification and apposition only a few lines later, when the Beowulf's war-band arrives at Heorot. Again our attention is drawn to the warrior's armour.

> Gūðbyrne scān
> heard handlocen;   hringīren scīr
> song in searwum   þā hīe tō sele furðum
> in hyra gryregeatwum   gangan cwōmon.

'War-mail shone, hard and hand-locked; the bright iron rings sang on byrnies as they first came marching to the hall in their awesome gear' (ll.321b–324).

As in the description of the boar-helms cited above, what is striking is the use of apparently inanimate entities as the subjects of verbs which we would normally associate with more animate agents. Here we have the vivid image of the byrnie of ringmail 'singing' as the warriors march along. In the prior passage, we have the more curious image of the sign of the boar 'guarding' the warrior's lives.

As subject of the transitive clause *ferhwearde hēold* (l.305b), the boar-emblem is presented as the primary protective agency of the helmet.[90] This otherwise curious attribution for the inanimate figure of the boar seems best explained as a realisation of the ancient belief in its powers. The Roman historian Tacitus, writing in the latter part of the first century A.D., recorded in his *Germania* how the Baltic tribe of the *Aestii* used the boar-emblem.

> They worship the Mother of the gods, and wear, as the distinguishing mark of this cult, the emblem of a wild boar. This serves instead of armour as a protection against all and provides the worshipper with a sense of security even among his foes (ch.45).[91]

The indications are, moreover, that this belief was maintained for many centuries throughout the Northlands.[92] Arguably of ultimately totemic

---

[89] F. Robinson, *Beowulf and the Appositive Style*, p. 68.
[90] The use of *ferhweard* may also entail a pun on *fearh*, 'farrow'.
[91] R.P. Robinson (ed.), *The Germania of Tacitus*.
[92] See also Hatto, "Snake-swords and Boar-helms in *Beowulf*", pp. 155–160.

origin,[93] such a belief could have motivated the presentation of the boar-figure as the subject of the transitive clause *ferhwearde hēold* (ll.303b–306a). If so, it would be a good example of the way in which the language of the poem can reveal what Wormald has called "the otherwise closed and unknown thought-world of the Anglo-Saxon warrior classes".[94] In terms of linguistic theory, transitivity structures represent the function of language to realise what one scholar has described as "the speaker's experience of the external world, and of his own internal world, that of his own consciousness".[95] In other words, the structure of the *Beowulf* clause in question may have been determined by a deeply-held belief in the protective potential of the boar-emblem.

A more explicit statement concerning the power of a boar-helm is contained in the description of Beowulf's own head-gear as he prepares for his sub-aquatic confrontation with Grendel's mother:

> ... se hwīta helm   hafelan werede,
> sē þe meregrundas   mengan scolde,
> sēcan sundgebland   since geweorðad,
> befongen frēawrāsnum,   swā hine fyrndagum
> worhte wǣpna smið,   wundrum tēode,
> besette swīnlīcum,   þæt hine syðþan nō
> brond nē beadomēcas   bītan ne meahton.

> 'The bright, head-guarding helm which would seek the surging water to stir up the depths of the mere, was adorned with jewellery and encircled in lordly links (*befongen frēawrasnum*),[96] just as the weapon-smith had wrought it in ancient days, who formed it by wondrous powers (*wundrum tēode*) and beset it with boar-images, so that thenceforth no blade or battle-sword was able to pierce it' (ll.1448–1454).

We are told unequivocally that the setting of boar-images on the helm prevents penetration by point or edge (ll.1453–1454). As the phrase *wundrum tēode* (l.1452b) may be translated as 'formed by wondrous powers', that is, construing 'wonder' in its miraculous or magical sense, then it is also suggested that supernatural forces are used in the making of the helm.

Now, in relation to the matter of the origin of *Beowulf*, the question is

[93] I mean *totemic* in the sense that its powers can be seen to be derived from faith in the deity whose relations to mankind it symbolised and mediated; see Glosecki, "The Boar's Helmet in *Beowulf*: Reflexes of Totemism and Exogamy in Early Germanic Literature".
[94] Wormald, "Bede, *Beowulf* and the Conversion", p. 58.
[95] Halliday, *Language as a Social Semiotic*, p. 45.
[96] On the phrase *befongen frēawrasnum*, and its relation to the use of chain-mail on helmets from pre-Viking period burials from Valsgärde and Vendel in Sweden, see Cramp, "*Beowulf* and Archaeology", pp. 61–62.

this: does the apparent willingness to describe the functioning of this pre-Christian sacred symbol imply that the beliefs associated with it were still a reality at the time of composition? It is certainly arguable that the descriptions of boar-helms in the poem contain such a degree of apparent realism as to imply that knowledge of them could have been derived from current usage. As noted above, there is no archaeological evidence that boar-helms were in use in England after the latter part of the seventh century, the latest known example being that from the mound at Benty Grange. That the recently discovered helm from Coppergate, York, perhaps of eighth-century date, lacks any distinctively betusked figures of boars could suggest that the fashionability of the type decreased after the seventh century. It also seems to be the case that not one of the poem's references to boar-helms (ll.303[b]–306[a], 1111[b]–1112[a], 1286[b], 1328[a] and 1448–1454) is qualified by accompanying references to Christianity.

The belief in the power of the boar-image, however, appears not to have been as inconsistent with Christian faith as might be assumed. This is shown, for example, by the Benty Grange boar-helm, which bears a silver cross on its nose-guard. The sign of the cross is, of course, also a powerful protective symbol. It also appears in association with the boar-sign in the Old English poetic version of the legend of St Helen, Cynewulf's *Elene* (ll.76, 255–260).[97] As well as this, a relief-carved tympanum from St Nicholas's Church, Ipswich, Suffolk, reveals that boar and cross were regarded as compatible as late as the eleventh century.[98] Moreover, the possibility that detailed knowledge of the boar-helm could have been derived from a tradition associated with a particular heirloom cannot be ruled out. War-gear was certainly robust enough to endure for several generations, as the references in some late Anglo-Saxon wills show. For example, one of the bequests contained in the will of Æþeling Æþelstan, dated 1015, refers to a sword which is said to have belonged to King Offa of Mercia (757–796), which at that time must have been well over two hundred years old.[99] Perhaps there could have been a famous boar-helm in Anglo-Saxon England to compare with the legendary one named *Hildisvin*, 'Battle-swine', in Northern poetic tradition, originally belonging to the Swedish king, Onela (ON *Áli*), and later owned by his nephew and dynastic opponent, Eadgils (ON *Aðils*).[100] Nor can we be sure that the emphasis on boar-power was not part of a deliberate design to locate the story firmly in the past. In other words, the presentation of the boar-

---

97 Gradon (ed.), *Cynewulf's Elene*; Cramp, "*Beowulf* and Archaeology", pp. 59–60.
98 Galbraith, "Early Sculpture at St Nicholas's Church, Ipswich"; and "Further Thoughts on the Boar at St Nicholas's Church, Ipswich".
99 Sawyer no. 1503, dated 1015.
100 Snorri Sturluson, *Edda: Skáldskapamàl*, ch. 44; Ellis Davidson, *Gods and Myths of Northern Europe*, p. 99.

emblem as the animate agent of a warrior's protection (ll.303ᵇ–306ᵃ) need not have been innocently motivated by a belief in its supernatural power; rather, its deployment as the subject of a transitive clause may have been an artistic device intended to create an antique effect. However apparently realistic the descriptions of boar-helms may seem to us then, we cannot be confident that they were still in active use at the time. Nevertheless, it does seem significant that Old English poetry known to have been composed in the tenth century, or later, such as *The Battle of Brunanburh*, *The Capture of the Five Boroughs* and *The Battle of Maldon*, contain no references to boar-helms or to the boar-emblem. The contrastingly detailed presentation of boar-helms and their ultimately pagan protective function in *Beowulf* may imply, therefore, that the poem drew on an earlier, pre-Viking tradition of Old English verse.

Let us now turn to the poem's three accounts of unequivocally pre-Christian funeral rites. These comprise two cremations (ll.1107–1124; 3134–3155) and a royal ship-funeral (ll.26–52). It may be asserted immediately that there is nothing anywhere else in Old English poetry to compare with the detail and vividness of these descriptions. Consider, for example, the cremation of the Hocing prince, Hnæf (ll.1107–1124).

> Wand tō wolcnum   wælfyra mǣst,
> hlynode for hlāwe;   hafelan multon,
> bengeato burston,   ðonne blōd ætspranc,
> laðbite līces.   Līg ealle forswealg,
> gǣsta gīfrost,   þara ðe þǣr gūð fornam
> bēga folces . . .

'[Smoke] rose to the clouds as the greatest of fires of the slain roared before the mound; heads melted and wounds burst open as the blood sprang out from the grievously-bitten body. The fire, greediest of spirits, there swallowed up all those whom battle had taken from the two folk' (ll.1119–1124ᵃ).

The grimly detailed realism in this description could imply that it was informed by a first-hand account of such a rite. As Dr Hilda Ellis Davidson observed, it "is hardly likely to have been based on vague traditions of a forgotten ritual".[101] The account of the siting and building of King Beowulf's burial-mound by his bereaved folk, following his own cremation (ll.3137–3148ᵇ), also shows a high degree of apparently realistic detail.

---

[101] Ellis Davidson, "Archaeology and *Beowulf*", p. 361. The tragic tale of the *Frēswæl* (ll.1071–1159), which provides the context for this passage, is to be discussed in Chapter Four.

Geworhton ðā　　Wedra lēode
hl(æw) on [h]līðe,　　sē wæs hēah 7 brād,
(wǣ)glīðendum　　wīde g(e)sȳne,
7 betimbredon　　on tȳn dagum
beadurōfes bēcn,　　bronda lāfe
wealle beworhton,　　swā hyt weorðlīcost
foresnotre men　　findan mihton.

'Then the Weder people built a mound on the hill, high and
broad, widely visible to wave-farers; and in ten days the battle-
leader's beacon was constructed. They surrounded the pyre's
ashes with a rampart [*i.e.* a mound], the worthiest that the wisest
of men could devise' (ll.3156–3162).

This passage suggests a knowledge of the art of barrow-building which
again could imply that it was based on a report of the construction of
such a mound. The siting of the barrow itself follows the heroic ideal
realised in King Beowulf's last speech. As he lies mortally wounded from
his victory over the dragon, he says,

"Hātað heaðomǣre　　hlǣw gewyrcean
beorhtne æfter bǣle　　æt brimes nosan;
sē scel tō gemyndum　　mīnum lēodum
hēah hlīfian　　on Hronesnæsse,
þæt hit sǣliðend　　syððan hātan
Bīowulfes biorh . . ."

' "Bid the famed-in-battle build me a splendid mound on the
headland after my pyre; it shall be a reminder to my people,
rising high on *Hronesnæsse*, so that seafarers will call it Beowulf's
Barrow" ' (ll.2802–2807b).

Something of the ideal which this passage realises has clearly motivated
the siting of, for example, the East Anglian royal barrows at Sutton Hoo
in Suffolk. Here, several large mounds dating from the from the late sixth
and early seventh centuries still stand on high ground overlooking the
upper estuary of the River Deben.[102] As most of them would have stood
originally much higher, as recent work has shown, several may have
been more widely visible.[103]

---

[102] The Sutton Hoo mounds are charted on the 1845 Admiralty Hydrographic Survey
map of the Deben (Hoppitt, "Sutton Hoo 1860").
[103] The recent re-excavation of Mound Two, for example, has revealed how much
higher it would originally have been (Carver and Evans, "Anglo-Saxon Discoveries at
Sutton Hoo, 1987–8, at p. 5). It is possible, therefore, that Sutton Hoo would have been
seen from the site of Ramsholt church, just over four miles away. It may also have been
just visible from the Roman Saxon Shore fortress at Walton, formerly situated some
eight miles to the south on a cliff commanding the river's mouth (now lost through
coastal erosion), and the possible site of the first East Anglian episcopal minster of

Sutton Hoo is also of interest here for another reason, for at least two of the barrows, Mounds One and Two, covered rich ship-burials.[104] The former in particular offers unique English corroboration for the poetic account of the royal rite of ship-funeral in *Beowulf* (ll.26–52). On the present evidence, attested Anglo-Saxon examples of the rite on the scale of this account are to be found only in East Anglia, especially in southeast Suffolk, at Sutton Hoo on the River Deben and at Snape on the River Alde.[105] As these big ship-burials appear to be archaeologically distinguishable by quantities of hull-rivets, even where seriously disturbed, as at Mound Two at Sutton Hoo, there may be a case for regarding East Anglia as a possible source for the *Beowulf* account. Indeed, the way in which the rite is represented in that account seems to come so close to the ceremony implied by the contents of Mound One at Sutton Hoo that some scholars have suspected that it may have been ultimately based on early seventh-century East Anglian practice.[106] Others, however, have expressed serious doubts about such a possibility.[107] A reappraisal, therefore, is required.

Him ðā Scyld gewāt   tō gescæphwīle
felahrōr fēran   on Frēan wǣre;
hī hyne þā ætbǣron,   tō brimes faroðe.
swǣse gesīþas,   swā hē selfa bæd,
þenden wordum wēold   wine Scyldinga
lēof landfruma,   lange āhte.
Þǣr æt hyðe stōd   hringedstefna
īsig 7 ūtfūs,   æþelinges fær;
ālēdon þā   lēofne þēoden,
bēaga bryttan   on bearm scipes,
mǣrne be mæste.   Þǣr wæs mādma fela

Dommoc (Rigold, "The Supposed See of Dunwich"; and "Further Evidence about the Site of *Dommoc*").

[104] On Mound One, see Bruce-Mitford, *SHSB*, vol.1 (some of the contents of this mound have already been discussed in this chapter); on Mound Two, see Carver and Evans, "Anglo-Saxon Discoveries at Sutton Hoo, 1987–1988".

[105] On Snape, see Bruce-Mitford, *Aspects of Anglo-Saxon Archaeology*, pp. 114–140; and Filmer-Sankey, "The Snape Anglo-Saxon Cemetery and Ship-Burial". Charles Green noted slight evidence for other possible Anglo-Saxon ship-burials at Ashby, Suffolk, and Catfield, Norfolk (*Sutton Hoo*, pp. 60–63).

[106] Wrenn, "Sutton Hoo and *Beowulf*"; O'Loughlin, "Sutton Hoo: the Evidence of the Documents", p. 12; Bruce-Mitford, "Sutton Hoo and the Background of the Poem"; and *SHSB*, vol. 1, pp. 716–717; Ellis Davidson, "Archaeology and *Beowulf*", p. 358; and even Meaney, "Scyld Scefing and the Dating of *Beowulf*", p. 25.

[107] See Farrell, *Beowulf, Swedes and Geats*, pp. 43–54; and "*Beowulf* and the Northern Heroic Age", pp. 196–197. Farrell argued that there need be "no direct connection" (*Beowulf, Swedes and Geats*, p. 53); see also Stanley, "The Date of *Beowulf*: Some Doubts and No Conclusions", pp. 202–205, who has maintained that "in the excitement of the discovery, the connection of Sutton Hoo with *Beowulf* has almost certainly been made too specific" (*ibid.*, p. 205).

of feorwegum   frætwa gelǣded;
ne hȳrde ic cȳmlīcor   cēol gegyrwan
hildewǣpnum   7 heaðowǣdum,
billum 7 byrnum;   him on bearme læg
mādma mænigo,   þā him mid scoldon
on flōdes ǣht   feor gewītan.
Nalæs hī hine lǣssan   lācum tēodan,
þēodgestrēonum   þon þā dydon,
þē hine æt frumsceafte   forð onsendon
ǣnne ofer ȳðe   umborwesende.
Þā gȳt hīe him āsetton   segen g(yl)denne
hēah ofer hēafod,   lēton holm beran,
gēafon on gārsecg;   him wæs geōmor sefa,
murnende mōd.   Men ne cunnon
secgan tō sōðe,   selerǣden*de*,
hæleð under heofenu*m*,   hwā þǣm hlæste onfēng.

'Then at the destined time, after many brave deeds, Scyld went his way to the Lord's keeping. His dear companions then bore him out to the water's side, as he himself had bidden while he still could, that much-loved Scylding lord and founding-chief who had ruled for so long. There at the quay lay the noble's ferry, with ring-adorned bows, cold and ready. Amidships they laid their beloved folk-king, lord of rings, the mighty one by the mast. There was much treasure, a fortune fetched from afar; never have I heard of a keel more comely decked with battle-weapons, war-gear, blades and ring-mail; on his breast lay many precious things that with him would fare afar in the sea's keeping. In no way did they endow him with lesser gifts and folk-treasures than did they who, in the beginning, had sent him forth as a child, alone over the waves. There now they set up for him a golden sign, high over head, and let the waters bear him, gave all to *gārsecg*; sad were their hearts and mournful was their mood. No man, whether the wise under the hall's roof, or heroes under the heavens', can know and truly say who received that lading' (ll.26–52).

At least one major discrepancy between this poetic description and the archaeological reality of Mound One is immediately apparent: Scyld's funeral-ship appears to be allowed to drift out to sea, whereas the Sutton Hoo vessel was interred beneath a large mound. One might thus argue that the *Beowulf* description derives from an account of a sea-burial. Although it is not impossible that the Sutton Hoo ship could have sailed its ceremonial last voyage prior to reaching its final berth,[108] the notion that a great treasure-laden, royal funeral-ship like that described in *Beowulf* would ever have been allowed simply to drift off with the tide

---

[108] As Ellis Davidson suggested, "Archaeology and *Beowulf*", p. 358.

THE QUESTION OF THE POEM'S ORIGIN

(ll.40^b–42, 48^b–49^a) is simply unrealistic, especially when considered from the point of view of the king's bereaved *gesīþas*. We hear of their affectionate obedience in bearing the body of the much-loved old king to the water-side (ll.28–29), *swā hē selfa bæd*, 'as he himself had bidden' (l.29^b), in laying it to rest amidships (ll.34–35), surrounded by treasures (ll.36^a–46), and of their great sadness (ll.49^b–50^a) as the royal funeral-vessel is gently committed to *gārsecg* (ll.48^b–49^a). The committal of the vessel forms the climactic event in a whole series of acts of giving (ll.36^a–42).[109] It thus seems unlikely that such a gift-laden royal funeral-ship, the focus of such deep emotion, would be simply abandoned to the tides, as the king's *swǣse gesīðas* could be subsequently faced with the rather catastrophic anti-climax of discovering the vessel beached with the next tide.[110] Such an outcome is pre-empted in the later Norse legendary accounts of royal ship-funeral by the dramatic depiction of the cremation of the vessel as it sails off into eternity.[111] Yet even allowing for the difficulties of detecting evidence for sea-burial archaeologically, mound-inhumation in ship-funeral ceremonies may have been the norm rather than the exception. The rich ninth-century ship-burial at Oseberg in Vestfold was actually moored to a large stone inside its mound.[112] This may well have been customary in the Northlands, as the explicit reference to the use of a rock to secure a burial-ship in the Old Norse *Gísla saga* (ch. 17) implies.[113] Indeed, providing the treasure-laden royal funeral-ship with the secure final berth of a burial-mound can have only furthered the ideological resonance of the rite, for the king's burial-mound was probably regarded as a place of veneration for subsequent generations.[114] The rich contents of the royal mound can be seen thus to have functioned as an eternal statement of the quality and renown of the dynastic line.[115]

If, moreover, the *Beowulf* account is considered in its context, that is, as

---

[109] Irving argued similarly that this description "suggests most strongly a deliberate and conscious sacrificial act, not in propitiation to any defined and formalized supernatural power so much as in simple gratitude for the gifts (unaccountable) that life may send, gratitude that outweighs the natural and deep sorrow felt at the loss of Scyld, gratitude that at last finds its best expression in the free 'giving' of Scyld back to his original source" (*A Reading of Beowulf*, p. 240).

[110] As Owen noted, *Rites and Religions of the Anglo-Saxons*, p. 97.

[111] For example, the sea-cremation of Sigurd Ring (*Skjǫldunga saga*, ch. 26); that of Haki (*Ynglinga saga*, ch. 27); and, most spectacular of all, that of the beautiful god, Baldr (*Edda: Gylfaginning*, ch. 49).

[112] Brøgger, Falk and Shetelig, *Osebergfundet*, vol. 1, especially fig. 31, p. 51.

[113] Þórólfsson (ed.), *Vestfirðinga Sǫgur*; for discussion, see Major, "Ship-burials in Scandinavian Lands", pp. 134–135.

[114] Chaney, *The Cult of Kingship in Anglo-Saxon England*, pp. 80–81, 96–97, 101–105.

[115] P.B. Taylor has pointed out that "the pagan Anglo-Saxon understood the *galdor* inherent in treasure hoards as a preserver of both the blood strain and the fame of their possessors" ("The Traditional Language of Treasure in *Beowulf*", p. 199). Similarly, A.Ya. Gurevich argued that "silver and gold in the ground remained at the perpetual

the culmination of the legendary life of Scyld Scefing (ll.4–52), the references to the voyage of the funeral-ship (ll.40ᵇ–42, 48ᵇ–49ᵃ) can be seen to
be more symbolic than literal. In purely artistic terms, as Scyld's legend
concerns the deliverance of the Danes from suffering by a boat-borne
saviour, it can be seen also to anticipate Beowulf's own arrival by sea
similarly to liberate the Danes from affliction. The funeral of Scyld Scefing at the culmination of the opening movement of the poem can be seen
also to mirror the latter's at the culmination of its closing movement.
Similarly, the lordlessness of the Danes, prior to the coming of Scyld
(ll.14ᵇ–16ᵃ), can be seen to foreshadow the situation of the Geats following King Beowulf's death.[116] Yet these literary implications must not be
taken to imply that the legend itself is entirely an artistic fabrication.
Ultimately, it appears to be based on ancient fertility-myth,[117] but in the
form in which we have it in *Beowulf* it is essentially a genealogical origin-
myth, intended to provide an idealised beginning for the Scylding dynasty which is sanctioned by destiny, thus legitimising the family's royal
authority.[118]

Apart from the account of his ship-funeral, which is relatively detailed,
the legend of Scyld is merely alluded to in *Beowulf*. Nevertheless, the
allusions are not so vague that we cannot retrieve its outline: Scyld first
appears as a foundling; ǣrest wearð / feasceaft funden, 'he was first found
helpless' (ll.6ᵇ–7ᵃ),[119] but later becomes a great warrior-king who leads
the Danes to power and glory (ll.4–6ᵃ, 9–11) and who fathers the Danish
royal family (ll.12–14ᵃ, 53–63). Another allusion to his advent is made in
the account of his ship-funeral. As the vessel is being laden with treasures and with war-gear (ll.36ᵇ–42), we hear that

---

posthumous disposal of their owner and kin, and was, as it were, the realization of their
success and happiness, their personal and family prosperity" ("Wealth and Gift-
Bestowal among the Ancient Scandinavians", p. 133).
[116] See similarly T.D. Hill, "Scyld Scefing and the *Stirps Regia*", p. 44; and also Bonjour,
The Digressions in Beowulf, pp. 1–11; and E.R. Anderson, "A Submerged Metaphor in the
Scyld Episode". On these narrative structural parallels in general, see further, Niles,
"Ring-Composition and the Structure of *Beowulf*", pp. 929–930, especially diagram 6, p.
930; and *Beowulf: the Poem and Its Tradition*, pp. 152–162. Of course, because it is thus
structurally integral, the opening movement is unlikely to be a later addition to *Beowulf*,
as Sisam ("Anglo-Saxon Royal Genealogies", pp. 339–340) and Meaney ("Scyld Scefing
and the Dating of *Beowulf*", pp. 37–39) have conjectured.
[117] Olrik, *Heroic Legends of Denmark*, pp. 411–412; Chambers, *Introduction*, pp. 68–86;
Klaeber, pp. 121–124; and especially Fulk, "An Eddic Analogue to the Scyld Scefing
Story".
[118] As T.D. Hill also has described it as "an archaic Germanic etiological myth which
concerns the problem of the origin of kingship" ("Scyld Scefing and the *Stirps Regia*", p.
41).
[119] Note that *feasceaft* here seems to be intended in the sense of 'helpless', or perhaps
'homeless', rather than 'destitute', as ll.43–46 imply below. For discussion, see Olrik,
Heroic Legends of Denmark, pp. 388–393; Bauschatz, *The Well and the Tree*, pp. 103–104;
and Meaney, "Scyld Scefing and the Dating of *Beowulf*", p. 14.

nalæs hū hine læssan   lācum tēodan,
þēodgestrēonum   þon þā dydon,
þē hine æt frumsceafte   forð onsendon
ǣnne ofer ȳðe   umborwesende.

'in no way did they endow him with lesser gifts and folk-
treasures than did they who, in the beginning, had sent him
forth as a child, alone over the waves' (ll.43–46).

These lines establish a direct relationship between Scyld's legendary
advent and his ship-funeral. He first appears as a foundling in a treasure-laden vessel, having been sent by mysteriously unspecified agencies
æt frumsceafte, 'in the (destined) beginning' (l.45ª), just as he later leaves
the world, also alone in a boat laden with treasures, *tō gescæphwīle*, 'at the
destined time' (l.26ᵇ). In other words, the form of his departure mirrors
the form of his arrival; the one explains the other. We thus have an
elegant parallel, in which the symbolic roles of the ship and its voyages
to and from the unknown are primary; having originally functioned as
Scyld's cradle, bearing him from the unknown over the sea to the Danes,
it becomes at the end his funerary vessel, returning him to the unknown.
The implication is that the references to the sea in the legend are more
symbolic than literal. In its context, therefore, Scyld's last voyage clearly
realises a *return* to his mysterious place of origin.

Reference to this place is also made in the culminating lines of the
ship-funeral account:

                    Men ne cunnon
secgan tō sōðe,   selerǣdende,
hæleð under heofenum,   hwā þǣm hlæste onfēng.

'No man, whether the wise under the hall's roof, or heroes
under the heavens', can know and truly say who received that
lading' (ll.50ᵇ–52).

These lines state explicitly that the ultimate destination of Scyld's
funeral-ship is beyond the knowledge of the wisest and the strongest of
men. The limits of mere human knowledge are similarly defined a little
later in the poem when we hear of the supernatural movements of
helrūnan like the monster Grendel: *men ne cunnon / hwyder helrūnan hwyrf-
tum scrīþað*, 'no man can know whither such wending demons glide',
(ll.162ᵇ–163). As with the ultimate destination of Scyld's funeral-ship,
Grendel's wendings are beyond the understanding of men. Although
applied to knowledge of the legendary past, in both of these instances
the verb *cunnan* is written in the present tense, which implies that the
statements are also of continuing concern in the poem's own time.[120] The

---

[120] Greenfield, "The Authenticating Voice in *Beowulf*", p. 60.

possible chronological significance of this, however, is uncertain, as both statements can be seen to be of perennial relevance to men.

The ultimate destination of Scyld's funeral-vessel is thus unknowable precisely because it is beyond mortal cognition, the limits of which are bounded by the unchartable waters of *gārsecg* (l.49a). The cosmological significance of *gārsecg* here has been well described by Tolkien, who wrote that the poem's audience saw "the *eormengrund*, the great earth, ringed with *gārsecg*, the shoreless sea, beneath the sky's inaccessible roof".[121] *Gārsecg* is used in the same sense in the Old English *Genesis* (l.117b) to refer to the Ocean encircling God's Creation.[122] The same unfathomable waters are referred to in the Creation song in *Beowulf* (l.90b–98): we hear . . . *þæt se Ælmihtiga eorðan worh(te)* . . . *swā wæter bebūgeð*, 'that the Almighty wrought the earth . . . beringed with water' (ll.92–93). A comparable statement articulating this essential theme is voiced in Bede's report of a debate by the counsellors of the Northumbrian king, Edwin (617–632), on the wisdom of adopting Christianity.[123] One of the king's *ealdormenn* compares the transience of the mortal life of man to the brief flight of a sparrow through the royal hall in wintertime:

". . . so this life of man appears but for a moment; what follows or indeed what went before, we know not at all".[124]

The little sparrow's flight through the great hall here becomes a powerful symbol of the journey of the soul of man through life. The royal hall itself can be seen to represent the totality of human life and achievement, beyond the walls of which lies the unknown, a conceptual metaphor which seems to have been fundamental to the Anglo-Saxon worldview.[125] In the legend of Scyld Scefing in *Beowulf*, the ship's voyage into and out of the mortal world, across the encircling waters of *gārsecg*, can be seen similarly to symbolise such a journey. That the legend also appears to be underpinned throughout by the metaphoric equation of the royal mead-hall with Scyld's kingdom only reinforces the suggested symbolic congruence of his voyage and the sparrow's flight.[126]

[121] Tolkien, "*Beowulf*: the Monsters and the Critics", p. 260.
[122] Krapp (ed.), *The Junius Manuscript*.
[123] The similarity of concern of the two was also pointed out by J. Earl, "*Beowulf* and the Sparrow", a paper delivered at the 1985 annual meeting of the Modern Language Association of America.
[124] Bede, *HE*, II, 13.
[125] On the symbolic significance of the royal hall in OE poetry, see P. B.Taylor, "Heorot, Earth and Asgard: Christian Poetry and Pagan Myth"; Irving, *A Reading of Beowulf*, pp. 90–91; Lee, *The Guest-Hall of Eden*, pp. 171–223; Hume, "The Concept of the Hall in Old English Poetry"; and Earl, "The Role of the Men's Hall in the Development of the Anglo-Saxon Superego".
[126] E.R. Anderson, "A Submerged Metaphor in the Scyld Episode".

All of this means that the references to Scyld's last voyage should be understood as a realisation of a poetic ideal of royal ship-funeral, within which the function of the *æpelinges fær* to cross the unfathomable ocean of *gārsecg* forms an essential metaphor. This notion of the ship as a means of crossing the boundary between worlds seems likely to be realised in most variations of the rite of both ship- and boat-funeral.[127] Certainly it seems to apply in the majestic ceremony implied by the contents of Mound One at Sutton Hoo, even though the vessel here was interred. Indeed, as I suggested above, eventual interment may well have been the norm in such royal ship-funerals, a berthing arrangement which need not have contradicted the suggested symbolic function of the vessel at all. The possibility that the account of Scyld's ship-funeral ceremony in *Beowulf* could have been ultimately based on an East Anglian rite cannot be ruled out, therefore, just because examples of the latter are all interments.

Although the suggested symbolism of Scyld's last voyage is not incompatible with Christian thought,[128] the context here – royal ship-funeral – is primarily pagan. The question again then is this: does the richness and realism of the account of royal ship-funeral in *Beowulf* imply that the ceremony was practiced near to the time of the poem's composition? As Dr Ellis Davidson has argued, "this section of the poem is hardly likely to have been composed at a time when Christians had repudiated the practice of ship-burial and forgotten the mythological basis for it".[129] Yet a ship-funeral ceremony on the scale of that entailed by the contents of Mound One at Sutton Hoo is likely to have been a memorable event. Like Snorri Sturlusson's account of the ship-borne cremation of the Swedish king Haki, it may well have been "much talked about for a long time after".[130] The late Mr George Arnott, a much respected authority on the history of the River Deben, had heard during his childhood – many years before its discovery – that there was a ship buried at Sutton Hoo. Writing in the 1940s, he recalled that

---

[127] For a discussion of this notion, see Bauschatz, *The Well and the Tree*, pp. 55–57. It has been queried by Schönbäck, however, who has argued that "although many grave-boats appear to be furnished and stocked for a long journey there is much to suggest that the ship was not a means of transport for the dead . . . many graves contained either incomplete boats, or boats turned upside-down over the burial or even placed on top of it" ("The Custom of Burial in Boats", p. 129). Mound Two at Sutton Hoo, for example, appears to have contained a vessel placed over the burial chamber (Carver and Evans, "Anglo-Saxon Discoveries at Sutton Hoo, 1987–8", pp. 7–11). Yet surely the very presence of a nautical vessel in a burial, in whatever form, suggests the notion of a symbolic voyage.

[128] As Irving observed, "The Nature of the Christianity in *Beowulf*", p. 21.

[129] Ellis Davidson, "Archaeology and *Beowulf*", p. 361.

[130] Snorri Sturluson, *Ynglinga saga*, ch. 23; probably written in the second quarter of the thirteenth century, this saga forms the opening of his *Heimskringla* (ed. Aðalbjarnasson).

my father told us about the ship, a tradition he had learnt from the
countryside and it became so much part of my childhood's surround-
ings that I never really thought much about it. I took it all for granted.
We used often to row across to Sutton cliff and walk over to the tumuli
and my father would describe the long-ship which lay buried there. . . .
We had no doubt about the burial mounds in our own minds and never
questioned it. When on that great day in the summer of 1939, the largest
mound was opened, I felt no surprise that there had been a ship there,
and I think that it would have come as quite a shock if nothing had
been found.[131]

Although the story which the young George Arnott heard could have
been no more than a product of his father's imagination – a truly percep-
tive imagination, as it turned out – the possibility that it was based on a
genuinely ancient local tradition, as George Arnott himself appears to
have believed, cannot be denied.

Information on royal burials, moreover, may well have been preserved
in the form of dynastic genealogical poetry for any number of generations. As J.E. Turville-Petre observed in her study of *Ynglingatal*, a classic of this kind of verse,

the dominant theme is the death of the king and his place of burial. The
social correlative of this literary genre is a grave-cult.[132]

In other words, genealogical verse and funeral rites can be seen as com-
plementary media realising similar dynastic ideological concerns.
Ynglingatal is attributed to the late ninth-century court poet Þjóðólfr of
Hvin by Snorri Sturluson, who used it as one of his main sources for
Ynglinga saga.[133] *Ynglingatal*, which may be translated literally as 'The
Tally of the Ynglings', celebrates the ancestry of King Rǫgnvaldr, chief of
the Yngling dynasty of the southern Norse kingdom of Vestfold during
the late ninth century, the poem providing regular information on the
circumstances of the deaths and places of burial of many of his line.
Archaeology has revealed the close correlation between some of its historically more credible verses and the royal burial-rites practised in Vestfold at the time. According to *Ynglingatal*, for example, Halfdan II ("the
Mild") was buried in a mound at the royal burial-site at Borre, overlooking the waters of Oslofjord, and this does not seem unlikely.[134] It has been
also thought possible that the famous Oseberg ship-burial, some eight

---

131 Arnott, *Suffolk Estuary*, p. 49.
132 J.E. Turville-Petre, "On *Ynglingatal*", p. 51.
133 Despite a recent attempt to date this poem to the twelfth century by Claus Krag
(*Ynglingatal og Ynglingesaga*) there is no compelling reason why we should reject this
attribution. *Ynglingatal* is discussed further in the next chapter.
134 Snorri Sturluson cites the verse in question in *Ynglinga saga*, ch. 47. On the Borre site,
see Bjørn Myhre, "The Royal Cemetery at Borre, Vestfold".

kilometres to the south of Borre, is the possible last resting-place of Halfdan the Mild's formidable daughter-in-law, Ása, the mother of the Yngling king Halfdan III ("the Black").[135] Another probably historical Yngling king named in Þjóðólfr's verse-tally is Rǫgnvaldr's father, Óláfr of Geirstaðir, whom some scholars have considered may have been buried in the Gokstad ship-burial, further south in Vestfold near Sandefjord.[136]

Conditions in the late ninth-century Norse kingdom of Vestfold, therefore, suggest a correlation between dynastic burials and genealogical verse. Analogy with the early seventh-century kingdom of East Anglia, where very similar burial-rites were practised, permits us to infer the existence of genealogical poetry concerning the ruling family there. Other indications for the existence of this kind of verse in Anglo-Saxon England are to be considered independently in subsequent chapters. The point I seek to make here, however, is that information on pre-Christian royal burial-rites like that of Scyld in *Beowulf* could have been preserved in such a medium for at least as long as the ruling family endured, even after the cessation of such practices. This means, of course, that in an English context, the detailed accounts of pre-Christian burial-rites in *Beowulf* do not necessarily imply early composition for the poem. Nevertheless, their degree of realism is such as to suggest that the sources which lie behind them were themselves of early origin. We may also claim that, at least on the present Anglo-Saxon archaeological evidence, there is a case for regarding East Anglia as the possible source for the royal ship-funeral account. A thorough consideration of the genre of Old English genealogical verse is necessary, however, before such a case can be advanced any further.

So far, then, we have to admit that none of the indications discussed – linguistic, comparative, historical or archaeological – constitute compelling evidence for the date or location of the composition of *Beowulf*. Yet taken together, they do offer independently converging arguments pointing to the much greater likelihood of composition before, rather than after, the establishment of Scandinavian culture in England in the latter part of the ninth century.

---

[135] G. Jones, *A History of the Vikings*, pp. 84–85.
[136] Smyth, *Scandinavian Kings in the British Isles*, pp. 109–110; though note the cautionary words of Þorleif Sjøvold, *The Viking Ships in Oslo*, p. 77.

CHAPTER THREE

BEOWULF AND THE OLD ENGLISH
ROYAL PEDIGREES

IT SEEMS CURIOUS that *Beowulf* should preserve apparently accurate details
– both historical and philological, insofar as they can be established –
from sixth-century Scandinavia. Its great interest in the fortunes of three
Northern dynasties of this period, the Danish *Scyldingas*, the Geatish
(Gothic) *Hrēðlingas*, and the Swedish *Scylfingas*, is a prominent characteristic which has yet to be satisfactorily explained. Klaeber questioned
"why such a minute attention to Northern dynasties continued to be
manifested in the epic" and pointed out the need to explain

> the ubiquitous Scandinavian elements in the Old English poem . . . it is
> not their mere presence but their curiously historical character that has
> to be accounted for.[1]

The hero of the poem refers to himself as a Geatish Hrēðling, which he is
through his mother, the daughter of King Hreðel (ll.373–375ᵃ), at whose
royal hall he had been fostered from the age of seven (ll.2428–2431).
Beowulf is especially endeared to his uncle, Hygelac, to whom he refers
as *"Hygelāc mīn"*, ' *"my* Hygelac" ' (l.2434ᵇ). Yet it is in the Danish Scyldings that the audience of *Beowulf* appear to have had the greatest interest.
As I pointed out in the previous chapter, the senior status of the Danes in
Beowulf is clear from the very first lines of the poem:

> Hwæt, wē Gār-Dena   in gēardagum,
> þēodcyninga,   þrym gefrunon,
> hū ðā æþelingas   ellen fremedon.

> 'Hwæt! We have heard of the renown of the spear-Danes' folk-
> kings in days of yore, and of how those nobles achieved deeds of
> courage' (ll.1–3).

We may infer from these lines that the fame of the Scylding *þēodcynings*
was well established in Anglo-Saxon England. As we shall see, the
poem's use of allusion to stories of these early Danish kings implies that
its original audience was already familiar with tales concerning the

---

[1] Klaeber, p. cxv.

renowned Scyldings. This familiarity with matters Danish appears to be in contrast to Geatish and Swedish matters, references to which seem to require more explication, as, for example, in the account of the fall of the Scylfing king, Ongenþeow (ll.2921–2998).[2]

We hear first of the coming of the eponymous founding-father of the Danish royal family, Scyld Scefing, the account of whose legendary life and death (ll.4–52) forms the poem's opening movement. Some aspects of Scyld's legend were considered in the previous chapter, where I suggested that it functions in *Beowulf* essentially as a dynastic origin-myth, providing an idealised model of Scylding beginnings. We hear next that his son, **Beow*, succeeded him,[3] and that he in turn was succeeded by *heah Healfdene* (ll.56[b]–57[a]). Healfdene had *feower bearn* – Heorogar, Hroðgar, Halga, and a daughter (ll.59–63).[4] Attention is then focussed on one of these four children, namely, Hroðgar, who becomes one of the major characters in the poem: we hear of the outstanding success of his reign (ll.64–67[a]), of his building of the great hall of Heorot to celebrate it (ll.67[b]–85), and of the consequent coming of the monster Grendel (ll.86–89[a]). It is thus apparent that the opening movement of *Beowulf* is structured on a version of the genealogy of the Scyldings. That the variously stated relationships between Scylding family-members throughout the poem are nowhere contradictory implies that this was a coherent genealogy, which can be represented as follows:

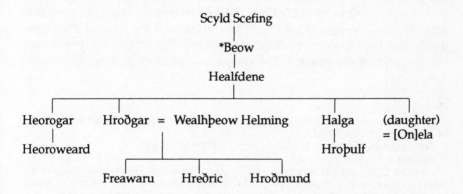

[2] As Whitelock pointed out (*The Audience of Beowulf*, pp. 34–38). Magoun ("*Beowulf B*: A Folk-Poem on Beowulf's Death", pp. 132–133) and A. Campbell ("The Use in *Beowulf* of Earlier Heroic Verse", p. 290, note 2) have also commented on this contrast.

[3] This name appears in the manuscript as *Beowulf* (ll.18[a], 53[b]), a form which seems best explained as a consequence of scribal confusion with the eponymous hero of the poem. See Klaeber, p. xxvi; Chambers, *Introduction*, pp. 87–88; Sisam, "Anglo-Saxon Royal Genealogies", p. 340; Kelly, "The Formative Stages of *Beowulf* Textual Scholarship: Part II", p. 240; and Fulk, "An Eddic Analogue to the Scyld Scefing Story", p. 314, note 4.

[4] For a discussion of the question of the name of the daughter and her marriage to the Swedish king, Onela, see Klaeber, p. 128; and Malone, "The Daughter of Healfdene".

Genealogy also appears to have underpinned the later Icelandic account of the family, *Skjǫldunga saga*, insofar as we may tell from our only record of it, a sixteenth-century Latin epitome by the scholar Arngrímur Jónsson.[5] This saga appears to have been originally compiled, probably in the twelfth century, by someone well-versed in the pedigree traditions of an Icelandic family which considered itself to be descended from the *Skjǫldungar*. Benediktsson argued that the Icelandic "interest in old heroic tales did not develop suddenly; it must have had old roots in a family, proud of its ancestry and endowed with historical interests".[6] He suggested that the family in question may have been the *Oddaverjar*, a line of chieftains from Oddi in southern Iceland during the twelfth and thirteenth centuries, who claimed descent from both the *Ynglingar* and the *Skjǫldungar*.[7] The Old English interest in the Danes in *Beowulf* may have been similarly sustained by the ancestral pride of an Anglo-Saxon aristocracy which claimed descent from the *Scyldingas*.[8] This would suggest that the genealogical context of the poem was assumed rather than stated explicitly.

In a seminal study published in 1917, Schücking attempted to account for this concern with the hypothesis that *Beowulf* was composed at the court of a baptised lord of the Danelaw during the late ninth century.[9] Klaeber described Schücking's study as being of "distinct merit", in that it tried "to find a substantial motive for the very remarkable interest taken in matters Scandinavian", a matter "still calling for adequate explanation".[10] Although Schücking appears to have accepted the view that *Beowulf* drew on specifically English traditions,[11] the flaw of his hypothesis was that it did not adequately explain the apparently pre-Viking background of the poem.[12] The question, therefore, is this: which pre-

---

5   Benediktsson (ed.), *Arngrimi Jonae*, vol. 9; see also Benediktsson, "Icelandic Traditions of the Scyldings", pp. 59–62.
6   Benediktsson, "Icelandic Traditions of the Scyldings", p. 65.
7   Benediktsson, *ibid.*, pp. 63–65.
8   As H.M. Chadwick observed many years ago, "the account of the early kings of the Danes seems to be in the nature of a tribal or family tradition . . . [the origin of which] is to be sought in the particular locality or family with which they are concerned. . . . it is natural enough that a poet who was well acquainted with some royal family, whether that of his own nation or not, would also know its traditions" (*The Heroic Age*, pp. 35–36).
9   Schücking, "Wann entstand der *Beowulf*? Glossen, Zweifel und Fragen" (1917).
10 Klaeber, p. cxxiii.
11 Schücking, "Die Beowulfdatierung: Eine Replik" (1923).
12 This point was also made by Chambers, *Introduction*, pp. 322–323. Similarly, Jacobs, describing Schücking's study as an "improbably ingenious hypothesis", pointed out that "the absence of any traditions of demonstrably Viking date and the genuine survival of some proper names in their earlier English form must argue against composition for or at the court of a late ninth-century Danish potentate" ("Anglo-Danish Relations, Poetic Archaism and the Date of *Beowulf*", pp. 26, 28–29). These factors appear to have

Viking Anglo-Saxon aristocracy might have fostered the curiously de-
tailed genealogical concerns with the Scyldings which we find in
Beowulf? Klaeber, following a hypothesis originally proposed by
Morsbach,[13] suggested

> that there may have existed close relations, perhaps through marriage,
> between an Anglian court and the kingdom of Denmark, whereby a
> special interest in Scandinavian traditions was fostered among the
> English nobility.[14]

He did not, however, consider the question of which of the Old English
noble families could have considered itself to be related to the Danes in
this way. We might expect such relations to have been signalled genealogically. As certain Danish royal names in *Beowulf* are also listed in some
surviving Old English royal pedigrees, I shall explore the question by
examining the status and significance of these names in both contexts. If
an Old English genealogical connection is identifiable in the background
of *Beowulf*, we might be able to establish the possible source of the
poem's Danish dynastic concern, and so perhaps provide a clue as to its
origin. First of all, however, a consideration of the Old English royal
pedigree genre is necessary.

THE OLD ENGLISH ROYAL PEDIGREES

Our main source for genealogical material pertaining to the West Saxon
royal family, the predominant dynasty in Southumbrian England from
the latter part of the ninth century onwards, is incorporated in the *Anglo-
Saxon Chronicle*.[15] The most important West Saxon pedigree preserved
therein, from which all later ones stem, is that of King Æþelwulf (839–
856). Æþelwulf's genealogy is listed in the entry for the year 855. Its
earliest surviving copy is contained in the section of the A manuscript of
the *Chronicle* which was written around the end of the ninth century or
the beginning of the tenth.[16] An older West Saxon pedigree, that of King
Ine (688–726), is included in a separate set of Old English royal records,

---

been overlooked by Poussa in her recent defence of Schücking's hypothesis ("The Date
of *Beowulf* Reconsidered: the Tenth Century?").
[13] Morsbach, "Zur Datierung des *Beowulf* Epos", p. 277.
[14] Klaeber, p. cxv.
[15] *Two of the Saxon Chronicles Parallel*, ed. Plummer. New editions of the manuscripts of
the *Anglo-Saxon Chronicle* are in preparation. Completed volumes which are relevant
here are Manuscripts A (ed. Bately) and B (ed. S. Taylor).
[16] For a discussion of the date of the handwriting of the early section of Manuscript A,
see Bately, *The Anglo-Saxon Chronicle: MS A*, pp. xxiv–xxv. The relationship between this
version of Æþelwulf's pedigree and those contained in Asser's *Life of King Alfred* (ed.
Stevenson) and the *Chronicon* of Ealdorman Æþelweard (ed. A. Campbell) is considered
later in this chapter.

known as the Anglian Collection.[17] This collection, which forms the earliest surviving group of Old English genealogies, also documents ancestral lists for the kingdoms of Deira, Bernicia, Mercia, Lindsey, Kent and East Anglia. Its earliest surviving manuscript, Cotton Vespasian B.vi, seems likely to have been written in Mercia in the early ninth century.[18] The group of pedigrees contained in this manuscript appears to stem from an archetype from which others in the collection independently derive.[19]

An older version of this archetype appears to have informed sections of the Cambro-Latin *Historia Brittonum* (chs 57–61), which contains a part of the Anglian Collection preserved in late eleventh- or early twelfth-century manuscripts.[20] Significant differences between these and the earlier manuscripts of the Anglian Collection imply that at least some of the Old English pedigrees had been compiled before 787.[21] Within the Collection itself, the pedigrees for rulers of the three southernmost kingdoms – Ine of Wessex (688–726), Æþelberht II of Kent (725–762), and Ælfwald of East Anglia (713–749) – appear to form an even earlier sub-group. A comparison of the relative dates of these kings suggests that this sub-group may have been compiled as early as 725 or 726.[22] Bede's citing of an almost identical version of the Kentish royal pedigree provides corroboration for this point.[23] The compilation of the sub-group could have been motivated by the need to assert the independence of these kingdoms from the power of Mercia at that time.

The fact of preservation in writing indicates that these royal pedigrees were products of clerical literacy. Many of them appear to have been originally structured on a format of fourteen generations, reckoning from subject to the required divine progenitor, Woden, inclusive.[24] This

17 There are four manuscripts in the collection (ed. Dumville, "The Anglian Collection of Royal Genealogies and Regnal Lists"): London, British Library, Cotton Vespasian B.vi; Cambridge, Corpus Christi College 183; London, British Library, Cotton Tiberius B.v, vol.I; and Rochester, Cathedral Library, A.3.5 (the *Textus Roffensis*). The collection includes lists of bishops, popes and disciples.
18 Dumville, "The Anglian Collection", pp. 24–25.
19 See Sisam, "Anglo-Saxon Royal Genealogies", pp. 290–292; and Dumville, "The Anglian Collection", pp. 38–40 and fig. 1, p. 46.
20 The *Historia Brittonum* (ed. Mommsen) seems likely to have been originally written by an unknown author in 829 x 830; see Dumville, " 'Nennius' and the *Historia Brittonum*"; and "Some Aspects of the Chronology of the *Historia Brittonum*". We await the forthcoming new edition by David Dumville.
21 Dumville, "The Anglian Collection", pp. 48–49; and "Kingship, Genealogies and Regnal Lists", p. 90.
22 Dumville, "The Anglian Collection", p. 40, note 2.
23 Bede, *HE*, I, 15; II, 5.
24. As was first pointed out by Sisam, who noted that the OE pedigrees conform to a "recognised length of fourteen names, including the ultimate ancestor" ("Anglo-Saxon Royal Genealogies", pp. 326–328). That Woden was regarded as the original founding-father of many OE royal families is stated by Bede (*HE*, I, 15).

does seem to be the case, even though in some pedigrees – such as those for Kent and Deira – there is over a century and half between kings who are in the same genealogical position.[25] This format is also apparent in the pedigree of the East Saxon king, Offa (abdicated 709), which has fourteen names from its subject to its progenitor, *Seaxnet*,[26] as well as in some of the pedigrees preserved in the version of the Anglian Collection incorporated in the *Historia Brittonum*. That for East Anglia, for example (ch. 59), does not show the beginnings of a tendency for retrospective genealogical accretion beyond Woden that we find in the Collection (such as in Cotton Vespasian B.vi), a tendency which finds its most extreme form in the late ninth-century pedigree of the West Saxon king Æþelwulf listed in the *Chronicle, s.a.* 855.

It seems likely that the precedent for this fourteen-generation format in Old English royal pedigrees was the genealogy of Jesus as given in the opening chapter of the first gospel of the New Testament, that of St Matthew (vv. 1–17). This is summarised in three fourteen-generation sections as follows:

> so all the generations from Abraham to David *are* fourteen generations; and from David until the carrying away into Babylon *are* fourteen generations; and from the carrying away into Babylon unto Christ *are* fourteen generations (v. 17).

This fourteen-generation format is also evident in some Northern genealogies. It can be seen, for example, to have determined the structure of the pedigree of the *Oddaverjar* in twelfth-century Iceland, which appears to have numbered twenty-eight generations from the ultimate ancestor, *Skjǫldr*, to its probable compiler and possible subject, Sæmundr the Wise, inclusive.[27] Another example is the pedigree of King Rǫgnvaldr of Vestfold as contained in *Ynglingatal*, 'The Tally of the Ynglings',[28] which Snorri Sturluson cites as one of his main sources for *Ynglinga saga*, the opening section of his great saga of the Norse kings, *Heimskringla*.[29] As Snorri presents it, *Ynglingatal* enumerates twenty-eight generations from Rǫgnvaldr to its eponymous progenitor, whom he names as *Yngvi-Freyr*

---

[25] As Dumville noted, "Kingship, Genealogies and Regnal Lists", pp. 89–90.

[26] The pedigree of Offa of Essex is preserved, in London, British Library, Additional ms. 23211; Ker, *Catalogue*, p. 160; see also Yorke, "The Kingdom of the East Saxons", pp. 3–4, 22–23.

[27] Bjarni Guðnasson, *Um Skjöldungasögu*, pp. 152–163, 315–317; and J. Turville-Petre, "On *Ynglingatal*", p. 62.

[28] I am indebted to Bjørn Myhre for this observation.

[29] Bjarni Aðalbjarnason (ed.), *Heimskringla*. I am grateful to Professor Bjørn Myhre for a copy of the English summary of recent research by Claus Krag (*Ynglingatal og Ynglingesaga*). As I noted in the previous chapter, Krag has contended that *Ynglingatal* may be a twelfth-century work, but none of his arguments compel us to doubt the veracity of Snorri Sturluson's attribution to the late ninth-century Norse poet, Þjóðólfr of Hvin. The classic study of the poem remains that by Åkerland, *Studier över Ynglingatal*.

in *Ynglinga saga* (ch. 11) and in his preface to *Heimskringla*.[30] The twenty-eight generations of Ynglings appear to be arranged in three groups, as follows:

(1) Yngvi-Freyr (ch. 10) to Dómarr (ch. 16) – seven generations;
(2) Dyggvi (the first in his race to be called king [ch. 17]) to Ingjaldr (chs 36–40: the last of the Ynglings to rule in Uppsala [ch. 41]) – fourteen generations; and
(3) Óláfr (chs 42–43) to Rǫgnvaldr (ch. 50) – seven generations.

This structuring is probably a consequence of the influence of Irish or English – and thus indirectly biblical – models on Northern genealogy from the ninth century.[31]

We are primarily concerned here, however, with earlier, Old English pedigrees. As I have argued, their original fourteen-generation format can be seen to have been determined by a literary precedent, although other features suggest that much of their content may have been drawn from orally maintained genealogical tradition. For example, the use of alliteration to bind together groups of ancestral names mnemonically may be seen in several of the pedigrees. The apparent use of symbolic filiation – the deployment of genealogical conventions in stereotypical father-to-son succession – may also point to an oral background.[32] A clear instance of symbolic filiation in the Anglian Collection appears in the East Anglian royal pedigree, where *Caser* (Caesar) is listed as the 'son' of Woden. These observations suggest that Old English royal pedigrees were not necessarily intended to function as chronologically accurate records;[33] rather, they were meant as a realisation of what was officially deemed to be the dynastic past at the time of their

---

[30] Although Snorri states in his preface that *Ynglingatal* names thirty of Rǫgnvaldr's forefathers, he quotes verses for only twenty-seven generations. He may, however, have paraphrased the opening verse concerned with the family eponym, as Vigfússon and Powell once suggested (*Corpus Poeticum Boreale*, vol.1, pp. 520–521), unless *Yngvi-Freyr* was an inference of later genealogists, as J. Turville-Petre has argued ("On *Ynglingatal*", pp. 53–55; but see also Faulkes, "Descent from the Gods", pp. 96–97). Moreover, at least two of the verses which Snorri cites from *Ynglingatal* were concerned with pairs of brothers, Alrekr and Eiríkr (ch. 20), and Yngvi and Alfr (ch. 21); he also names another pair, the sons of Yngvi, Jǫrundr and Eiríkr (chs 23–24), all of whom may have been included in his reckoning of thirty forefathers. If so, as presented in *Ynglinga saga*, the ancestral tally of the Ynglings seems to have numbered twenty-eight generations from subject to eponymous ancestor.

[31] As J. Turville-Petre suggested, "On *Ynglingatal*", pp. 49–50. For alternative interpretations of the structure of *Ynglingatal* and other OE and ON pedigrees, see J. Turville-Petre, "On *Ynglingatal*", pp. 49–50; and T. Hill, "Woden as 'Ninth Father': Numerical Patterning in some Old English Royal Genealogies", especially pp. 169–170.

[32] On symbolic filiation, see Henige, "Oral Tradition and Chronology", pp. 378–383.

[33] See also the arguments of Miller, "Date-Guessing and Pedigrees".

compilation.[34] Bede's account of how the Northumbrian regnal list was rewritten to exclude the unfortunate reigns of Eanfrith in Bernicia and of Osric in Deira during the year-long occupation by Cædwalla of Gwynedd shows how royal records could be manipulated according to need.[35]

> To this day that year is still held to have been ill-omened and hateful to all good men . . . So all those who compute the dates of kings have decided to abolish the memory of those perfidious kings and to assign this year to their successor Oswald, a man beloved of God.[36]

As with this instance of retrospective adjustment of a regnal list, so royal pedigrees could be selectively edited to maintain the ideological interests of the dynastic line which was in power at the time of compilation. As Dumville has put it,

> genealogy allowed the ruling dynasties to present the past (and, by implication, the future) in terms of their own history; such total exclusion of other lines was a powerful propaganda weapon. . . . Encapsulated in verse (particularly praise-poems), in heroic tales, and in the less literary genealogical records, . . . dynastic propaganda could be broadcast via the learned classes whose responsibility it was to maintain 'knowledge' of this type.[37]

The existence of such genealogical learning among the Anglo-Saxons is indicated by the reference to the lineages of the twelve tribes of Israel in the Old English poetic version of the Old Testament *Exodus*:

> swā þæt orþancum   ealde reccað
> þā þe mægburge   mǣst gefrūnon
> frumcyn fēora,   fæderæþelo gehwæs.

> 'so elders who have studied deeply the tribal genealogies reckon skilfully the ancestry of living kin, the noble forefather of each' (ll.359–361).[38]

The suggestion is then that Old English royal pedigrees should be regarded as ancestral *tallies*, originally based on a fourteen-name format, of names reckoned by royal genealogists to be ideologically necessary to dynastic authority at the time of their compilation.

Many of the listed ancestors, moreover, were probably selected from a

---

[34] As Dumville pointed out, "Kingship, Genealogies and Regnal Lists", pp. 73–74, 77–79, 85–86.
[35] Dumville, *ibid.*, p. 81.
[36] Bede, *HE*, III, 1.
[37] Dumville, "Kingship, Genealogies and Regnal Lists", p. 83.
[38] Tolkien, *The Old English Exodus*, ed. J. Turville-Petre.

pre-literary genre of royal genealogical verse, the prior existence of which has already been suggested. Evidence for the maintenance of such verse in early Anglo-Saxon England may be found in the *Vita Sancti Guthlaci*, which was written in East Anglia during the reign of King Ælfwald (*ca* 713–749).[39] Its author, Felix, introduces his saintly hero genealogically. We are told that St Guthlac's father, Penwalh, is *de egregia stirpe Merciorum*, 'from a distinguished line of Mercians' (ch. 1). We then hear that

> huius etiam viri progenies per nobilissima inlustrium regum nomina antiqua ab origine Icles digesto ordine cucurrit.

> 'the descent of this man was traced in set order through the most noble and ancient names of illustrious kings, back to *Icel* in whom it began in days of old' (ch. 2).

The reference to the name *Icel* and the explicit status of its bearer as the founder of the line suggests that Felix was alluding to an authentic version of the Mercian royal pedigree. *Icel* is listed as the seventh name in the version of the Mercian royal pedigree which is preserved in the Anglian Collection, a genealogical position which appears popular with dynastic founding-figures. For example, the seventh name in the East Anglian pedigree is *Wehha*, whom the *Historia Brittonum* seems to identify as the 'first' to rule over the East Angles (ch. 59); in the Deiran ancestral list it is *Soemel*, whom the *Historia Brittonum* says was the 'first' to separate Deira from Bernicia (ch. 61); and in the Bernician list it is *Oesa*, said to be the 'first' to come to Britain.[40] These examples may suggest that seventh place was a conventional position for founding figures because it is pivotal in a pedigree which follows a format of fourteen generations. That Felix refers to a version of the Mercian royal pedigree in which *Icel* is given the status of a founding father, and that other forebears enjoy reputations for nobility and illustriousness, suggests that this version was more than just a list of names. Another indication that this was the case arises from a later reference to Guthlac's lineage. In his account of the young saint's conversion, Felix relates how, in the aftermath of the success of a nine-year career as the leader of a war-band, Guthlac had become increasingly anxious over the transitoriness of mortal life

> cum antiquorum regum stirpis suae per transacta retro saecula miserabiles exitus flagitioso vitae termino contemplaretur.

> 'when he contemplated the miserable deaths and shameful ends of the ancient kings of his line in the course of past ages' (ch. 18).

---

[39] *Felix's Life of St Guthlac*, ed. Colgrave. The earliest ms. has been dated to the late eighth or early ninth centuries (Colgrave, *ibid.*, pp. 26–54).
[40] See Dumville, "A New Chronicle-Fragment of Early British History".

That Guthlac knew of the circumstances of the deaths of his ancestors again implies that his royal genealogy was more than just a bare list of names.[41] As I noted at the end of the last chapter, this kind of information seems to have been a distinctive feature of the genre of royal genealogical verse. This is shown especially well by the aforementioned Old Norse *Ynglingatal*, 'The Tally of the Ynglings', perhaps the best surviving example of the genre, with, it appears, a verse or so allotted to each generation. Like the Icling genealogy to which young Guthlac is said to have listened, *Ynglingatal* is a poem concerned with a royal line in which regular attention is devoted to the circumstances of the deaths of the kings of the line.[42] Analogy with the probably late ninth-century *Ynglingatal* may then suggest that the Icling ancestral tally referred to by the author of the early eighth-century *Vita Sancti Guthlaci* was maintained in verse.

Another hagiographic source which appears to refer to the maintenance of royal genealogical poetry in Anglo-Saxon England is the twelfth-century *Passio Sancti Athelberhti*.[43] This work is concerned with the life, death and associated miracles of Æþelberht, king of East Anglia in the late eighth century. His assassination near Hereford, the cathedral of which still bears his dedication, is recorded in the *Chronicle, s.a.* 792. The unique text of the *Passio* is written in a twelfth-century hand, but because of its peculiarly abrupt style, the authentically Anglo-Saxon forms of its personal names, and its knowledge of local place-names, the extant manuscript is believed to be based, in part at least, on Old English vernacular or homiletic traditions which arose in the vicinity of Hereford in the aftermath of the Æþelberht's murder.[44] In other words, despite the relatively late date of its manuscript, there are indications that the *Passio* contains potentially authentic information from the late eighth century.

It was on his way to Hereford, according to the *Passio*, that King Æþelberht asked to hear 'royal songs'.

"Itinerantibus non modica crebro leticia, dum illic diua poemata modulando recitantur. Ergo nobis qui ediderit carmina regio armilla donabitur." Nec mora, duo canendi prediti scientia in cordis leticia psallere ceperunt. Erant carmina de regis eiusdem regia prosapia. Quibus ille

[41] This important point has been elucidated by Moisl, "Anglo-Saxon Royal Genealogies and Germanic Oral Tradition", p. 232.
[42] As J. Turville-Petre pointed out, the principal theme of *Ynglingatal* "is the death of the king and his place of burial. The social correlative of this literary genre is a grave-cult" ("On *Ynglingatal*", p. 51).
[43] *Passio Sancti Athelberhti* is preserved in the Cambridge, Corpus Christi College MS.308 (ed. James, "Two Lives of St Ethelbert, King and Martyr").
[44] See James, "Two Lives of Ethelbert", pp. 218–219; C. Wright, *The Cultivation of Saga in Anglo-Saxon England*, pp. 96–97, 106; and R. Wilson, *The Lost Literature of Medieval England*, pp. 98–99.

delectatus abstracta brachio protinus armilla modulantes carmina donat, dum repatriat plurima spondet.

' "Often it is enjoyable for wayfarers when divine poems are recited melodiously. Therefore an arm-ring shall be given by me to whomever can perform royal songs." Without delay, two skilled in the art of song started to make music with glad hearts. They were songs about the royal line of that same king. Delighted by them, he took a bracelet from his arm and gave it to those who had sung the songs, and pledged more on returning home'.[45]

As Moisl has pointed out, the way that the East Anglian court poets are rewarded here resembles closely the way that the eponymous narrator of *Widsith* is rewarded with arm-rings on more than one occasion (ll.65b, 73b–74a, 90–98).[46] The 'songs about the royal line' of Æþelberht, moreover, seem likely to have been none other than genealogical poetry concerning the East Anglian royal family.[47] The *Passio Sancti Athelberti* thus provides some degree of corroboration for the point advanced in the last chapter that the existence of East Anglian dynastic verse may be inferred from archaeology. It also reinforces the suggestion that poetry was a major medium for the maintenance of royal genealogical tradition.

The overall conclusion of this section is that the Old English royal pedigrees were originally based on a fourteen-name biblical format of ancestral names which were probably derived largely from a pre-literary genre of genealogical verse. In the light of all this, we may now consider the significance of certain royal names which are common to both *Beowulf* and some of the surviving Old English royal pedigrees. The aim is to see if an Old English genealogical connection – especially one involving Danes – is identifiable in the background of *Beowulf*, so providing a clue as to its origin.

THE PEDIGREE OF KING OFFA

Perhaps the most well-known example in *Beowulf* of a name which is listed in an Old English pedigree is that of Offa, legendary king of Angel, the ancestral home of the English, which appears to have been in what is now Schleswig.[48] This could provide a context for the poem's Scandina-

---

[45] James, "Two Lives of Ethelbert", p. 238.

[46] Moisl, "Anglo-Saxon Royal Genealogies and Germanic Oral Tradition", pp. 238–242.

[47] The significance of this reference has been noted by Wright, *The Cultivation of Saga*, p. 31, note 1; Wilson, *Lost Literature*, pp. 24–25; and Moisl, "Anglo-Saxon Royal Genealogies", pp. 231–234, 238–239.

[48] See especially Chambers, *Widsith*, pp. 71–75; and Jankuhn, "The Continental Home of the English".

vian concerns, for Offa is also a figure of Danish legend.[49] He is, however, not directly connected with the Scyldings in *Beowulf*, and appears to belong to an earlier period.[50]

Offa is referred to in a brief eulogy (ll.1955–1962) at the end of one of the poem's more problematic passages. Beowulf has just returned by ship from his triumphant adventures in *Scedeland* to the hall of his uncle and lord, King Hygelac. We are told how he and his men disembark and proceed towards Hygelac's nearby high hall (ll.1920–1926[a]). We then hear about Hygelac's queen, Hygd (ll.1926[b]–1931[a]), until the narrative seems to shift very abruptly from Hygd to another queenly figure (l.1931[b]). The murderous reputation of the latter is then described in some detail (ll.1931[b]–1943), and we learn that she was eventually tamed by her marriage to Offa (ll.1944–1954). Whether the suddenness of the shift is intended or not is unclear. If intentional, it could be seen as being consistent with the poem's tendency to contrast and compare its characters with figures from Germanic legend, as, for example, when Beowulf is compared with the most famous dragon-slayer of the Northlands, Sigemund (ll.874[b]–897), or when he is contrasted with the notorious Heremod (ll.899–915; 1707[b]–1723[a]). In this sense, the sudden digression to the infamous wife of the legendary hero Offa could have been intended as an instructive contrast to Hygelac's queen. Yet as the passage stands we cannot be sure of this, for it is artistically so awkward that one may legitimately suspect the possibility of interpolation, or, perhaps more likely, scribal error.[51]

Either way, we hear unequivocally high praises for King Offa (ll.1954–1962), before narrative attention returns to Beowulf's journey on foot from the beach to the hall of Hygelac (ll.1963–1976). In Klaeber's edition, this part of the passage is as follows:

> hīold hēahlufan wið hæleþa brego
> ealles moncynnes mīne gefrǣge
> þone sēlestan bī sǣm twēonum,
> eormencynnes; forðām Offa wæs
> geofum 7 gūðum, gārcēne man,
> wīde geweorðod, wīsdome hēold
> ēðel sīnne; þonon Eomǣr wōc
> hæleðum tō helpe, Hem[m]inges mǣg,
> nefa Gārmundes, nīða cræftig.

---

[49] His legend is told by both Sven Aageson and Saxo Grammaticus (Garmonsway and Simpson, *Beowulf and Its Analogues*, pp. 222–233); for a discussion of Anglo-Danish relations during the Migration Age, see Chambers, *Widsith*, pp. 75–79.

[50] Offa seems to belong to the latter part of the fourth century (Chadwick, *The Origin of the English Nation*, pp. 134–136); the Scyldings to the beginning of the sixth, as was inferred in Chapter Two.

[51] As Whitelock thought, *The Audience of Beowulf*, pp. 58–59; see also the discussion by Chambers, *Introduction*, pp. 539–543.

'She held high love for the heroes' lord, he of mighty kin, who,
as I have learnt, was the best of all mankind between the two
seas; because Offa was widely honoured in gift-giving and in
warfare, that spear-brave man ruled his ancestral seat with wisdom; from him sprung Eomer, the ally of heroes, skilled in
battle, the kinsman of Hemming and the grandson of Garmund'
(ll.1954–1962).

This passage reads as if eulogy for the legendary king of Angel is the
principal purpose for digressing from the account of Beowulf's homecoming.[52] It is therefore potentially significant that the genealogical
sequence included here (Garmund – Offa – Eomer) bears some measure
of agreement with a section of the Mercian royal pedigree from the
Anglian Collection. The best surviving example is preserved in Cambridge, Corpus Christi College 183:

> Icel Eomæring
> Eomær Angengeoting
> Angengiot Offing
> Offa Wærmunding
> Wærmund Wihtlæging.[53]

The version preserved in the oldest manuscript of the Collection, the
British Library, Cotton Vespasian B.vi is as follows:

> Icil Eamering
> Eamer Angengeoting
> [An]gengeot Offing
> Offa Uærmunding
> Uermund Uihtlaeging.[54]

The degree of agreement between this section of the Icling pedigree and
the *Beowulf* passage in question has been regarded by some scholars as a
possible indicator that the poem could have been composed in Mercia
during the second half of the eighth century. Following a suggestion first
made in 1892 by J. Earle,[55] Whitelock tentatively advanced the possibility
that the extravagant praise of King Offa of Angel here could have been
"in compliment to a descendant and namesake", King Offa of Mercia
(757–796).[56]

Although the extent of the agreement between the two is sufficient to
suggest that both probably derive ultimately from a common genealogi-

---

[52] As Whitelock also observed, *The Audience of Beowulf*, p. 60.
[53] Dumville, "The Anglian Collection", p. 33.
[54] Dumville, *ibid.*, p. 30.
[55] Earle, *The Deeds of Beowulf*, pp. lxxvi ff.
[56] Whitelock, *The Audience of Beowulf*, p. 63.

cal source, it does not in itself warrant an exclusively Mercian claim to the composition of *Beowulf*. To begin with, the artistic awkwardness of the passage containing the poem's reference to the line of Offa of Angel renders its significance equivocal. If it was intended to function as a complimentary allusion to the forebears of the Mercian royal family, moreover, it would seem odd that the compliment was made in such a seemingly abrupt manner nearly two-thirds of the way through the story. As it is, Offa appears to be quite peripheral to the poem's principal narrative concerns.[57] A more serious difficulty, however, concerns the emendation of the manuscript reading *gēomor* to the name *Eomēr*, or *Eomǣr* (l.1960[b]). Although there does appear to have been almost universal scholarly agreement over this emendation,[58] Kiernan has argued reasonably that editors may well have been unduly influenced by the sequence of names in the Mercian royal pedigree.[59] Certainly, this same influence seems to have led Klaeber to propose that *nefa* (l.1962) can mean 'grandson', rather than 'nephew'.[60] Yet as Kiernan also argued, following the arguments of Rickert and Malone,[61] the manuscript reading for line 1960, although perhaps metrically awkward, makes sense without emendation. Only a slight adjustment, which does not change a single letter of the line, is necessary to satisfy alliterative requirements. The Malone-Kiernan reading of this passage thus runs as follows:

> . . . forðām Offa wæs
> geofum 7 gūðum,   gārcēne man,
> wīde geweorðod,   wīsdōme hēold
> ēðel sīnne   þon ongēomor wōc
> hæleðum tō helpe,   Heminges mǣg,
> nefa Gārmundes,   nīða cræftig.

'. . . because Offa was widely honoured in gift-giving and in warfare, that spear-brave man ruled his ancestral seat with wisdom when he, the sad one, awoke as the ally of heroes, skilled in battle, the kinsman of Heming and the nephew of Garmund' (ll.1957[b]–1962).

[57] Eliason, following an idea advanced by Matthes ("Hygd"), argued that Offa may have been the first husband of Hygelac's queen, Hygd ("The 'Thryth-Offa Digression' in *Beowulf*"), thus establishing an implicitly close connection between the Angles and the *Gēatas*. Yet this theory requires some very special pleading indeed. Particularly dubious is Eliason's method of attempting to date historically the reign of Offa of Angel on the basis of calculating back through the names listed in the Mercian royal pedigree, alotting an average of 25–30 years per generation (*ibid.*, pp. 129–130).
[58] Kelly, "The Formative Stages of *Beowulf* Textual Scholarship: part II", p. 255.
[59] Kiernan, *Beowulf and Beowulf Manuscript*, pp. 184–185.
[60] Klaeber, p. 379; Malone, "Swerting", pp. 25–236.
[61] Rickert, "The Old English Offa Saga"; Malone, "Swerting".

As Malone pointed out,[62] the retention of the adjective *gēomor* is particularly felicitous here as it is consistent with the legendary reputation of Offa in Denmark as recorded by Saxo Grammaticus:[63]

> for from his first years he never used to play or make merry, but was so void of all human pleasure that he kept his lips sealed in a continual silence, and utterly restrained his severe appearance from the business of laughter (Malone's translation).

Although the story of Offa's grim silence which Saxo inherited could have developed from a misconstrual of the personal name *Eomēr*, there may be a case for not rejecting the manuscript reading of line 1960. If not, the name *Eomēr* might not belong in the passage at all, which would somewhat lessen the degree of agreement between *Beowulf* and the Mercian royal pedigree.

Within the pedigree itself there are features which suggest that its compilers used a different version of the line of Offa of Angel to that is given in *Beowulf*. As Malone observed, the name of Offa's father in the pedigree, *Uermund* or *Wærmund*, is not necessarily a straightforward variant of the name *Garmund* in the poem.[64] Moreover, the names *Offa* and *Eomēr* are presented in the pedigree as being grandfather and grandson, whereas in *Beowulf*, at least according to the Klaeber version, they are father and son. The intervening generation in the pedigree, the ninth on the list, is occupied by the name *Angengēot* (or *Anglegēot*), which does not occur in *Beowulf*. One possibility is that it could be a genealogical convention, perhaps reflecting an Anglo-Geatish political connection.[65] Yet the significance of the form *Angengēot* remains unclear. The presence of the exactly the same form – also in the ninth position – in the pedigree-list for the main line of the Bernician dynasty shows that the name *Angengēot* was not necessarily exclusively Mercian. The parallel occurrence of this name could perhaps express political relations between Mercia and Bernicia at the time of the compilation of the pedigrees,[66] but even this possibility is far from certain. As a royal genealogical convention, it could also be interpreted as being of ethno-religious significance, as Malone argued.[67]

Let us turn now to Offa himself. To begin with, that he was well-known figure in the Danish tradition preserved by Saxo Grammaticus and Sven Aageson implies that Mercia was not the only place where tales

---

62 Malone, "Swerting", p. 235.
63 Olrik and Raeder (ed.), *Saxonis Gesta Danorum*, Book 4.
64 Malone, "Swerting", pp. 235–236, note 1.
65 A conjecture developed by Eliason ("The 'Thryth-Offa Digression'", pp. 130–131) and Malone ("Humblus and Lotherus", p. 203).
66 See Dumville, "Kingship, Genealogies and Regnal Lists", pp. 79–80.
67 Malone, *Widsith*, 2nd edition, p. 189.

of the famous deeds of Offa were fostered.[68] That his reputation was also widespread in England is indicated by the eulogistic reference to him in *Widsith* (ll.35–44).

> Offa wēold Ongle,   Alewīh Denu*m*,
> sē wæs þāra manna   mōdgast ealra;
> nō hwæþre hē ofer Offan   eorlscype fremede,
> ac Offa geslōg   ǣrest monna
> cnihtwesende   cynerīca mǣst,
> nǣnig efeneald him   eorlscipe māran
> on ōrette,   āne sweorde
> merce gemǣrde   wið Myrgingu*m*
> bī Fīfeldore;   hēoldon forð siþþan
> Engle 7 Swǣfe,   swā hit Offa geslōg.

'Offa ruled Angel, Alewih the Danes: he was the boldest of all of these men, yet he did not outdo Offa in deeds of courage; for Offa, first of men, gained at a stroke the greatest of kingdoms while still a boy; no one of his age achieved greater deeds of valour in battle: with one sword he marked the boundary with the Myrgings at *Fifeldore*: just as Offa struck it, Engle and Swæfe have henceforth held it' (ll.35–44).

This eulogy refers to Offa's famous single-handed victory at *Fīfeldor*, securing the southern marches of Angel against the Myrgings.[69] Those who would argue that the praise for Offa in *Beowulf* suggests a Mercian origin have to acknowledge the corollary that the eulogy for Offa in *Widsith* would suggest similarly that that poem was of possible Mercian origin. This was indeed acknowledged by Whitelock and Wrenn.[70] Yet surely the reference to Offa in *Widsith* constitutes no basis for a claim to its Mercian origin. Certainly, such a claim would require some very special pleading as the poem's narrator, the eponymous Widsið, is himself one of the Myrgings (ll.4ᵇ–5ᵃ), the very folk who were Offa's enemies at *Fīfeldor*.

The extant pedigree of an East Saxon king called Offa,[71] who appears to have abdicated around the year 709,[72] shows that the Mercian royal family was not the only one in early Anglo-Saxon England which maintained a claim to descent from a legendary figure named Offa.

---

[68] For a convenient translation of these sources, see Garmonsway and Simpson, *Beowulf and Its Analogues*, pp. 222–233.

[69] *Fīfeldore* appears to be what is now the River Eider (Magoun, "Fifeldore and the Name of the Eider").

[70] Whitelock, *The Audience of Beowulf*, pp. 63–64; and Wrenn (in Chambers, *Introduction*), p. 540.

[71] London, B.L., Add. MS.23211; see Ker, *Catalogue*, p. 160; and Yorke, "The Kingdom of the East Saxons", pp. 3–4.

[72] Bede *HE* v, 19; Yorke, "The Kingdom of the East Saxons", pp. 22–23.

1.   <u>Offa</u> Sighering
2.   Sighere Sigberhting
3.   Sigberht S[aweard]ing
4.   Saweard Saberhting
5.   Saberht Sledding
6.   Sle[dd] Æscwining
7.   Æscwine Offing
8.   <u>Offa</u> Bedcing
9.   Bedca [Sigefugling]
10. Sigefugl Swæpping
11. Swæppa Antsecging
12. Ants[ecg] Gesecging
13. Gesecg Seaxneting
14. (Seaxnet)

The legendary Offa is listed here as the grandfather of the East Saxon king, Sledd.[73] It has been suggested that Offa here was a genealogical convention reflecting the political dominance of Mercia in the later seventh and eighth centuries.[74] This does not necessarily follow, however, for the name occurs in the surviving pedigrees for none of the other kingdoms similarly subordinated to Mercian power at the beginning of eighth century.

The allusion to Offa in *Beowulf* appears thus not to be necessarily of exclusively Mercian significance; rather, as the references to his fame in Danish sources and in *Widsið* imply, the allusion relates more probably to Offa's legendary reputation as one of the earliest of English heroes. As Klaeber observed, "the only conclusion to be drawn from it with reasonable certainty seems to be that the poet was interested in the old Anglian traditions".[75] All that we can be sure of is that the claim to descent from Offa the Angle in the Mercian pedigree realises the official view of the dynastic past at the time of compilation, that is, during the latter half of the eighth century. The claim to descent from Offa may have been monopolised retrospectively by his Mercian namesake at that time, perhaps seeking to constitute the legitimacy of either his hold on the Mercian throne in the aftermath of his succession in 757 or his later aspiration to be the leading ruler over the English. The claim that Offa was a Mercian dynastic forebear need not necessarily have been operative any earlier and it may be significant that Offa is mentioned neither in the version of the Mercian royal pedigree referred to by Felix in the earlier eighth-

---

[73] On Sledd, see Yorke, *ibid.*, pp. 15–16.
[74] Yorke, *ibid.*, p. 15.
[75] Klaeber, p. 198.

century *Vita Sancti Guthlaci*, nor in any referred to by Bede at around the same time.

All of this suggests that what measure of agreement there is between a version of the line of King Offa of Angel in a late eighth-century Mercian royal pedigree and one of the more editorially awkward passages in *Beowulf* does not warrant an exclusively Mercian claim to be the source of the poem's Northern dynastic concerns. It is not impossible, however, that a version of *Beowulf* could have been known in Mercia in the late eighth or early ninth centuries, where it may have inspired royal name-giving, as may be suggested by the names of the Mercian kings at that time, such as *Beornwulf*, *Wīglāf*, and *Wīhstān*.

THE PEDIGREE OF KING ÆÞELWULF OF WESSEX

The entry in the *Anglo-Saxon Chronicle* for the year 855 shows that the kings of Wessex, at least from the time of King Ælfred (871–899), considered themselves to be descended from the same Danish royal family which we meet in *Beowulf*. The genealogy of King Æþelwulf (839–856), father of Ælfred, claims descent ultimately from the biblical Adam by means of a series of genealogical accretions beyond the original fourteen generations from subject to the traditional Germanic progenitor, Woden. Among the names in this upper series are *Scēaf*, *Sceldwa* and *Bēaw*.

The earliest written version of Æþelwulf's pedigree is contained in the *A* manuscript of the *Chronicle*, which appears to date from around the end of the ninth century.[76] Although the name *Scēaf* does not appear in this version,[77] it must have been present in the lost archetype of the *Chronicle* (*Æ*) for it is listed in the version which appears in the late tenth-century *B* manuscript of the *Chronicle*, s.a. 856.[78] Another version of Æþelwulf's pedigree is given in Asser's biography of King Alfred, *De Rebus Gestis Ælfredi*, which was written in 893 and is thus contemporary with *A*.[79] This includes forms of names not listed in *A* and in this respect is virtually identical with the version preserved in the *B* manuscript of the *Chronicle*.[80]

The *Æ* version of the Danish section of Æþelwulf's pedigree shows similarities to the genealogy of the Scyldings in *Beowulf*. The former presents *Bēaw* as the son of *Sceldwa*, just as the latter names the son and heir of Scyld as *Bēowulf* (ll.18–22, 53–56ᵃ), which is almost certainly

---

[76] Bately (ed.), *The Anglo-Saxon Chronicle: MS A*, pp. xxi–xxv.
[77] Bately, *ibid.*, pp. 45–46.
[78] S. Taylor (ed.), *The Anglo-Saxon Chronicle: MS B*, pp. 32–33.
[79] Stevenson (ed.), *De Rebus Gestis Ælfredi*.
[80] For a convenient comparison of these versions of the West Saxon royal pedigree, see Chambers, *Introduction*, pp. 202–203.

scribal error for *Bēow*.[81] Yet *Sceldwa* and *Scēaf* are not represented as father
and son as they seem to be in *Beowulf*; rather, they are separated by five
generations, namely, *Heremōd, Itermon, Hathra, Hwala* and *Bedwīg*. The B
manuscript seems to suggest, moreover, that it is *Scēaf* – and not Scyld as
in *Beowulf* – who is associated with a nautical advent: *se wæs geboren on
þære earce Noes*, 'he was born in Noah's Ark', and lists Adam as Æþelwulf's ultimate ancestor. The version of Æþelwulf's pedigree included in
the late tenth-century Latin *Chronicon* of the West Saxon ealdorman,
Æþelweard, s.a. 857,[82] however, agrees with *Beowulf* in listing *Scēf*, father
of *Scyld*, as the ultimate forebear. Æþelweard's version of Æþelwulf's
pedigree thus does not include the five names between *Sceldwa* and *Scēaf*
which are listed by Asser and probably in the Æ version of the *Chronicle*.
The differences between these versions of Æþelwulf's pedigree may be
represented in ascending order as follows:

THE Æ CHRONICLE	ÆÞELWEARD'S CHRONICLE
Bēaw Sceldwaing	Bēo
Sceldwea Heremōding	Scyld
Heremōd Itermoning	
Itermon Hraþraing	
Hraþra Hwalaing	
Hwala Bedwīging	
Bedwīg Scēafing	
	Scēf

As his Prologue suggests, Æþelweard took a special interest in his own
family's pedigree, and the absence of the five names from his version is
unlikely to have been a mistake because he numbers the generations
beyond Cerdic. Yet whether Æþelweard's source was an earlier, pre-Æ
text of the *Chronicle* or royal family genealogical tradition,[83] there can be
little doubt that his late tenth-century *Chronicon* preserves an older and
more authoritative version of Æþelwulf's pedigree than those listed by
Asser and in the surviving manuscripts of the *Chronicle*.[84]

---

81 Kelly, "The Formative Stages of *Beowulf* Textual Scholarship: Part II", p. 240; Björkman, "Bēow, Bēaw und Bēowulf"; Sisam, "Anglo-Saxon Royal Genealogies", pp. 339–
342; and Meaney, "Scyld Scefing and the Dating of *Beowulf* – Again", pp. 21–22. For a
recent and penetrating consideration of this name and its implications, see Fulk, "An
Eddic Analogue to the Scyld Scefing Story".
82 A. Campbell (ed.), *Chronicon Æthelweardi*, p. 33.
83 On the former possibility, see Meaney, "St Neots, Æthelweard, and the *Anglo-Saxon
Chronicle*"; and "Scyld Scefing and the Dating of *Beowulf*", pp. 14–20; on the latter, see
Chambers, *Introduction*, pp. 318–319; and Sisam, "Anglo-Saxon Royal Genealogies",
p. 317.
84 As Meaney pointed out in her discussion of these differing versions of Æþelwulf's
pedigree, "as a rule, shorter genealogies are earlier than longer ones: once a prestig-
iously long set of ancestors has been claimed, none of them is likely to be discarded

Indeed, the resemblances between the upper section of the West Saxon pedigree in Æþelweard's *Chronicon* and that of the Scylding genealogy in *Beowulf* are remarkably close. Unlike any other surviving early source, both contain a version of a Danish royal pedigree showing the names *Scēf, Scyld* and *Bēo-* in exactly the same relationship to one another. Both pedigrees, moreover, stem from *Scēf*, about whom Æþelweard adds the following information:

> Ipse Scef cum uno dromone aduectus est in insula oceani que dicitur Scani, armis circundatus, eratque ualde recens puer, et ab incolis illius terræ ignotus. Attamen ab eis suscipitur, et ut familiarem diligenti animo eum custodierunt, et post in regem eligunt; de cuius ordinem trahit Aðulf rex.

> 'And this Sceaf arrived with one light ship in the island of the ocean which is called Skáney, with arms all round him. He was a very young boy, and unknown to the people of that land, but he was received by them, and they guarded him with diligent attention as one who belonged to them, and elected him king. From his family King Æþelwulf derived his descent.'

There are striking similarities between this version of the boat-borne advent of the royal progenitor and the legend of Scyld Scefing in *Beowulf*, both of which locate that advent unequivocally in the Northlands. Both also present the hero as a foundling; like Æþelweard's *Scēf*, Scyld Scefing appears in *Beowulf* as a very young boy, *umborwesende* (l.46[b]), alone in a similarly equipped ship, as is made clear in the account of his boat-borne funeral:

> Nalæs hī hine læssan   lācum tēodan,
> þēodgestrēonum   þon þā dydon,
> þē hine æt frumsceafte   forð onsendon
> ænne ofer ȳðe   umborwesende.

> 'In no way did they endow him with lesser gifts or folk-treasures than did they who, in the beginning, sent him forth as a child, alone over the waves' (ll.43–46).

Æþelweard's *Scēf* is said to be surrounded by arms, just as Scyld Scefing is presented as being surrounded by *þēodgestrēon*, 'folk-treasures' (l.44[a]), including weapons (ll.39–40[a]), for his last voyage, which, as the above passage states (ll.43–46) is laden in the same manner as the vessel in which he had arrived as a child.[85] These resemblances must be more than coincidental. Both contain English versions of a section of an identifiably

---

deliberately – only by accidental omission" ("Scyld Scefing and the Dating of *Beowulf*", p. 13). See also Fulk, "An Eddic Analogue to the Scyld Scefing Story", p. 321.
[85] This passage was also discussed in Chapter Two.

Danish royal pedigree showing three almost identical forms in precisely the same relationship to one another. Despite differences of emphasis, moreover, both versions present the legend of the boat-borne foundling-hero as royal origin-myth. The final statement of Æþelweard's account of the hero, *de cuius ordinem trahit Aðulf rex*, leaves no doubt that in his day Æþelweard believed that his family derived its origin from this boat-borne founding-father. It is clear, therefore, that ultimately the two must share a common genealogical source.

We seem thus to have evidence that the West Saxon kings of the late ninth and tenth centuries regarded themselves as descendants of the same Danish royal family which we meet in *Beowulf*. However, the degree of agreement between Æþelweard's version of the Danish section of King Æþelwulf's pedigree and the upper part of the Scylding genealogy in *Beowulf* is insufficient to warrant a West Saxon claim to the composition of the poem.[86] To begin with, the agreement between the two on the spellings of *Scyld*, *Scēf* and *Bēo-* is not of compelling significance, since both were written or copied in the same period and show the expected late West Saxon forms in these instances. Both agree also that the legendary boat-borne founder of the line sailed into the world of men in Scandinavia, but Æþelweard uses the name *Scani* whereas *Beowulf* uses *Scedeland* (1.19b) and *Scedenīg* (1.1686a). Æþelweard's *Scani* seems to be a Latinised version of the form current in tenth-century Wessex, which appears originally to have stemmed from OE *Scōneg*. The latter, which is used in the late ninth-century Old English translation of the work of Orosius,[87] probably derives from the borrowed ON *Skáney*. *Scedeland* and *Scedenīg*, however, seem to represent more ancient Old English forms, for they retain the consonant *d* which appears to have been lost in Old Norse – leading to the subsequent lengthening of the preceding vowel – before the Viking period.[88] The suggestion is then that the *Beowulf* forms were not derived from a ninth-century Old Norse loan-word as Æþelweard's *Scani* seems to have been, but from an older English source.

There are also significant differences of emphasis between Æþelweard's account of the founder of the line and that told in *Beowulf*.

---

[86] For a contrary view, see Murray, "*Beowulf*, the Danish Invasions and Royal Genealogy"; and Meaney, "Scyld Scefing and the Dating of *Beowulf*". Some scholars have seen significance in certain potentially early West Saxon place-names, as evidenced by charters. Yet all that can be maintained on the basis of these place-names is that it is possible that a version of the poem could have been known in the vicinity of Malmesbury before the early tenth century, as Lapidge concluded his discussion of the point ("*Beowulf*, Aldhelm, the *Liber Monstrorum* and Wessex", pp. 179–184).

[87] Bately (ed.), *The Old English Orosius*, p. 16, l.24.

[88] This point was also made in Chapter One; see Noreen, *Altisländische und Altnorwegische Grammatik*, § 292; Gordon, *An Introduction to Old Norse*, §§ 53, 66, 230; Björkman, "Scedeland, Scedenig"; de Vries, *Altnordisches etymologisches Wörterbuch, s.v. Skáney*; Svennung, *Scadinavia und Scandia*, pp. 36–51; and Fulk, "Dating *Beowulf* to the Viking Age", pp. 343–344.

Æþelweard attributes the mythic boat-borne origin to Scef, whereas *Beowulf* attributes it to Scyld. Æþelweard, moreover, does not refer to the hero's departure, a matter which *Beowulf* richly describes in the form of a pre-Christian royal ship-funeral (ll.26–52). This difference is even more pronounced in the *B* manuscript of the *Chronicle*, which rationalises the myth of the boat-borne foundling-hero with the Old Testament legend of Noah's Ark by identifying him as a son of Noah who *wæs geboren on þære earce*. This reads like a clerical attempt to synthesise Christian and Germanic legend so as to provide a retrospective genealogical link with the Old Testament. The reference to the hero's birth in Noah's Ark parallels the allusion to his boat-borne appearance in *Beowulf* (ll.43–46), and draws attention to the symbolic significance of the ship as a vessel of birth and renewel.[89] The emphasis on the hero's advent by Æþelweard and its representation in Old Testament terms in the *Chronicle* may well have been prompted by religious considerations, insofar as a full-scale royal ship-funeral may have been considered to be unacceptably pre-Christian by West Saxon genealogists. These differences suggest that late ninth-century Wessex was not the source of the legend of the royal boat-borne founding-hero as we have it in *Beowulf*.

The legend itself was probably not native to Wessex. Its nautical character suggests that it is more likely to have been fostered by a seafaring people.[90] Wessex appears to have been a land-locked realm, with an old heartland centred on the upper Thames valley, until its expansion southwards in the latter half of the seventh century.[91] The hero does not appear to be included in the fourteen-generation ancestral list of the West Saxon king, Ine (688–726), preserved in the Anglian Collection.[92] King Æþelwulf's pedigree seems to be a late ninth-century expanded version of King Ine's list, with the legend of Scyld Scefing forming part a retrospective extension of ancestral names beyond the original progenitor, *Woden*.[93] This extension probably reflects West Saxon power-politics of that time.[94] Despite Æþelweard's noted use of a form (*Scani*) of

---

[89] T. Hill, "The Myth of the Ark-Born Son of Noe and the West-Saxon Royal Genealogical Tables".

[90] As Olrik noted, *The Heroic Legends of Denmark*, p. 409.

[91] Yorke, *Kings and Kingdoms in Early Anglo-Saxon England*, p. 132.

[92] Ine's pedigree is preserved in the early tenth-century Cambridge, Corpus Christi College MS 183, fols 65ʳ-67ʳ (ed. Dumville, "The Anglian Collection", pp. 32–34). Like others in the collection, this manuscript seems likely to have derived from a late eighth-century archetype. Ine's pedigree forms part of the sub-group which may have been compiled in 725 or 726, as Dumville noted (*ibid.*, p. 40, note 2).

[93] In his analysis of the upper section of Æþelwulf's pedigree ("Anglo-Saxon Royal Genealogies", pp. 314–322), Sisam concluded that it is "a late and artificial composition, developed by well-marked stages in such a way that, as a rule, the remotest names represent the latest accretions" (*ibid.*, p. 321).

[94] There may have been a need to sanction West Saxon authority over Danes settled in England (Murray, "*Beowulf*, the Danish Invasions and Royal Genealogy", p. 106; and

apparently Old Norse derivation, however, we need not assume that the story of the hero's nautical arrival and departure stemmed from Northern sources of the Viking Age. Although the rite of ship-funeral was practised in the pagan Northlands during the period,[95] none of the surviving Scandinavian sources concerned with the Skjǫldungar present the dynasty's eponymous progenitor in this way.[96] The origin-legend of the hero from over the sea, moreover, appears to have incorporated aspects of ancient English fertility myth,[97] so was probably developed in an English dynastic context long before the ninth century. What degree of agreement there is between the West Saxon version of the legend and that in Beowulf, therefore, is probably a consequence of their ultimate derivation from a common Old English source, perhaps a genealogy maintained in verse.[98]

It appears thus that the question of the source of the poem's detailed concern with the Scyldings is not satisfied by the late ninth-century West Saxon dynastic claim to Danish ancestry. There is, however, one other possible Scylding forebear in a surviving Old English royal pedigree still to be considered, namely, Hrōðmund, who is listed in the pedigree of Ælfwald, king of East Anglia during the first half of the eighth century. The dynastic traditions of the pre-Viking East Anglian kingdom have already been noted as a potential source for the royal ship-funeral account of Scyld Scefing in Beowulf. In the following chapters I shall explore the possible relations between Beowulf and King Ælfwald's pedigree in detail.

Frank "Skaldic Verse and the Date of Beowulf", pp. 127–128). One might add that the extension could also reflect the claims of Wessex over other English kingdoms.

[95] Müller-Wille, "Boat-Graves in Northern Europe", fig. 10, p. 196.

[96] See Garmonsway and Simpson (ed. and tr.), Beowulf and its Analogues, pp. 118–123, for convenient translations of the sources in question. An indirect association with the sea may be inferred from Skjǫldr's marriage to the goddess Gefjon in Ynglinga saga (ch. 5), on which see Chadwick, The Origin of the English Nation, pp. 258–268; Ellis Davidson, Gods and Myths of Northern Europe, pp. 45, 113–114.

[97] On the hero's pre-Christian cult origins, including his connection with the deity Ing, see Chadwick, The Origin of the English Nation, pp. 274–296; Chambers, Widsith, pp. 66–79; Olrik, The Heroic Legends of Denmark, pp. 411–412, 416–421; Chambers, Introduction, pp. 68–86; Klaeber, pp. 121–124; Ellis Davidson, Gods and Myths of Northern Europe, pp. 104–105; Halsall, The Old English Rune Poem, pp. 146–147; and Fulk, "An Eddic Analogue to the Scyld Scefing Story".

[98] As Lapidge pointed out in the case of Æþelwulf's pedigree ("Beowulf, Aldhelm, the Liber Monstrorum and Wessex", pp. 187–188); see further the arguments of Fulk, "Dating Beowulf to the Viking Age", p. 342; and "An Eddic Analogue to the Scyld Scefing Story", p. 320.

CHAPTER FOUR

THE ROYAL NAME *HROÐMUND*

THE OCCURRENCE OF the royal name *Hroðmund* in both *Beowulf* and the pedigree of King Ælfwald of East Anglia has been noted by scholars before,[1] but has yet to receive detailed consideration. Let us first look at the Hroðmund listed as an East Anglian dynastic ancestor.

HROÐMUND IN KING ÆLFWALD'S PEDIGREE

The pedigree of King Ælfwald of East Anglia, who ruled *ca* 713–749, is contained in the Anglian collection of royal genealogies, the earliest surviving manuscript of which, the British Library, Cotton Vespasian B.vi, appears to date from the early ninth century.[2] His original fourteen-generation ancestral tally is reckoned there as follows:

1. Aelfwald alduulfing
2. Alduulf eðilricing
3. Eðilric ening
4. Eni tyttling
5. Tyttla wuffing
6. Wuffa wehing
7. Wehha wilhelmimg
8. Wilhelm hryping
9. Hryp hroðmunding
10. Hroðmund trygling
11. Trygil tyttmaning
12. Tyttman casering
13. Caser wodning
14. Woden.

As was noted in Chapter Three, Ælfwald's pedigree can be seen to form part of a sub-group of genealogies within the collection, the original

---

[1] Sarrazin, "Neue *Beowulf*-Studien"; Arnold, *Notes on Beowulf*, p. 43; and O'Loughlin "Sutton Hoo . . .", pp. 7–8.
[2] Dumville, "The Anglian Collection", p. 31; Ælfwald's pedigree is listed on folio 109ᵛ, col. 3.

compilation-date of which may have been as early as 725 or 726.³ As
Ælfwald appears to have ruled East Anglia from around 713 until his
death in 749,⁴ his pedigree can be seen thus to have been committed to
writing around the end of the first third of his reign. His interest in
literary endeavours is also indicated by the *Vita Sancti Guthlaci*, which, as
its author, one Felix, states in his Prologue, was written in East Anglia at
the behest of King Ælfwald, to whom it is dedicated.⁵ Felix addresses
Ælfwald here as one who 'rules *by right* over the realm of the East
Angles', which may be an implicit reference to his lord's royal pedigree.
That East Anglian royal genealogy had been committed to writing by
around the first quarter of the eighth century is also implied by Bede,
who quotes a section of the pedigree of Rædwald, king of East Anglia
during the early seventh century. Bede states that Rædwald was *filius
Tytili, cuius pater fuit Uuffa*, 'the son of Tytil, whose father was Wuffa'.⁶
The last two names here are listed in the same order in Ælfwald's pedigree, which suggests that both were compiled using the same East Anglian genealogical sources.

   Hrōðmund is listed as the tenth name on Ælfwald's ancestral tally, a
position well beyond the pedigree's horizon of historical credibility. The
name occurs there in exactly the same form as that borne by a Scylding
prince in *Beowulf*. As far as I am able to ascertain, apart from the place-
name *Rodmundes Dæn*, which occurs in the description of a Hampshire
estate boundary in a suspicious tenth-century charter,⁷ the only other
known Old English instance of this royal compound-name is that belonging to the son of Hroðgar in *Beowulf*. In keeping with the patterns of
name-giving found in early Germanic aristocracies, the front element
hrōð- occurs in the names of other members of the Danish royal family in
Beowulf, such as *Hrōðgār, Hrōþulf* or *Hrēðrīc*.⁸ It also occurs in the name of
the Geatish royal eponym *Hrēðel*. Schütte observed that the element *hrōð*
appears to be a "privilege of early kings".⁹ Although relatively prominent in *Beowulf*, it appears to be rare in attested Anglo-Saxon dynastic
epithets.¹⁰ One possible example, however, is the aforementioned East

---

3 Dumville, "The Anglian Collection, p. 40, note 2.
4 On the dates of Ælfwald's reign, see Stenton, "The East Anglian Kings of the Seventh
Century", p. 46.
5 Colgrave (ed.), *Felix's Life of St Guthlac*.
6 Bede *HE*, II, 15. Bede completed his great work in 731.
7 Searle, *Onomasticum Anglo-Saxonicum*, p. 303; Sawyer no. 427; the text of the charter is
printed by Earle, *A Handbook of Land-Charters and other Saxonic Documents*, pp. 355–360 –
Rodmundes Dæne appears on p. 357.
8 On the variation of elements of compound-names, see Woolf, *The Old Germanic
Principles of Name-Giving*, pp. 1–2.
9 Schütte, *Our Forefathers: the Gothonic Nations*, vol. 2, p. 348.
10 One instance, the non-royal, presumably female, *Hrothwaru*, appears in an apparently authentic charter concerning land at Withington, Gloucestershire, by Milred,

Anglian royal name *Rædwald*.[11] As this form is only known from Bede's Latin, its Old English form could have been **Hrǣðwald*, 'glorious ruler'.[12] If so, it would have been linked with the name *Hrōðmund* by back-variation. As both front- and back-variation appear to have been established principles of name-giving among the *Wuffingas* this would suggest that the latter could have been numbered as an East Anglian dynastic forebear as early as the beginning of the seventh century.[13]

Within Ælfwald's ancestral tally, the bearer of the name *Hrōðmund* is reckoned as the 'son' of *Trygil*. Yet deep into the prehistoric section of the pedigree as we are here, this filiation is more likely to be symbolic than chronographic in significance.[14] The fact that Hrōðmund's father in *Beowulf* has a different name thus does not rule out the possibility that this prince of Denmark may be somehow identifiable as an ancestor of King Ælfwald of East Anglia. That the name *Hrōðmund* is alliteratively paired with *Hryp* (these are in fact the only two names in Ælfwald's tally which alliterate on *hr-*) may in itself be significant, for such pairing is a characteristic form which would imply that the two could have been associated with an East Anglian dynastic foundation-legend. Pairs of founding-fathers with alliterating names, depicted as either brothers or as fathers and sons, appear to have been a distinctive convention in early Germanic royal tradition, the most well-known pair in Anglo-Saxon England being Hengest and Horsa.[15] Other Germanic legendary founder-pairs include *Ibor* and *Agio*, a pair of brothers who are said to have led the Langobard migration from Scandinavia;[16] and two Vandal royal pairs, *Ambri* and *Assi*,[17] and *Raos* and *Raptos*.[18] As early as the first century A.D., the Roman historian Tacitus described a Germanic folk called the *Naharvali* and their cult of twin deities, the *Alci*.[19] These twins were worshipped as young brothers, which led J. Turville-Petre to argue that the twinning convention we find in the genealogies may have had

Bishop of Worcester, written in Latin and dated 774 (Sawyer no. 1255). Another example could be the patronymic **Hrōðingas* on which the Essex *Roding* place-names may have been based.

[11] Bede, *HE*, II, 5, 12, 15.

[12] Alternatively, the first element of this name could have been OE *rǣd*, 'nimble', although this seems not to have been as royal a title as *hrōð*.

[13] Woolf, *The Old Germanic Principles of Name-Giving*, pp. 8–16.

[14] On symbolic filiation, see the discussion of the OE pedigree genre in Chapter Three, and the references cited there. For a discussion of the potential significance of the name *Trygil*, see Chapter Six.

[15] This pair is the main subject of J. Turville-Petre's study of the convention, "Hengest and Horsa".

[16] Bethmann and Waitz (ed.), *Scriptores Rerum Langobardicarum*, I, ii, iii.

[17] Bethmann and Waitz, *ibid.*, I, vii.

[18] Cary (ed. and tr.), *Dio Cassius: Historia Romanorum*, § lxxii.

[19] Robinson, R.P. , (ed. and tr.), *The Germania of Tacitus*, 43.

an ultimately religious origin.[20] Another Anglo-Saxon royal example is provided by the West Saxon founding-father and son pair, Cerdic and Cynric.[21] In the alliteratively paired Hroðmund and Hryp, therefore, we may have an instance of this twinning convention, assimilated, like Cerdic and Cynric, in the stereotypical 'father-son' form of the pedigree genre. If so, as the second name of the founder-pair is usually the more shadowy of the two,[22] the name Hryp here may have been no more than a suitably alliterating counterpart for Hroðmund. As J. Turville-Petre pointed out, the genealogical function of the pairing of ancestral names may have been partly "rhythmic . . . to authenticate by repetition, or to multiply names to a desired number".[23]

The name Hryp is itself etymologically problematic as it stands.[24] If it is an Old English personal name, it may be related to the first element of the Yorkshire place-name Ripon.[25] The same first element may also occur in the Derbyshire place-name Repton.[26] The form Hrype (or Hreope) in these place-names appears to be an otherwise unknown Old English folk-name. As Repton was a place of burial for some of the kings of Mercia in the eighth and ninth centuries,[27] the possibility arises that the name Hryp in Ælfwald's pedigree could have signalled East Anglian solidarity with Mercia. At least by 731, all the kingdoms south of the Humber were subject to King Æþelbald of Mercia, as we know from Bede's contemporary statement.[28] At about the same time, Felix, the author of Vita Sancti Guthlaci, implies that his lord Ælfwald was indeed subject to Æþelbald, but that the relationship between them was

---

20 Turville-Petre, "Hengest and Horsa", pp. 274–276.
21 This pair is referred to in the Chronicle (Manuscripts A and E, s.a. 495, 508, 527, 530 and 534). They are also listed in the version of the West Saxon royal pedigree preserved in the Anglian collection, that of King Ine (688–726), where their legend appears to be interwoven with that of another West Saxon founding-figure, Ceawlin. Ceawlin is assimilated there as a son of Cerdic, while Cynric is listed as his grandson. On the ideological significance of these West Saxon foundation-legends, see Yorke, "The Jutes of Hampshire and Wight and the origins of Wessex".
22 Myres noted that Cynric is "not a figure in whom historians have felt much confidence" (The English Settlements, p. 153). Similarly, Sims-Williams observed that Hengest's legendary brother, Horsa, referred to in the Chronicle (Manuscripts A and E, s.a. 449, 455), "could be an accretion, either taken from an independent tradition or simply invented by storytellers to provide Hengest with a similarly named companion-in-arms (compare Romulus and Remus, or Cerdic and Cynric)" ("The Settlement of England . . .", p. 23).
23 J. Turville-Petre, "On Ynglingatal", p. 65.
24 As Redin noted, Studies in Uncompounded Personal Names in England, p. 31.
25 Smith (ed.), The Place-Names of the West Riding of Yorkshire, vol. 5, p. 165.
26 K. Cameron (ed.), The Place-Names of Derbyshire, vol. 3, p. 653.
27 The Chronicle (Manuscripts A, D, E and F s.a. 755) states that King Æþelbald (716–757) was buried there; two other Mercian kings, Wiglaf (827–840) and his grandson, St Wihstan (850), are also known to have been given a crypt-burial at Repton.
28 Bede, HE, V, 23.

friendly.[29] There is nothing to suggest that relations between East Anglia and Mercia were radically different in 725 or 726, the possible date of compilation for Ælfwald's pedigree. Perhaps the cult of St Guthlac helped to provide a unifying focus for the continuity of goodwill between East Anglia and Mercia, at least during the second quarter of the eighth century. The presence of the name *Hryp* in Ælfwald's pedigree, therefore, if significant, could have related to some aspect of the common background of the two kingdoms indicated by some sources.[30]

The suggestion is then that the name *Hroðmund* in King Ælfwald's pedigree may have been regarded as being associated with an East Anglian dynastic origin-legend, at least at the time of the compilation of Ælfwald's fourteen-name pedigree, if not earlier. Let us now examine the place of Hroðmund the Scylding *æþeling* in *Beowulf*. As will become clear, although he may seem a minor figure in *Beowulf*, he can be seen to be more central a character than either Offa or Scyld.

HROÐMUND IN *BEOWULF*

Hroðmund is named just once in *Beowulf*, where he is mentioned together with his brother, Hreðric (l.1189[a]). The order of their names here, *Hreðrīc 7 Hroðmund*, might suggest that Hroðmund is the younger of the two. They are the young sons of the venerable Hroðgar, and are further referred to, but not named, in line 2013.[31]

It is Hreðric who appears to be identifiable in Scandinavian sources. He is referred to in the late twelfth-century *Gesta Danorum* of Saxo Grammaticus,[32] where two apparently unconnected figures named *Røricus* are mentioned (Book 2, § 62, and 3, §§ 82–85), *Røricus* being a Latinized philological equivalent of OE *Hreðrīc*. Malone has argued – not unconvincingly – that these two figures both derive from traditions concerning the same Scylding prince.[33] Saxo's first *Røricus* is named in his version of the *Bjarkamál* as 'Rørik, son of the avaricious Bøk' (Book 2, § 62). The father's name here, *Bøki avari*, seems satisfactorily explicable as a consequence of the misconstrual of one of Hreðric's Old Norse epithets,

---

29 Colgrave, *Felix's Life of St Guthlac*, pp. 16, 176.

30 Martin, "The *Iclingas*"; Davies, "Annals and the Origin of Mercia", pp. 22–24. and Rumble, " 'Hrepingas' Reconsidered", pp. 170–171.

31 There is one other reference to Hreðric in the poem (l.1836[a]), which appears to require emendation (ms. *hreþrinc*). Emendation to the personal name *Hreðrīc* was first proposed by Grundtvig and has been followed by all editors (see Birte Kelly, "The Formative Stages of *Beowulf* Textual Scholarship: part II", p. 246).

32 Olrik and Raeder (ed.), *Saxonis Gesta Danorum*.

33 Malone, "Hrethric", pp. 274–286.

hnøggvanbaugi, "ring-stingy", a version of which seems likely to have appeared in the lost text of the *Bjarkamál* which Saxo was presumably following. Such an epithet is to be found in a twelfth-century Icelandic edition of the pedigree of the *Skjǫldungar* in *Langfeðgatal*,[34] which lists a *Hrærekr Hnauggvanbaugi* as successor to *Rolfr Kraki*. It seems likely, therefore, that Saxo misunderstood the form *baug* as a personal name.[35] Saxo's second *Røricus* has a related title, for he is named *Røricus Slyngebond*, 'ring-slinger' (Book 3, §§ 82–85).[36] He also appears as one of the successors of the famous Hrólfr, and is described as a son of the latter by another late twelfth-century Danish historian, Sven Aageson, and as his kinsman in *Skjǫldunga saga*.[37]

A Scylding prince with a name corresponding to OE *Hrōðmund*, however, does not seem to be identifiable in surviving Northern traditions of the family. A single remote echo could be the *Hrómundr harði* who is listed as the first of the twelve champions of Hrólfr in the probably fourteenth-century *Hrólfs saga kraka*, although no kindred relations are given and he appears nowhere else. Because nowhere in Northern sources do we have a brother of Hreðric such as we find in *Beowulf*, we may wonder if Hroðmund is no more than a convention intended to complement the youthful status of Hreðric.[39] As we have seen, there does seem to be a convention in heroic legend for princes to appear in pairs, often with alliterating names. Yet as the form of the name *Hrōðmund* implies that its bearer was part of Old English Scylding tradition at an early stage of development,[40] and given the indications that some aspects of the Scylding story in *Beowulf* may be based in history,[41] it is not unreasonable to regard Hroðmund in *Beowulf* as a proto-historical figure who came to be forgotten in later Scandinavian tradition.[42]

---

[34] Kålund (ed.), *Alfræði Íslenzk*, vol. 3.
[35] As was pointed out by Olrik, *The Heroic Legends of Denmark*, pp. 68–70, 73–74; and Malone, "Hrethric", p. 275. Jones described this as "one of Saxo's more obvious muddles" (*Kings, Beasts and Heroes*, p. 134); see also Ellis Davidson, *Saxo Grammaticus*, vol. 2, p. 48, note 64.
[36] Saxo tells the story of how this name was earned. Other versions of this story appear elsewhere in Northern sources; some Old Icelandic genealogies, for example, list a *Hrærekr* with the epithet *slaungvanbaugi*, 'ring-slinger'; see Garmonsway and Simpson (ed. and tr.), *Beowulf and its Analogues*, pp. 124–125, 206–211.
[37] Sven Aageson, *A Brief History of the Kings of Denmark*, ch. 1; *Skjǫldunga saga*, ch.14; see Garmonsway and Simpson (ed. and tr.), *Beowulf and its Analogues*, p. 207.
[38] Slay (ed.), *Hrólfs saga kraka*, ch. 49; Garmonsway and Simpson (ed. and tr.), *Beowulf and its Analogues*, p. 198.
[39] As Olrik (*The Heroic Legends of Denmark*, pp. 62–63) and Chambers (*Introduction*, p. 27) have also noted, though neither considered it a serious possibility.
[40] As with other names borne by the Scyldings in *Beowulf*; see the discussion of these forms in Chapter One.
[41] See the discussion of the historical horizon of the poem in Chapter Two.
[42] Olrik reached a not dissimilar view: "We may . . . take him to be a historic personage who was afterwards lost from poetic tradition" (*The Heroic Legends of Denmark*, p. 62). A

If we now look closely at the part Hroðmund plays in *Beowulf*, we shall see that both he and his brother are focal figures in the poem's depiction of the Danish royal family. As Malone argued in 1927, Hreðric and Hroðmund "are central and unifying figures in an episode so fraught with pity and terror that even now, after twelve centuries, we read and are deeply moved".[43] This episode is worth examining closely.

The episode in question occupies Fits XV–XVIII of the manuscript (ll.991–1250). It describes the great feast in the hall of Heorot held to celebrate Beowulf's victory over Grendel. The scene is jubilant, as we might expect after the defeat of the murderous *scucca* who had haunted Heorot for so long:

> Ne gefrægen ic þā mǣgþe mā̆ran weorode
> ymb hyra sincgyfan sēl gebǣran.
> Bugon þā tō bence blǣdāgande,
> fylle gefǣgon; fægere geþǣgon
> medoful manig mā̆gas þā̆ra
> swīðhicgende on sele þām hēan,
> Hrōðgar 7 Hrōþulf. Heorot innan wæs
> frēondum āfylled; nalles fācenstafas
> Þēod-Scyldingas þenden fremedon.

> 'I have never heard of a folk, of a greater troop, bearing themselves better around their treasure-giver. The renowned ones then sat down at the bench and rejoiced at the feast; Hroðgar and Hroþulf, those bold-minded kinsmen, handsomely partook of many a full mead-cup in that high hall. Heorot was filled within with friends; not at all did the *Þeod-Scyldingas* then frame *facenstafas*' (ll.1011–1019).[44]

A close reading of this description of harmony among the Scyldings within Heorot reveals that it is underpinned by patterns of alliteration: *mā̆gas*, 'kinsmen' (l.1015[b]), are united over *medoful manig*, 'many a full mead-cup' (l.1015[a]), *swīðhicgende on sele þām hēan*, 'bold-minded in that high hall' (l.1016). At the same time, these alliteratively collocated words are lexically congruous, a stylistic device creating an effect which may be reckoned to be consistent with what an Old English audience might have expected to be part of the conventional poetic representation of so ideal a heroic scene as this victory-feast. It was Randolph Quirk who first drew scholarly attention to the presence and function of these collocations in *Beowulf*. He argued that

possible explanation for the absence of Hroðmund in Northern sources will be advanced below.

43 Malone, "Hrethric", p. 268.
44 On the term *facenstafas*, see below.

an expectation of the congruous and complementary, expressed through recurrent collocations, is built into the poetic system of Old English, and . . . that this is close to the starting point in estimating the original audience's pleasurable experience . . . There is evidently a prime satisfaction in the propriety of like belonging with like, of traditional correspondences being observed.[45]

The use of this device is also observable, for example, in the very opening lines of *Beowulf*, where the collocation of *þeodcyning*, 'folk-king' (1.2ᵃ), with *þrym(m)*, 'renown' (1.2ᵇ), and of *æþeling* 'noble' (1.3ᵃ), with *ellen*, 'courage' (1.3ᵇ), sets up the required heroic tone. The use of the same device in the description of the Scyldings at the feast in Heorot (ll.1015–1016) is similarly effective, the heroic ideal being "enshrined in the metrical and lexical system", as Quirk put it.[46] Line 1017 maintains this alliterative and lexical pattern by emphasising the unity of Hroðgar and Hroþulf together in Heorot. Hroþulf is Hroðgar's nephew, as we learn later, when the two are described as *suhtergefæderan*, 'uncle and nephew' (1.1164ᵃ). In Northern sources concerned with the *Skjǫldungar*,[47] Hroþulf (ON *Hrólfr*) is said to be the son of Hroðgar's younger brother Halga (ON *Helgi*), although he seems to be older than his cousins, Hreðric and Hroðmund, as we shall see.

Line 1018 of the episode suddenly departs from this pattern of alliterative collocations by metrically linking *frēondum*, 'friends' (1.1018ᵃ), with the lexically incongruous *fācenstafas* (1.1018ᵇ). The latter compound, which only occurs in *Beowulf*, is usually translated as 'deceit', 'treachery', or 'evil'. Yet these are the same terms used to translate the uncompounded form, *fācen*, so we may wonder if a specific kind of *fācen* is implied by the compound *fācenstafas*. The plural of the second element, *stæf*, 'staff', can also mean 'letter' or 'writing', a meaning probably deriving from the use of wooden staves with smoothed sides for the transmission of runic messages; hence OE *rūnstæf*, 'runic letter'.[48] The compound *fācenstafas* could then involve the malevolent use of runes, as with the equivalent Old Norse compound, *feiknstafir*, one of the meanings of which is 'baleful runes'.[49] The alliterative collocation of *frēondum* (1.1018ᵃ) with *fācenstafas* (1.1018ᵇ) thus subverts the patterns of

---

45 Quirk, "Poetic Language and Old English Metre", p. 153. Quirk's work utilised the poetic theory of Jakobson ("Closing Statement: Linguistics and Poetics"). The central theoretical point here is that the equivalence in sound which is produced by parallelism, such as alliteration, prompts the possibility of a semantic relation. For an attempt at exploring the text of *Beowulf* in terms of Quirk's pioneering approach, see Reinhard, *On the Semantic Relevance of the Alliterative Collocations in Beowulf*.
46 Quirk, *ibid.*, p. 153.
47 For references to these sources see the section on the Danes in Chapter Two of this study.
48 On *runstafas*, see Page, *An Introduction to English Runes*, pp. 96–118.
49 As Klaeber noted in his glossary (*s.v. fācenstafas*).

lexically congruous collocations to describe the victory-feast in Heorot in lines 1013, 1015, 1016 and 1017. In other words, the bright harmony of the feast is counterpointed by a lexical incongruity stressed by the metre. This counterpoint seems to anticipate the culminating statement of the passage: *nalles facenstafas / Þeod-Scyldingas þenden fremedon*, 'not at all did the Folk-Scyldings *then* frame *facenstafas*' (ll.1018ᵇ–1019). This statement, with its qualifying temporal adverb *þenden* (l.1019ᵇ), appears to forebode some future intrigue among the *Þeod-Scyldingas*. We may infer from this that the current show of harmony among the leading members of the Danish royal family is destined *not* to be permanent.

The last two lines of the passage (ll.1018–1019) thus seem to sound an ironic note of latent discord among those present at the victory-feast in Heorot. As these lines immediately follow the first occurrence in *Beowulf* of the name *Hroþulf* (l.1017ᵃ), we may suspect its bearer to be implicated as a potential source of this latent discord.[50] This implication is reinforced later in the episode by another statement implying that the current solidarity of Hroðgar and Hroþulf is merely temporary:

> þær þa godan twegen
> sæton suhtergefæderan;   þa gyt wæs hiera sib ætgædere,
> æghwylc oðrum trywe.

'There the two good ones sat, uncle and nephew; there yet was their sibship united, each was to the other true' (ll.1163ᵇ–1165ᵃ).

Again, the use of a temporal adverb – in this case *gyt* (l.1164ᵇ) – implies that the existing *sib*, 'sibship' (l.1164ᵇ) between the *suhtergefæderan*, 'uncle and nephew' (l.1164ᵃ), is to be of limited duration only.[51] This passage thus also imbues the current show of harmony between the *þa godan twegen*, namely, Hroðgar and Hroþulf, with some irony.

Remarkably, the same implication also arises from the reference to Hroðgar and Hroþulf in *Widsith*:

> Hroþwulf ond Hroðgar   heoldon lengest
> sibbe ætsomme   suhtorfæderan
> syþþan hy forwræcon   Wicinga cynn
> ond Ingeldes   ord forbigdan
> forheowan æt Heorote   Heaðobeardna þrym.

'Hroþwulf and Hroðgar, uncle and nephew, had kept sibship together for a very long time, when they drove off the Viking

[50] That Hroþulf is named for the first time in the poem here is seen by many scholars as being significant. Irving, for example, has suggested that the naming of Hroþulf at this point "would lack purpose if the audience did not know of later violence associated with Hroþulf" (*A Reading of Beowulf*, p. 133).
[51] So Quirk also pointed out, "Poetic Language and Old English Metre", p. 167.

folk and humbled Ingeld's vanguard, hewing down at Heorot
the Heaðobard force' (ll.45–49).[52]

Yet again, as in the *Beowulf* passages (ll.1018b–1019; 1163b–1165a) cited
above, it is the use of a temporal adverb – here, *lengest*, 'for a very long
time' (l.45b) – which implies that the *sib* of the same *suhterfæderan* is not
to remain harmonious *æt Heorote* in perpetuity. In both poems, then, a
temporal adverb is deployed which has precisely the same effect in
implying that the *sib*, 'sibship' (*Widsith*, l.46a; *Beowulf*, l.1164b), between
the *suhterfæderan*, 'uncle and nephew' (*Widsith*, l.46b; *Beowulf*, l.1164a)
was not destined to last. The compound *suhterfæderan*, formed from two
substantives, is especially rare, occurring *only* in these passages from
Beowulf and *Widsith* in the entire corpus of Germanic poetry.[53] That references to the same two *Þeod-Scyldingas* and the same royal hall – even
using the same vocabulary and syntax – should appear in two independent Old English poetic sources points to the existence of an established Old English verse tradition concerned with the Scyldings which
told of an eventual schism within the dynasty. It would have been
through such a source that the intended audience of *Beowulf* would have
acquired the competence to respond to such allusions. Both *Beowulf* and
Widsith seem to imply knowledge of later conflict between Hroðgar's
side of the family and that of Hroþulf.[54] The implication seems to be that
the 'very long time' of sibship between Hroþulf and Hroðgar referred to
in *Widsith* (l.45b) coincides with their relationship of apparent solidarity
as it is presented in *Beowulf*, and that the sundering of their sibship is to
take place at some point after the fall of *Ingeldes ord*.[55]

If we also consider surviving Northern sources concerned with the
Scyldings (ON *Skjǫldungar*), we find that the allusions to future conflict
between Hroðulf and Hroðgar's branch of the dynasty which seem to
arise from the two Old English poems are amplified sharply, particularly
by a passage in the Saxo's twelfth-century Latin paraphrase of the *Bjarkamál*.[56] In this source, it is clearly stated that *Rolf* (Hroþulf) killed *Rørik*
(Hreðric):

---

[52] I follow Deutschbein in translating the main verbal clause in this passage, *heoldon
lengest*, in the pluperfect tense ("Beowulf der Gautenkönig", p. 296). The pluperfect
tense in OE is theoretically signalled by an auxiliary construction of the past preterite of
habban and the participle of the required verb, but actually examples of this are rare in
OE poetry. The past preterite, however, can be construed as pluperfect, especially when
it is accompanied by a temporal adverb, as it is here.
[53] Carr, *Nominal Compounds in Germanic*, pp. 40–41.
[54] In Chambers's words, "equally with the poet of *Widsith*, the poet of *Beowulf* cannot
mention Hroþulf and Hroðgar together without foreboding evil" (*Widsith*, p. 83).
[55] On the possible sequence of events implied here, see Malone, "Hrethric"; and "The
Tale of Ingeld".
[56] Saxo, *Gesta Danorum*, Book 2, § 62. The *Bjarkamál* itself is certainly older, and may
have originated in the tenth century, or earlier, as was noted in Chapter Two.

[Rolf] . . . qui natum Bøki Røricum strauit auari,
Implicuitque uirum leto uirtute carentem;
'[Rolf] . . . who laid low Røric, son of the avaricious Bøk, killed the man
who lacked virtue'.[57]

This statement is widely regarded as an allusion to Hroþulf's killing of
Hreðric in the context of an internecine struggle for the Danish throne
following the death of Hroðgar.[58] If this tragic event was also told of in
the Old English tradition of the Scyldings, it would account for the
suspicions which *Beowulf* seems to focus on the shadowy Hroþulf.

Let us return now to *Beowulf*. Following the dramatic allusions to future
family discord in lines 1018–1019, the narrative continues with an account of Hroðgar's ceremonial giving of victory-gifts to Beowulf and his
men (ll.1020–1054). Implicit in this account may be a further allusion to a
tale of tragic internecine conflict among the Scyldings. The gifts include a
banner (ll.1021^a, 1022^a), a helm, a mailcoat, and a sword (ll.1022^b–1023).
In Beowulf's later report of his adventures in *Scedeland* to his lord,
Hygelac, we learn the history of these gifts:

> "Mē ðis hildesceorp   Hrōðgār sealde,
> snotra fengel;   sume worde hēt,
> þæt ic his ærest ðē   ēst gesægde;
> cwæð þæt hyt hæfde   Hiorogār cyning,
> lēod Scyldunga   lange hwīle;
> nō ðy ær suna sīnum   syllan wolde,
> hwatum Heorowearde,   þēah hē him hold wære,
> breostgewædu. . . ."

> ' "Hroðgar, the wise king, gave me this war-gear; in one speech
> he ordered that I should tell you first about his gift; he said that
> King Heorogar, the Scylding chief, had possessed it for a long
> while; even so, he would sooner not give the body-armour to his
> son, to brave Heoroweard, loyal to him though he was . . ." '
> (ll.2155–2162^a).

It is not clear why the war-gear which had once belonged to Heorogar

---

[57] On this reference to Hreðric as "Rørik, son of the avaricious Bøk", see the note earlier
in this chapter.
[58] See Olrik, *The Heroic Legends of Denmark*, pp. 68–74; Malone, "Hrethric", pp. 275–282;
Chambers, *Introduction*, pp. 25–27. For Klaeber, lines 1018–1019 of *Beowulf* were, in the
light of Saxo's reference, "unquestionably an allusion to Hroþulf's treachery in later
times" (p. 169, note to ll.1018–1019). Sisam (*The Structure of Beowulf*, pp. 35, 81) and
Morgan ("The Treachery of Hrothulf", pp. 25–26) have argued against this widely held
view on strictly limited textual grounds. Yet both ignore the potentially subversive
significance of the incongruous alliterative collocation in line 1018, which seems to
trigger the initial sense of irony.

had not been given to his son. Yet whatever the reason may have been, it may be significant that the description of this gear provides the opportunity for the one and only reference to Heoroweard in *Beowulf*. He is said here to be both *hwæt*, 'brave' (1.2161ª), and loyal (1.2161ᵇ), which suggests that it was not through lack of honour that he did not receive the war-gear once owned by his father. In Scandinavian sources, Heoroweard is identifiable as *Hjǫrvarðr*,[59] who brought about the eventual downfall of Hrólfr (Hroþulf), at his own royal hall at Lejre, despite the valiant last stand of the latter's followers.[60] This seems to have been one of the most famous battles in Northern heroic legend, for it inspired the composition of the *Bjarkamál* and is celebrated in *Hrólfs saga kraka* (chs 32–34) and *Skjǫldunga saga* (chs 12–13).[61] Northern sources suggest then that Heoroweard was also to become a major figure in Scylding family legend. So although he is not actually named in the episode of the victory-feast in *Beowulf*, he may be implicitly invoked through the later descriptions of his father's war-gear. The gifts which Hroðgar gives to Beowulf may also allude thus to knowledge of subsequent internecine strife among the Scyldings. For Whitelock, there was no question of this:

> the poet . . . has only to mention Heoroweard's name – and he goes out of his way to do so – and the whole of the final act of the Scylding drama would leap into his audience's minds, one of the most famous events in northern story, . . . namely the slaying of Hrothulf by his cousin Heoroweard.[62]

Following the account of Hroðgar's ceremonial gift-giving, a further indication that the current solidarity of the *Þeod-Scyldingas* is in potential jeopardy emerges from the structural parallel which we appear to have between the situation in Heorot and that in the Frisian royal hall in the ensuing song of the *Frēswæl* by *Hroðgares scop* (ll.1071–1159).[63] For this tale of past tragedy concerning Scylding forebears appears to have been intended as a deliberate contrast to the present, apparently peaceful, situation in Heorot. It may thus anticipate the possibility of a tragic future. The focal figure in the song of the *Frēswæl* is the Danish princess Hildeburh, *Hōces dohtor* (1.1076ᵇ), sister of the *Hnæf Scyldinga* (1.1069ᵇ)

[59] Lind, *Norsk-isländska dopnamn, s.v. Hjǫrvarðr*.
[60] Brodeur thought it probable that the allusion to the burning of Heorot in *Beowulf* (ll.82ᵇ–83ª) could refer to the great battle there between Hroþulf (*Hrólfr*) and Heoroweard (*Hjǫrvarðr*), rather than to that between the Danes and Heaðobards, as most scholars assume (*The Art of Beowulf*, p. 77, note 5).
[61] It is also described in the *Chronicon Lethrense* (ch.7), and in the *Annales Ryenses*; see Garmonsway and Simpson (ed. and tr.), *Beowulf and its Analogues*, pp. 156–177, 179–204, 206.
[62] Whitelock, *The Audience of Beowulf*, p. 36.
[63] *Frēswæl* is the name given to the story in *Beowulf* (1.1070ª), as Tolkien pointed out in his study of its relation to the fragmentary *Finnsburh* (*Finn and Hengest*, pp. 9, 53).

and wife of the Frisian king, Finn Folcwalding. Her marriage is clearly of importance to the whole tale in that it implies an allegiance between Danes and Frisians.[64] Her tragedy is that the marriage fails because of circumstances beyond her control:

> unsynnum wearð
> beloren lēofum   æt þām lindplegan
> bearnum 7 brōðrum;   hīe on gebyrd hruron
> gāre wunde;   þæt wæs geōmuru ides!
> Nalles hōlinga   Hōces dohtor
> meotodsceaft bemearn,   syþðan morgen cōm,
> ðā hēo under swegle   gesēon meahte
> morþorbealo māga,   þær hē[o] ǣr mǣste hēold
> worolde wynne.

'Guiltless she was, yet bereft of her dear ones, her child and brother, at the shield-play; they were fated to fall, wounded by the spear: she was a tragic lady! Not without cause did the daughter of Hoc bewail destiny's decree, for when morning came, she could then see the baleful slaughter of her kin beneath the heavens, where before she had enjoyed the greatest of earthly bliss' (ll.1072b–1080a).

It appears that tension between the rival warriors of Finn and Hnæf precipitate a bitter fight in the Frisian royal hall, in which both Hildeburh's son and brother, Hnæf, are killed. Following a tactical stalemate, the Frisian king and the leader of the surviving Danes, Hengest, agree to terms (ll.1080b–1106). A vivid description of the cremation of Hnæf and his sister's son follows (ll.1107–1124). This grimly realistic account, part of which (ll.1119–1124a) was cited in Chapter Two of this study, underlines the tragic failure of the marriage-alliance of Hildeburh and Finn.[65]

> Hēt ðā Hildeburh   æt Hnæfes āde
> hire selfre sunu   sweoloðe befæstan,
> bānfatu bærnan, 7 on bǣl dôn
> ēame on eaxle.

'At Hnæf's pyre, Hildeburh then ordered her own son to be entrusted to the flames and his body was placed on the fire and burnt, shoulder-to-shoulder with his uncle' (ll.1114–1117a).

After a difficult winter for Hengest (ll.1125–1136a), fighting breaks out

---

[64] As Tolkien observed, *Finn and Hengest*, p. 53; for a full reconstruction of these events, see Tolkien, *ibid.*, pp. 159–162.
[65] As Glosecki observed, ideally, "favourable relations between uncle and uterine nephew reaffirm the existing peace-treaty" ("The Boar's Helmet in *Beowulf*, p. 291).

again (ll.1136ᵇ–1145), leading to the bloody slaying of Finn (ll.1146–1153), *æt his selfes hām*, 'in his own home' (l.1147ᵇ).

> Ðā wæs heal *r*oden,
> fēonda fēorum,   swilce Fin slægen,
> cyning on corþre,   7 sēo cwēn numen.

'Then the hall was reddened with the life-blood of foes, as Finn was slain, the king with his company, and the queen carried off' (ll.1151ᵇ–1153).

The Frisian royal hall is then plundered (ll.1154–1157ᵃ) and the lone figure of Hildeburh, homeless and bereft of her husband, son, and brother, is ferried back to the land of the Danes (ll.1157ᵇ–1159ᵃ).

With Queen Hildeburh's sad journey, this tale of past tragedy ends and we return to the contrastingly merry din of the feast in Heorot for the entry of the Scylding queen, Wealhþeow, the mother of Hreðric and Hroðmund.

> Lēoð wæs āsungen,
> glēomannes gyd.   Gamen eft āstāh,
> beorhtode bencswēg,   byrelas sealdon
> wīn of wunderfatum. Þā cwōm Wealhþēo forð
> gān under gyldnum bēage   þær þā gōdan twēgen
> sǣton suhtergefæderan;   þā gȳt wæs hiera sib ætgædere,
> ǣghwylc ōðrum trȳwe.   Swylce þǣr *Un*ferþ þyle
> æt fōtum sæt frēan Scyldinga;   gehwylc hiora his ferhþe
>   trēowde,
> þæt hē hæfde mōd micel,   þēah þe hē his māgum nǣre
> ārfæst æt ecga gelācum.

'Sung was the lay, the singer's tale. The mirth arose again, and the bench-din rang out as the cup-bearers served wine from wondrous vessels. Then Wealhþeow came forth, golden-crowned, to go to where the two good ones sat, uncle and nephew; there yet was their sibship united, each was to the other true. Also there sat *Un*ferþ the *þyle* at the feet of the Scylding lord; they each trusted his spirit, and that he had great courage, though in battle he had not been honourable to his own kin' (ll.1159ᵇ–1168ᵃ).

Although Wealhþeow has already been introduced once in *Beowulf* (ll.612ᵇ–642), the narrative juxtaposition of the two queens here prompts the possibility that a deliberate parallel is intended between the fate of Hildeburh in the *Frēswæl* and that of Wealhþeow in the immediately ensuing scene in Heorot. It is as if the sudden shift of Hildeburh's emotional state from peace to anguish (ll.1076–1080ᵃ) implies that the same *edwenden*, 'reversal', could be destined for Wealhþeow. As Malone pointed out, "the tragedy of the one reminds us of the tragedy of the other".[66]

As we have seen, the possibility of future internal strife in the Scylding royal hall has already been foreshadowed. The story of battle in the Frisian royal hall, with its themes of oathbreaking and the violent sundering of sibship, in spite of an outward show of solidarity, only increases the explosive potential within Heorot. The threatened sibship of Hroðgar and Hroþulf appears to be almost explicit in lines 1164–1165a.[67] As was noted in the discussion above of lines 1018a–1019, this is the second time that a temporal adverb construction is used in the episode to similarly imply that the current solidarity of the *suhtergefæderan* is destined not to last. The half-line *æghwylc ōðrum trȳwe*, 'each was to the other true' (1.1165a), emphasizes the mutual responsibilities involved in the maintenance of trust and peace between them. Yet the alliterative collocation of the first two words of this half-line with the name Unferþ (1.1165b), also implicates Hroðgar's *þyle* in maintaining this responsibility.

Although this name is spelt consistently throughout the manuscript as *Hunferð*, all editors seem to agree – on metrical grounds in every instance (ll.499a, 530b, 1165b and 1488a) – that it should be emended to Unferð.[68] Unferð is respected in the poem for his wisdom and courage (ll.589b, 1167a, 1489b). His special position at Hroðgar's feet, alluded to twice (ll.500, 1166a), signals his authority, as does his challenging exchange with Beowulf upon the latter's arrival in Heorot (ll.499–606).[69] Unferð is presented here as being loyal to both Hroðgar and Hroþulf: *gehwylc hiora*

---

[66] Malone, "Hrethric", pp. 268–269. This parallel has also been noted by Lawrence, *Beowulf and Epic Tradition*, pp. 126–127; Whitelock, *The Audience of Beowulf*, pp. 35–36; Brodeur, *The Art of Beowulf*, p. 141; and Shippey (*Old English Verse*, pp. 21–22. The suggested parallel does not appear to have been taken into account by Sisam (*The Structure of Beowulf*, p. 82) or Morgan ("The Treachery of Hrothulf", pp. 28–29, 34–35) in their excessively cautious comments on this episode.

[67] The abrupt change to hypermetric half-lines (ll.1164–1168) may also signal a deliberate increase in emotional intensity, as Nist pointed out (*The Structure and Texture of Beowulf*, p. 108). Even if Kiernan's proposed re-editing of these lines was acceptable (*Beowulf and the Beowulf Manuscript*, pp. 190–191), whereby three lines are each given an additional half-line (ll.1163, 1164 and 1168), this remains a metrically unusual section, producing a similarly intensifying effect.

[68] Kelly, "The Formative Stages of *Beowulf* Textual Scholarship: part II, pp. 243, 244, 246. Vaughan, however, has made a good case for accepting the manuscript reading by showing that the written form of a name with an initial *H* was not always dependent on its spoken form ("A Reconsideration of 'Unferð' ", pp. 40–45). For example, the personal name *Holofernes* in the poem *Judith* (which follows *Beowulf* in the Nowell Codex) is also written with an initial *H* and yet, like *Hunferð* in *Beowulf*, appears to consistently alliterate with a vowel (Vaughan, *ibid.*, pp. 40–41). There is, moreover, evidence that the name *Hunferð* was in use in England as early as the eighth century (Vaughan, *ibid.*, pp. 42–45). See further Scragg, "Initial *H* in Old English"; and Fulk, "Unferth and His Name".

[69] On this, the positive side of his character, see Hollowell, "Unferð the *þyle* in *Beowulf*". For a negative view, see Rosier, "Design for Treachery: the Unferð Intrigue".

his ferhþe trēowde, 'they each trusted his spirit' (l.1166ᵇ). Yet there seems to be something odd about the intimacy of the three men as it is depicted here.[70] We are immediately reminded of *Unferð*'s reputation for dishonour: . . . *hē his māgum nǣre / ārfǣst æt ecga gelācum*, 'he had not been honourable to his kin at the clashing of swords' (ll.1167ᵇ–1168ᵃ). Clearly, there is some notoriety associated with this deed which recalls the earlier condemnation of the character of *Unferð* by Beowulf: *". . . ðu þīnum brōðrum tō banan wurde, / hēafodmǣgum"*, ' ". . . but you were the bane of your brothers, your leading kinsmen" ' (ll.587–588ᵃ). The reiteration of the darker side of his character invites the suspicion that, despite the respect shown for him elsewhere in the poem, he may have been regarded as a potential threat to the sibship of the *Scyldingas*. Certainly, his status as a fratricide associates him with the curse of Cain, used in *Beowulf* to explain Grendel's malevolence in Heorot, as we are reminded explicitly with the coming of Grendel's mother (ll.1258ᵇ–1267ᵃ).[71]

Unferð's identification as a latently threatening figure may also be inferred from other aspects of his character in *Beowulf*. During his earlier exchange with the hero of the poem, he is said to have *onband beadurūne*, 'unbound the battle-rune' (l.501ᵃ), a phrase unique in Old English. If it refers to some sort of runic magic, it may connect *Unferð* with the malevolent use of runes which seems implicit in the ominously positioned term *fācenstafas* (l.1018ᵇ) which was noted earlier in this chapter. As the Scylding *þyle*, an office which appears to have been associated with the Old English god *Woden*, he may well have possessed knowledge of runic lore.[72] Woden was known in Old Norse as *Óðinn* and he is referred to twice in the ON poem *Hávamál* (strophes 80 and 142) as *fimbulþulr*, 'mighty *þulr*'.[73] Strophe 142 of *Hávamál* refers to runic counselling staves, the use of which is apparently initiated by the *fimbulþulr* himself. If so, the reputation of the divine *fimbulþulr* for runic wisdom may denote one of the main functions of the mortal *þulr*.[74] The Wodenic OE *þyle* may also have been regarded as some sort of arbiter of kingship, a function which may relate to the fact that descent from Woden was deemed a necessary prerequisite to any claim to kingship, as almost all Old English royal pedigrees show.[75] A consideration of the ON *þulr* suggests that the OE *þyle* may have been both the custodian and teacher of the knowledge

---

[70] We may recall, as Irving put it, how "the Finn story has shown us that the outward appearances of such a scene are not to be trusted" (*A Reading of Beowulf*, p. 138).

[71] See Hughes, "Beowulf, Unferð and Hrunting: an Interpretation", pp. 390–393.

[72] See, for example, Clarke, "The Office of *Þyle* in *Beowulf*"; Baird, "Unferð the *Þyle*"; and Hollowell, "Unferð the *þyle* in *Beowulf*.

[73] Neckel (ed.), *Edda*, pp. 29, 41.

[74] See Haugen, "The *Edda* as Ritual: Odin and his Masks"; and Hollowell, "Unferð the þyle in *Beowulf*", p. 244.

[75] The name seems to have been "a means of defining royalty", as Miller noted, "Bede's Use of Gildas", p. 254, note 1.

required by claimants to the throne.[76] Is so, we would have further reasons to suspect the involvement of *Unferð* the *þyle* in any question over the Scylding succession.

Ominous doubts thus seem woven into the background as our attention returns to the dignified figure of Wealhþeow approaching Heorot's high seat. With all due formality, she presents a full drinking vessel to her royal husband Hroðgar and states openly her approval for the generosity which he has shown to the *Geatas* (ll.1168[b]–1174), including his adoption of Beowulf as an honorary son (ll.1175–1176[a]).[77] She then continues:

> "Heorot is gefælsod,
> bēahsele beorhta; brūc þenden þū mōte
> manigra mēdo, 7 þīnum māgum lǣf
> folc 7 rīce, þonne ðū forð scyle,
> metodsceaft seȯn. Ic mīnne can
> glædne Hrōþulf, þæt hē þā geogoðe wile
> ārum healdan, gyf þū ǣr þonne hē,
> wine Scildinga, worold oflǣtest;
> wēne ic þæt hē mid gōde gyldan wille
> uncran eaferan, gif hē þæt eal gemon,
> hwæt wit tō willan 7 tō worðmyndum
> umborwesendum ǣr ārna gefremedon."

' "Heorot, the bright ring-hall, is cleansed; enjoy while you may the many blessings, and to your family leave throne and kingdom when you go forth to meet destiny's decree. I know that my gracious Hroþulf will keep the young ones in honour, if you, lord of the Scyldings, leave the world before him; I expect that he will repay our sons with good if he recalls all those favours we did for him earlier as a child, in goodwill and in honour." (ll.1176[b]–1187).

Now that *Heorot is gefælsod*, 'Heorot is cleansed' (l.1176[a]),[78] Wealhþeow raises the question which seems to have been at the heart of episode all along: the question of the Scylding succession in the event of the aged Hroðgar's death. She herself appears to be well aware of the potential for

---

[76] See Fleck, "*Konr – Óttarr – Geirroðr*: A Knowledge Criterion or Succession to the Germanic Sacred Kingship", pp. 46–49).

[77] I do not see that these lines (ll.1175–1176[a]) necessarily imply that Wealhþeow views Beowulf as a threat, as was first suggested by Schücking ("Heldenstolz und Würde im Angelsächsischen, mit einem Anhang: Zur Charakterisierungstechnik im Beowulfepos", p. 41) and, more recently, by J.M. Hill ("*Beowulf* and the Danish Succession: Gift Giving as an Occasion for Complex Gesture"). On the relation of Wealhþeow and Beowulf, see further below.

[78] That is, as far as she knows at this stage, though her statement will prove to be premature. On the use of the verb *(ge)fælsian*, see Hübener, "*Beowulf* and Germanic Exorcism".

future conflict over this question, for her words seem to be deliberately intended to neutralise it.[79] Naturally, her primary concern is for the welfare of her two boys, Hreðric and Hroðmund, a concern evident in her direct address to her husband: *"þīnum māgum lǣf / folc 7 rīce, þonne ðū forð scyle"*, ' "to your kin leave throne and kingdom when you go forth" ' (ll.1178b–1180a). The phrase *"þīnum māgum"*, ' "your kin" ' (l.1178b) would also include Hroðgar's nephew, Hroþulf, though of course the use of the plural form would rule out him alone. Hroþulf appears to be a more senior member of the family than Hreðric and Hroðmund, as his seating position in Heorot implies. He sits at King Hroðgar's side, rather than with the *geogoð*, where Hreðric and Hroðmund sit (ll.1188–1190a). The implication is that the future welfare of Wealhþeow's boys will come to be dependent on Hroþulf's good faith in the event of Hroðgar's death. This may be the reason why, although continuing to speak formally to her husband for the rest of her speech (ll.1180b–1187), she appears to be indirectly addressing Hroþulf. With the utmost delicacy, referring to him as *"minne . . . glædne Hroþulf"*, ' "my gracious Hroþulf" ' (l.1180b–1181a), she gently asserts that she *"can"*, ' "knows" ' (l.1180b), *"þæt hē þā geogoðe wile / ārum healdan"*, ' "that he will keep the young ones in honour" ' (ll.1180–1182a). She makes this assertion on the basis that Hroþulf is indebted to Hroðgar and Wealhþeow for the honour which he has received from them as a child (ll.1184–1187). She thus reminds Hroþulf of his own childhood, part of which appears to have been fostered by his uncle and aunt, as lines 1185b–1187 imply, and as her reference to Hroþulf as *mīnne* (l.1180b), suggesting endearment, may signal. Certainly, this is not at all unlikely, for the absence from the action of *Beowulf* of Hroþulf's father, Halga – apart from his single mention in the Scylding genealogy (l.61b) – is consistent with the references to his death in *Ynglinga saga* (ch. 29) at the time when his son was only eight years of age. In reminding Hroþulf of this debt, she publicly imposes upon him the duty to reciprocate the goodwill and generosity which he had been formerly granted.[80]

She then pauses and turns towards the seated and silent figures of

---

[79] In Irving's words,"the only way that Wealhþeow knows to prevent the explosion which seems imminent in this tense grouping is to resort to what one must call incantation" (*A Reading of Beowulf*, p. 139).

[80] "She hopes to win him by appealing to the better side of his nature", as Malone has put it ("Hrethric", p. 270). Irving has referred to her "fragile hopes" which are "cast over the uncontrollable future, a future that will be wholly dependent on Hroþulf's will" (*A Reading of Beowulf*, p. 141). The keyword here is *gyldan*, underlining Hroþulf's duty to reciprocate the gifts which he has formerly received from Hroðgar and Wealhþeow, as Glosecki argued ("The Boar's Helmet in *Beowulf*", p. 229 and note 53). In Robinson's words, "scholars who, following Kenneth Sisam [*The Structure of Beowulf*, p. 82]. . . , refuse to accept the dark implications here would seem determined to turn a deaf ear to the tone and words of the poem. Anyone who does not hear anxiety in Wealhþeow's speech about how Hroþulf will act toward her offspring must think that

Hreðric and Hroðmund, who are now named explicitly for the first time in the poem.

> Hwearf þā bī bence,   þǣr hyre byre wǣron,
> Hreðrīc 7 Hroðmund,   7 hæleþa bearn,
> giogoð ætgǣdere;   þǣr se gōda sǣt,
> Bēowulf Gēata   be þǣm gebroðrum twǣm.

She turned then to the bench where her boys were, Hreðric and Hroðmund, and the sons of heroes, youths together; and there the good one sat, Beowulf the Geat, beside the two brothers' (ll.1188–1191).

The importance of Hreðric and Hroðmund is implicitly signalled by the fact that at their side sits Beowulf himself. That the hero is seated here, among the *geogoð*, 'youths' (l.1190ᵃ), and not among the more senior *duguð*, may also reflect his status as an honorary son of Hroðgar. At the same time, it may also symbolise his solidarity with the interests of Hreðric and Hroðmund, rather than those of any other party in the Scylding household. Certainly, being assigned a seat with the sons of Hroðgar is regarded by Beowulf himself as a great honour, as he refers to it in his report to Hygelac later in the poem (l.2013).

Wealhþeow's anxiety for the future of her boys remains apparent as she presents the hero with a full drinking-vessel,[81] followed by some gifts of her own for him (ll.1192–1196). These include a unique *healsbēag*, 'neck-ring', so special that it is compared in quality to the legendary *Brōsinga mene*, 'the collar of the Brosings' (ll.1197–1201).[82] The subsequent history of this ring is then described: we hear how it is destined to be worn by Hygelac, Beowulf's uncle, when he meets his death some years later during his ill-fated raid against Frankish territories in Frisia (ll.1202–1214).[83] Following this description of a future scene of carnage,

---

Mark Antony genuinely believes Caesar's murderers to be honourable men" ("History, Religion and Culture", p. 109).

[81] It is possible that this was the same vessel which she had earlier offered to Hroðgar (l.1179ᵃ). If so, she would be symbolically binding Beowulf's allegiance to Hroðgar through the ritual of the sharing of the cup; it may also be significant that there is no reference to her offering the vessel to Hroþulf. For a discussion of the cup-bearing ritual, see Bauschatz, *The Well and the Tree*, pp. 76–78.

[82] This legendary allusion appears to be an euhemerisation of a mythic tale, as Ursula Dronke has shown ("*Beowulf* and Ragnarǫk", pp. 322–325). It may be intended to emphasize the fetish power, or luck, implicit in the gift-ring, which Wealhðeow hopes will be transferred with it to its new owner (on which see P.B. Taylor, "The Traditional Language of Treasure in *Beowulf*", p. 198). Damico ("*Sǫrlaþáttr* and the Hama Episode in *Beowulf*") has argued that the allusion becomes intelligible when it is compared to the narrative outline of the passage of the theft of the *Brísinga men* in the fourteenth-century *Sǫrlaþáttr* (in *Flateyjarbók*, ed. Vigfússon and Unger, vol. 1, pp. 275–283).

[83] This is one of the five references in the poem to this arguably historical event: see the discussion in Chapter Two.

the narrative shifts back to the sound of the feast in Heorot: *heal swēge onfēng.* / *Wealhðeo maþelode* 'the hall was filled with sound. Wealhþeow spoke' (ll.1214ᵇ–1215ᵃ). This shift from future tragedy in Frisia back to the narrative present is parallel to the earlier shift back from past tragedy in Frisia at the end of the *Frēswæl*: *gamen eft āstāh, beorhtode bencswēg. . . . Þā cwōm Wealhþēo forð,* 'the mirth arose again, and the bench-din rang out. . . . Then Wealhþeow came forth' (ll.1160ᵇ–1162). This structural parallel seems to emphasize further the fragility of the present situation within Heorot, framed in time as it is by narrative glimpses of a past and future of death and disaster.

> Wealhþēo maþelode, heo fore þǣm werede sprǣc:
> "Brūc ðisses bēages, Bēowulf lēofa,
> hyse, mid hǣle, 7 þisses hrægles nēot,
> þēo[d]gestrēona, 7 geþēoh tela,
> cen þec mid cræfte, 7 þyssum cnyhtum wes
> lāra līðe! Ic þē þæs lēan geman.
> Hafast þū gefēred, þæt ðē feor 7 nēah
> ealne wīdeferhþ weras ehtigað,
> efne swā sīde swā sǣ bebūgeð,
> windgeard, weallas. Wes þenden þū lifige,
> æþeling, ēadig! Ic þē an tela
> sincgestrēona. Bēo þū suna mīnum
> dǣdum gedēfe, drēamhealdende!
> Hēr is ǣghwylc eorl ōþrum getrȳwe,
> mōdes milde, mandrihtne hol[d],
> þegnas syndon geþwǣre, þēod ealgearo,
> druncne dryhtguman dōð swā ic bidde."

'Wealhþeow made a speech, before the men she spoke: "May this ring bring good luck, dear young Beowulf, and make use of this corslet and of the folk-treasures, and thrive well, assert yourself with skill, and to these boys be kind in counsels! I will reward you for it. You have brought it about that far and near all men shall forever esteem you, even as widely as the sea flows around the shores, the home of the wind. As long as you live, *æþeling*, may you be blest! I wish you well with your treasures. In your deeds be good to my sons, keeping them in bliss! Here each noble is true to the other, gentle in thought, and loyal to his lord; the thanes are in harmony, the folk all ready; having drunk [the royal mead], the lord's men do as I bid" ' (ll.1215–1231).

As she presents her victory-gifts to him, Wealhþeow addresses Beowulf with no less than seven direct imperatives (ll.1216ᵃ, 1217ᵇ, 1218ᵇ, 1219ᵃ, 1219ᵇ–1220ᵃ, 1225ᵃ, 1226ᵇ–1227). Two of these explicitly specify her wish that the hero will support the two boys sitting beside him: *"þyssum cnyhtum wes* / *lāra līðe"*, ' "to these boys be kind in counsels" ' (ll.1219ᵇ–1220ᵃ), and *"bēo þū suna mīnum* / *dǣdum gedēfe, drēamhealdende"*, ' "in your deeds be good to my sons, keeping them in bliss'" (ll.1226ᵇ–1227). The gifts and exhortations seem to be part of the same continuing strategy – to try to secure the future welfare of Hreðric and Hroðmund. She thus openly courts Beowulf, in the full glory of his triumph over Grendel and hence the strongest man in *Scedeland*, as her ally.

Beowulf responds to all of this in a later passage. Just before he leaves Heorot to return home, he says to Hroðgar,

> "gif him þonne Hreðric   tō hofum Gēata
> geþingeð þeodnes bearn,   hē mæg þær fela
> frēonda findan;   feorcȳþðe bēoð
> sēlran gesōhte   þǣm þe him selfa dēah."

> ' "if Hreðric, the king's son, ever determines to go to the halls of the Geats, he can find there many friends; it is well for one who himself is doughty to travel widely" ' (ll.1836–1839).

Beowulf seems to consider Hreðric to be a young man of worth here, and signals his solidarity with him by offering him friendship.[84] As such, Wealhþeow's efforts to enlist the hero's support on behalf of her sons can be seen to be not without some degree of success. Yet the emphasis which the poem places on her gift of the special *healsbeag* (ll.1195ᵇ–1214ᵃ), which she wishes will bring good luck to Beowulf and the *Gēatas* (ll.1216–1217ᵃ), counterpoints all of her hopes with a grim irony. For as we have already been made aware, the spell-binding power of this ring is destined to fail, as it will be worn by the Geatish king when he meets his end in a catastrophic defeat in Friesland. We are told that *hyne wyrd fornam*, 'fate carried him off' (l.1205ᵇ). The transitive structure of this clause, with *wyrd* as its active agent, implies that there is a background of powerful destinal agency at work here. The clear implication is that *wyrd* will weave its own patterns, in spite of Wealhþeow's best efforts.

The culminating lines of the Scylding queen's speech to Beowulf seem to be intended for other ears besides those of the hero.

> Hēr is ǣghwylc eorl   ōþrum getrȳwe,
> mōdes milde,   mandrihtne hol[d],
> þegnas syndon geþwǣre,   þēod ealgearo,
> druncne dryhtguman   dōð swā ic bidde."

> ' "Here each noble is true to the other, gentle in thought, and loyal to his lord; the thanes are in harmony, the folk all ready; having drunk [the royal mead], the lord's men do as I bid" '
> (ll.1228–1231)

---

84 Of this passage, Malone wrote that Beowulf "is definitely allying himself with Hroðgar and his son. . . . The queen, to that extent, has not exerted herself in vain. We leave Hreðric with the knowledge that he has in Beowulf a friend in time of need. There is no pathos in this picture" ("Hrethric", p. 273).

These lines assert the ideal of trust and loyalty within Heorot which Wealhþeow seeks to prolong.[85] Yet at the same time, her words echo an ironic note of discord, for her assertion that *"hér is ǽghwylc eorl óþrum getrýwe"*, ' "here each noble is true to the other" ' (1.1228), echoes the earlier statement that *ǽghwylc óðrum trýwe*, 'each was to the other true' (1.1165ᵃ). Her assertion thus reiterates the mutual responsibilities involved in the preservation of good faith between the same group of men. Yet it was the presence of *Unferþ*, with his past record of dishonourable violence toward his own family (ll.587–588ᵃ, 1167ᵇ–1168ᵃ) which implied that the earlier statement (1.1165ᵃ) was equivocal, and it is his continuing presence which now contradicts Wealhþeow's hopeful assertion (1.1228).

Despite her moving and diplomatic speech to Beowulf, it thus ends on an uncertain note which echoes earlier doubts, a note which is amplified almost immediately:

> Eode þā tō setle.   Þǽr wæs symbla cyst,
> druncon wīn weras.   Wyrd ne cūþon,
> geōsceaft grim*me*,   swā hit āgangen wearð
> eorla manegu*m*.

'She went then to the settle. That was the finest of feasts, the men drank wine. Of fate they knew nothing, of the grim destiny ordained long before, such as had come to pass to many a man' (ll.1232–1235ᵇ).

Again the poem refers to the power of *wyrd*, recalling that which brought Hygelac, wearing the special *healsbēag* imbued with Wealhþeow's blessings for good fortune, to his downfall (ll.1202–1214ᵃ): *hyne wyrd fornam*, 'fate carried him off' (1.1205ᵇ). We are told now that the feasters are anyway utterly oblivious to the unrelenting patterns woven by *wyrd*: *wyrd ne cūþon / geōsceafte grim*me*, 'of fate they knew nothing, of the grim destiny ordained long before' (ll.1233ᵇ–1234ᵃ). This statement only increases the note of irony which seems to have been undermining the queen's brave efforts to establish a secure future for Hreðric and Hroðmund all along. At the same time, the reference to *wyrd* anticipates the ensuing scene in *Beowulf*, in which another anxious parent enters Heorot, *Grendles mōdor* (1.1258ᵇ), seeking revenge for her son's mortal wounding the night before.

---

[85] Irving has described these lines as "pure incantatory prayer" (*A Reading of Beowulf*, p. 144). Similarly, Shippey has commented that Wealhþeow "is striving to evoke the *dream* for which she so desperately wishes. All spells proceed from the belief that if you say something the right way, it will come true, and that is what she is doing" (*Beowulf*, p. 39).

A close reading of the episode of the Scylding victory-feast, therefore, leaves us with ominous doubts as to the permanence of peace within the Danish royal family. As I have attempted to describe, these doubts seem to derive initially from the poem's counterpointing of its presentation of family harmony with ironic notes of latent discord. As the episode progresses, Wealhþeow emerges as the primary medium for the advancement of the question which appears to lie at its centre: the Scylding succession. She becomes thus the focal figure in Heorot, framed in time by narrative glimpses of a past and future of tragedy; and in her heart, motivating her efforts, is a profound concern for the fate of her two boys, Hreðric and Hroðmund. In Malone's words,

> the young princes themselves take no part in the action . . . and yet, everything hinges on them. . . . Their peril drives the queen to do all that she does. And their destiny, though unrecorded by the poet, gives to the episode the tragic undertone which makes it a thing of beauty. They remain in the background, but the background dominates the scene.[86]

Although the relations between the Northern sources concerned with the *Skjoldungar* can be confusing,[87] the degree of apparent agreement with the picture of the dynasty in *Beowulf* is remarkable.[88] They imply that the question of the Scylding succession raised in *Beowulf* is destined to have a tragic outcome, just as Wealhþeow herself seems to fear. Again, the words of Malone deserve to be cited fully:

> the poet's audience, the English of old, knew that her hopes were in vain. They listened to the mother, pleading for her son, and knew that her prayers were aimed at the man who was destined to slay him. Wealhþeow's speech, then, is a masterpiece of unconscious irony. But it is also pathetic, deeply moving. This Danish queen, with her hopes and fears, her premonition of what is to come and her brave fight against the dangers that are to beset her son, is a figure as tragic as any in English literature.[89]

The implicit knowledge that Hroþulf is destined to kill Hreðric in the process of securing his own claim to the throne of Denmark would

---

[86] Malone, "Hreðric", p. 271.
[87] See, for example, Olson, "The Relation of *Hrólfs Saga Kraka* and the *Bjarkarímur* to *Beowulf*"; and Jones, *Kings, Beasts and Heroes*, pp. 132–134.
[88] As Chambers put it, OE and Scandinavian traditions of the Danish royal family "interlock, dovetail into one another, and make a connected whole which, though it leaves details obscure, seems in its main outlines established beyond doubt" (*Introduction*, p. 427).
[89] Malone, "Hrethric", p. 270.

certainly account for much of the apparent irony in the episode, as well as suggesting why Hreðric and his brother appear to be focal figures in the episode of the victory-feast. It is their very existence in Heorot, vividly highlighted by their mother, which prompts the question of the Scylding succession, and so raises the spectre of internecine conflict.

Now if, as the sources seem to suggest, Hreðric is destined to be killed by his cousin Hroþulf in the course of a putative struggle for the succession, we may wonder if Hroðmund is to share the same fate. I pointed out in Chapter Two of this study how the sympathy shown for Hroðgar's side of the Danish royal family in *Beowulf* contrasts with the interest shown in Hroþulf (ON *Hrólfr*) in Scandinavian sources concerned with the dynasty. I noted earlier in this chapter that Hreðric appears to be identifiable in Saxo's paraphrase of the *Bjarkamál* as Hroþulf's opponent and victim, although he is not presented there as a cousin of Hroþulf. I also noted that there appears to be no reference in Northern sources to a brother of Hreðric such as we find in *Beowulf*.[90] The similarly contrasting treatments of another branch of the *Scyldingas*, the line of Hroðgar's elder brother, Heorogar, may suggest a motive for the obfuscation of Hroþulf's kinship with his dynastic opponents in Scandinavian sources. In *Beowulf*, Heorogar is praised unequivocally by Hroðgar (ll.467b–469), yet he appears not to be referred to at all in the North. Heorogar's son, Heoroweard (ON *Hjǫrvarðr*), however, does appear in Scandinavian sources, where he is depicted as Hroþulf's enemy and banesman.[91] In the light of *Beowulf*, the reign of Hroþulf can be seen to have begun and ended in the context of an internecine struggle for royal power between cousins. Such a view is not provided by the Northern sources, which give the impression that the rule of the son of Halga was without rival claims from collateral lines. Yet *Beowulf* suggests that there may have been at least two of these, that of Hroðgar and that of Heorogar. The Old English epic, therefore, would explain much that is omitted from the Northern picture of Hroþulf in supplying motives both for his killing of Hreðric and for Heoroweard's subsequent attack on Hroþulf.

The absence from Northern sources concerned with the family of a prince with a name corresponding to OE *Hroðmund* may result from this apparent tendency to obfuscate the kinship between the renowned Hroþulf and his dynastic rivals. Like his brother, Hroðmund could have fallen victim to Hroþulf, or even become his man, as may be implied by the name of one of his twelve champions in *Hrólfs saga kraka* (ch.49). Such an arrangement would not have been impossible; in mid-seventh-century England, for example, King Æþelhere of East Anglia was allied

---

[90] One of the twelve champions of Hrólfr bore a name corresponding to OE *Hroðmund*, on whom see further below.

[91] On Heoroweard, see the discussion in Chapter Two.

to King Penda of Mercia despite the fact that the latter had slain his brother and predecessor, Onna.[92] Equally plausibly, however, to avoid his brother's fate, Hroðmund could have escaped into exile. Analogy with *Beowulf*'s presentation of another dynastic feud certainly permits this supposition. It is later in *Beowulf* that we hear how two exiled Swedish princes, Eanmund and Eadgils, appear at the Geatish court, where young King Heardred, Hygelac's son, has only recently succeeded to the Hreðling throne (ll.2369–2379a).

> Hyne wræcmæcgas
> ofer sǣ sōhton,   suna Ōhteres;
> hæfdon hȳ forhealden   helm Scylfinga,
> þone sēlestan   sǣcyninga
> þāra ðe in Swīorīce   sinc brytnade,
> mǣrne þēoden.   Him þæt tō mearce wearð;
> hē þǣr [f]or feorme   feorhwunde hlēat,
> sweordes swengum,   sunu Hygelāces;
> 7 him eft gewāt   Ongenðīoes bearn
> hāmes nīosan,   syððan Heardrēd læg,
> lēt ðone bregostōl   Bīowulf healdan,
> Gēatum wealdan;   þæt wæs gōd cyning.
> Sē ðæs lēodhryres   lēan gemunde
> uferan dōgrum,   Eadgilse wearð
> fēasceaftum frēond;   folce gestēpte
> ofer sǣ sīde   sunu Ōhteres,
> wigum 7 wǣpnum;   hē gewræc syððan
> cealdum cearsīðum,   cyning ealdre binēat.

'Exiles, the sons of Ohthere, sought him [Heardred] out over the waters; they had rebelled against the lord of the Scylfings [Onela], the famous chieftain, the best of the sea-kings who distributed treasure in Sweden. That was for him [Heardred] his undoing; on account of his hospitality, the son of Hygelac received his death-wound from the stroke of a sword; and then, when Heardred lay dead, Ongenþeow's son [Onela] went back to seek his home, and let Beowulf hold the throne and rule the Geats; he was a good king! He [Beowulf] bore in mind the requital for his lord's fall, and at a later date became a friend to the helpless Eadgils; he supported the son of Ohthere with people, with warriors and weapons, across the wide waters; he [Beowulf] then took his revenge in cold and grievous raids; he deprived the king [Onela] of his life' (ll.2379b–2396).

Both Eanmund and Eadgils are driven into exile by their uncle, the Swedish king, Onela, *Ongenðīoes bearn* (l.2387b). It is clear that their conflict with Onela amounts to a dynastic struggle for the Scylfing

[92] Bede, *HE*, III, 18; III, 24.

throne. Heardred makes a fatal error in providing refuge for the two royal renegades, for it involves him directly in the Scylfing feud, and he is killed in the course of Onela's ensuing attack (ll.2384^b–2386). In this attack, as we learn later, Eanmund is also killed by Wihstan, Wiglaf's father, fighting in Onela's service (ll.2612^b–2619).[93] Onela then returns home, leaving Beowulf as king of the *Gēatas* (ll.2387–2390). In vengeance for the fall of Heardred, however, the hero subsequently supports Eadgils's war against Onela *ofer sǣ sīde*, 'across the wide waters' (l.2394^a), and, *cealdum cear-sīðum*, 'in cold and grievous raids' (l.2396^a), eventually kills the latter. The former, it appears, then becomes the Scylfing king. The culmination of this conflict between Eadgils (ON *Aðils*) and Onela (ON *Áli*) appears to be similarly referred to in *Ynglinga saga* (ch. 29), in *Skáldskaparmál* (ch. 54), and in *Skjǫldunga saga* (ch. 12), as a battle in the winter on the frozen surface of Lake Vänern.[94]

The situation of Eanmund and Eadgils in the feud over the Scylfing succession provides a parallel to that of Hreðric and Hroðmund in the putative struggle over the Scylding succession, as well as an insight into the nature of such dynastic conflicts. Both conflicts appear to be internecine power-struggles between two collateral lines, in which one of each of the two pairs of royal brothers involved is slain. In both feuds, moreover, a foreign power supports one or other of the rival factions. In *Beowulf*, Eanmund and Eadgils receives the support of the *Gēatas*, while in the allusions to the Scylfing feud in *Skáldskaparmál* and in *Skjǫldunga saga*, Eadgils (ON *Aðils*) is said to be aided by the twelve champions of Hrólfr. Indeed, foreign involvement appears to be a regular feature of such dynastic feuding, as Stjerna noted, describing it as an 'intervention principle'.[95]

The way in which the two conflicts are presented in *Beowulf*, moreover, signals a close sympathy with one of the factions involved. In the Scylding feud, insofar as it can be seen to be foreshadowed in *Beowulf*, sympathy with the sons of Hroðgar seems fundamental, as I have argued. In the Scylfing feud, the sympathy lies most explicitly with Onela, as I pointed out in Chapter Two. He is eulogised as *þone sēlestan sǣcyninga / þāra ðe in Swīorīce sinc brytnade,/ mǣrne þēoden*, 'the famous chieftain, the best of the sea-kings who distributed treasure in Sweden' (ll.2382–2384^a).[96] The formulaic phrase *þæt wæs gōd cyning* (l.2390^b) may also refer

[93] An explanation as to how Wihstan Wægmunding, a kinsman of Beowulf (ll.2813–2814^a), came to be fighting for Onela against the *Gēatas* is advanced in the next chapter.
[94] See Garmonsway and Simpson (ed. and tr.), *Beowulf and Its Analogues*, pp. 216–221.
[95] Stjerna, *Essays on Questions Connected with the Old English Poem of Beowulf*, p. 88.
[96] King Hroðgar is similarly described as *woroldcyninga / þǣm sēlestan be sǣm twēonum / ðāra þe on Scedenigge sceattas dǣlde*, 'the finest of world-kings between the seas who dealt out treasure in the Danish realm' (ll.1684^b–1686).

to Onela,[97] as the context implies, rather than to Beowulf.[98] If the most likely emendation to the scribal error in line 62[b] of *Beowulf* is accepted,[99] Onela's queen would have been the daughter of Healfdene, *Heaðo-Scilfingas healsgebedda*, 'the Battle-Scylfing's dear bedmate' (1.63). As this marriage may well have entailed an allegiance, through royal kinship, between the Scylfing and Scylding dynasties, Onela's faction within the Swedish ruling family may have been understood as pro-Danish, which may account for the poem's praise for him.[100] It also would have placed Beowulf in a difficult dilemma, for in spite of his own Scylding affinities, he appears to have been obliged to avenge the death of Heardred by supporting Eadgils against the respected Onela. The praise for Onela in *Beowulf* is in marked contrast to the way that Eanmund and Eadgils are described in the immediately preceding lines: they are *wræcmæcgas*, 'exiles' (1.2379[b]),[101] who had *forhealden helm Scylfinga*, 'rebelled against the Scylfing chief' (1.2381).

The analogy thus afforded by the Swedish dynastic feud in *Beowulf* permits us to infer the possibility that Hroðmund, like Eanmund and Eadgils, was obliged to go into exile. Certainly, exile appears not to have been unusual in the world of the poem, as is implied by the words of Wulfgar to Beowulf and his men at the doors of Heorot: *"Wēn' ic þæt gē for wlenco, nalles for wræcsīðum, / ac for higeþrymmum Hrōðgār sōhton"*, ' "I think that it is not because of exile, but because of courage and daring, that you have sought out Hroðgar" ' (11.338–339). Ecgþeow, the hero's father had himself visited Hroðgar as an exile (11.459–472), an affair discussed in the next chapter. There is no shortage of historical examples of *æþelingas* being forced into exile, as the feuding which might bring about such a fate appears to have been in the nature of Anglo-Saxon dynastic power politics. As Dumville has pointed out, the

> large numbers of collateral lines in many of the heptarchic kingdoms will have ensured that, where there was not a very strong . . . king, the existence of numerous æthelings caused a great deal of tension and

---

[97] Again, like Hroðgar (1.863[b]), as was noted in Chapter Two.

[98] As Farrell noted (*Beowulf, Swedes and Geats*, p. 7).

[99] As it is by the majority of scholars – see Kelly, "The Formative Stages of *Beowulf* Textual Scholarship: part II", p. 241).

[100] Allegiance between Scyldings and Scylfings would also account for the presence and senior rank of Wulfgar (*Wendla lēod* [1.348[b]]) in the service of Hroðgar at the Danish court. As both Stjerna (*Essays on . . . Beowulf*, pp. 50–63) and Belden ("Onela the Scylfing and Áli the Bold", p. 152, note 6) have argued, the *Wendlas* of *Beowulf* appear to have been connected with the Scylfing dynasty and may have dwelt around Vendel in the Swedish province of Uppland, where there is archaeological evidence for the early royal and aristocratic status of the area in the period *ca* 500 x 700.

[101] *Wræcmæcg* is used elsewhere in OE poetry to refer to devils, as in *Guðlac*, 11.231, 558, *Juliana*, 1.260, and *Christ*, 1.363. All of these instances clearly indicate the negative connotations of the term.

instability. Factional alliances must have been the natural condition of dynastic politics in these circumstances.[102]

Concomitantly, it would often have been necessary for a king to consolidate the strength of his position by the removal of rival claimants, either through assassination or through exile. For example, in the early seventh century, Eadwine of Deira was forced into exile by Æþelfrið of Northumbria.[103] Later, the latter's sons were obliged to go into exile when Eadwine won power after the Æþelfrið's death at the Battle of the River Idle in 616 or 617.[104]

It is not impossible, therefore, that Prince Hroðmund, like the many Anglo-Saxon *æþelingas* who found themselves in similar circumstances, may have been deemed to have followed the exile's path.

So, on the one hand, we have Hroðmund the Scylding prince, fate unknown, though perhaps in exile; and on the other, we have Hroðmund the East Anglian dynastic ancestor, perhaps associated with a royal origin-myth. Certainly, if the two are really the same proto-historical figure, we would have a most significant connection between an early English nobility and the background of *Beowulf*. Yet apart from the uniqueness of these two instances of the name *Hroðmund*, there is no reason why we should suppose that they should refer to the same figure. If, however, we return to King Ælfwald's pedigree, we shall see that there may be some grounds for identifying the two, as there are independent indications that Queen Wealhþeow, the mother of Hroðmund in *Beowulf*, may herself have been regarded as an East Anglian dynastic ancestor.

[102] Dumville, "The Ætheling", p. 29.
[103] Bede, *HE*, II, 12.
[104] Bede, *HE*, II, 12; III, 1.

CHAPTER FIVE

WUFFINGS AND WULFINGS

THE NAME *Wuffa* is listed both in King Ælfwald's pedigree and in Bede's version of King Rædwald's. Bede asserts that Rædwald was the son of Tyttla, whose father was Wuffa, *a quo reges Orientalium Anglorum Uuffingas appellant*, 'from whom the kings of East Anglia are called Wuffings'.[1] In other words, at least according to Bede, *Wuffa* was the East Anglian dynastic eponym. It is often assumed, perhaps because of the literal style with which Bede presents Rædwald's pedigree, that Wuffa was Rædwald's historical grandfather. Within Ælfwald's pedigree, however, although the names of his father (Ealdwulf), grandfather (Æþelric), and great-grandfather (Eni, the brother of Rædwald) may represent consecutive, historical generations,[2] the horizon of historical credibility, so far as the present evidence warrants, extends no further than the name *Tyttla*. Beyond this point, the order of ancestral names bear no necessary chronological significance whatsoever. Indeed, as recent work suggests, the pedigree's pre- and proto-historic 'generations' may be more accurately understood to represent symbolically filiated conventions and figures from origin-legends deemed to be relevant to dynastic authority at the time of compilation.[3] The bearer of the royal eponym *Wuffa* thus need not be regarded as the historical founder of the dynasty whose genealogical position came to be determined chronographically; rather, like the Kentish dynastic eponym, *Oisc*,[4] *Wuffa* may have been the East Anglian royal *cognomen*, the distinguishing family-name, the bearer of which is perhaps best understood as an emblematic figure personified from dynastic origin-myth.

Etymologically, the name *Wuffa* appears to be a diminutive variant of

---

1   Bede, *HE*, II, 15.
2   Bede, *HE*, II, 15; III, 18; see the discussions by Stenton, "The East Anglian Kings of the Seventh Century"; and by Glass, "The Sutton Hoo Ship Burial", pp. 180–182.
3   See the consideration of the OE royal pedigree genre in the previous chapter and the references cited there.
4   *Oisc* is mentioned by Bede (*HE*, II, 5); see Chadwick, *The Origin of the English Nation*, pp. 44–48; Redin, *Studies in Uncompounded Personal Names in Old English*, p. 33; Ström, *Old English Personal Names in Bede's History*, pp. 73–74; J. Turville-Petre, "Hengest and Horsa", pp. 284–286; Sims-Williams, "The Settlement of England in Bede and the *Chronicle*", pp. 22–23; and Brooks, "The Creation and Early Structure of the Kingdom of Kent", pp. 58–59.

Wulf,[5] and can thus be translated as 'Little Wolf'. The patronymic form *Wuffingas* seems similarly best explained as a variant of *Wulfingas*, 'the kin of the wolf', a folk-name which is mentioned in both *Beowulf* and *Widsith*. As O'Loughlin has pointed out,

> there are no linguistic obstacles to the equation of Bede's *Uuffingas* with the *Wulfingas* of *Widsith*, 1.29, and the *Wylfingas* of *Beowulf*, 1.471. The forms are etymologically identical, and the phonological variations irrelevant.[6]

The name *Wulfingas* (or *Wylfingas*) appears to be an old theriomorphic type of folk-name entailing an ultimately totemic affinity with the wolf,[7] an affinity also implicit in its variant form *Wuffingas*. Genealogically, therefore, *Wuffa*, 'Little Wolf', may have been an emblematic personification of the totemic founding-father and guardian-spirit of the East Anglian dynasty.[8]

Some scholars have argued that the suggested interpretation of the name *Wuffingas* can be seen to be strengthened by archaeological evidence, in that a wolf emblem is identifiable as one of the gold fittings from the possible ceremonial wand which had lain on the right side of the body-space beneath Mound One at Sutton Hoo (Fig. 5).[9] As this item lacks any parallels, however, it is not clear how much significance should be attached to it. The function of the potentially wolf-like forms on the "man between beasts" motif (Fig. 6) duplicated on the magnificent purse-lid from Mound One, itself an important item of royal regalia, is also uncertain.[10] A. M. Arent has argued that the motif represents some sort of warriorship initiation rite, perhaps ultimately shamanistic.[11] Others have extrapolated the possible lupine nature of the beasts on the

---

5 Redin, *Studies*, pp. 10, 73; and Ström, *Old English Personal Names*, p. 79.

6 O'Loughlin, "Sutton Hoo: the Evidence of the Documents", p. 4.

7 As Smithers has suggested, "The Geats of *Beowulf*", pp. 90–93.

8 On totemic ancestors, see Neuman, *The Origins and History of Consciousness*, pp. 144–146. The concept of totemic guardian-spirit may perhaps be expressed in the possible OE word *fæcce*, 'fetch' (*Corpus Glossary, ca* 800). Compare the later ON *fylgja*, 'wraith (double)' and its compound *kynfylgja*, 'family wraith' or 'inherited gift'; see E.O.G. Turville-Petre, *Myth and Religion of the North*, pp. 227–230; and Glosecki, "The Boar's Helmet in *Beowulf*", pp. 215–222.

9 For an account of this wood, bone or ivory wand (which may have functioned as a sceptre), see Bruce-Mitford, *SHSB*, vol. 2, pp. 394–402. The significance of the possible wolf emblem is noted on pp. 353–354, with a cautionary reference to the work of Hauck ("Herrschaftszeichen eines Wodanistischen Königtums", pp. 50–51). A similar interpretation for this emblem was suggested by Wrenn ("Sutton Hoo and *Beowulf*", pp. 512, 520).

10 See Bruce-Mitford, *SHSB*, vol. 2, pp. 353–4, 512–14; and A. Evans, *The Sutton Hoo Ship Burial*, pp. 87–88.

11 Arent, "The Heroic Pattern: Old Germanic Helmets, *Beowulf* and *Grettis saga*", pp. 133–136.

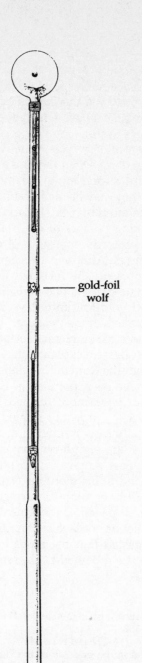

gold-foil
wolf

Figure 6
One of a pair of gold cloisonné
mounts with insets of garnet
and millefiori glass from the
purse-lid from Mound 1 at
Sutton Hoo (scale 2 to 1)

Figure 7
Bronze die from Torslunda,
Öland, Sweden (scale 1 to 1)

Figure 5
Rupert Bruce-Mitford's reconstruction
of the ceremonial wand from Mound 1
at Sutton Hoo, showing fittings of
gold foil, gold filigree, and cabochon
garnets (scale 1 to 3)

motif in relation to East Anglian kingship.[12] Iconographically, the 'man-between-beasts' motif is found elsewhere, such as on one of the four bronze helmet-plate stamping dies from Torslunda, on the Baltic island of Öland, which shows the figure of an armed man between what appear to be bears (Fig. 7).[13] In contrast, the beasts on the Sutton Hoo version are depicted with pointed ears, longer legs and prominent tails. Moreover, the necks and foreshoulders of the creatures are larger than the hips and rear quarters, suggesting that the former are supposed to be more powerful, as is the case with wolves. As such, they may be identifiable as lupine. If so, then the Sutton Hoo version of the motif may be susceptible to a totemic interpretation. The peculiar flanking posture of the beasts could be regarded as a representation of the protective presence of the putative ancestral guardian-spirit of the Wuffings. Although we cannot be sure what the motif was intended to represent, the fact that it is depicted in the especially rich medium of plate-garnets and millefiori glass, mounted in gold settings with stamped gold-foil underlays, implies that it was of special significance to the makers of the treasure.

That the wolf *could* have been an implicitly totemic emblem associated with an East Anglian royal family origin-myth offers an explanation as to why the emblem of the she-wolf and twins from the Roman foundation-legend of Romulus and Remus appears to have been popular in East Anglia. Numismatically, the Roman wolf-and-twins motif formed the pattern for the Anglo-Saxon sceatta series type V, probably minted in Canterbury in the eighth century.[14] An unusually clear rendering of the motif, however, appears on an example of a late eighth-century coin series from the reign of King Æþelberht of East Anglia.[15] Two other similarly outstanding depictions of the wolf-and-twins motif also come from pre-Viking East Anglia: one is on a late fifth- or sixth-century gold bracteate found at Undley, Suffolk.[16] The other appears on a fragment of a late eighth- or early ninth-century bone casket or book-cover found at Larling, Norfolk.[17] James Campbell has suggested that the motif may have been popular in East Anglia, at least on the Æþelberht coin series,

[12] Storms, "The Sutton Hoo Ship-Burial: An Interpretation", pp. 332–4; and K.Hauck, "Zum zweiten Band der Sutton Hoo-edition", pp. 351–359.

[13] Bruce-Mitford, *Aspects of Anglo-Saxon Archaeology*, pp. 214–222 and plate 58b.

[14] Metcalf, "Monetary Circulation in southern England in the first half of the Eighth Century", fig. 16. An East Anglian source for this series is also a possibility according to Marion Archibald (Webster and Backhouse, *The Making of England*, §§ 74a and 74b).

[15] Stewart, "The London Mint and the Coinage of Offa", plate 3; for a brief discussion of the historical significance of this series, see Blunt, "The Anglo-Saxon Coinage and the Historian", p. 4; and Webster and Backhouse, *The Making of England*, § 222a.

[16] West, "The Gold Bracteate from Undley, Suffolk"; Hines, *The Scandinavian Character of Anglian England in the pre-Viking Period*, pp. 204–9, 303–4; and C. Hills, "The Gold Bracteate from Undley, Suffolk: some further Thoughts".

[17] B. Green, "An Anglo-Saxon Bone Plaque from Larling, Norfolk", pp. 321–323.

because of the inclusion of the name *Caser* as a 'son' of Woden in Ælfwald's pedigree.[18] The presence of this name in the pedigree may indeed be construed as an expression of the Roman imperial aspirations of the Wuffings. Yet as other Old English dynasties must have had similar aspirations, it seems curious that only an East Anglian king explicitly numbered Caesar among his forebears. Perhaps the Wuffing claim to such ancestry was legitimate because the essentially totemic Roman foundation-legend of the she-wolf and twins[19] appeared congruent with East Anglia's own, arguably totemic, ancestral associations with the wolf. If so, then the symbolic potential of the wolf for the East Anglian royal family may be relevant to both the presence of the name *Caser* in an eighth-century royal pedigree and the prominent use of the wolf-and-twins motif on an eighth-century coin series.[20]

A belief in the totemic function of the wolf as a guardian-spirit for the kings of East Anglia may also explain why the wolf appears as such an intimate and protective creature in the Anglo-Saxon legend of the martyrdom of the last English king of East Anglia, St Edmund, who was killed on 20th November, 869. The earliest version of this legend is the tenth-century *Passio Sancti Eadmundi*, by Abbo of Fleury.[21] Although he claims to be informed by an authoritative source, Abbo's account is, as Antonia Gransden has shown, "little more than a hotch-potch of hagiographical commonplaces".[22] The famous scene in which a great wolf guards Edmund's severed head between its paws, however, appears to lack an exact hagiographic parallel.[23] It is thus tempting to view the wolf's miraculous function in this legend as deriving from a traditional association with the kings of East Anglia.

There are also archaeological indications that East Anglia had stronger Scandinavian affinities than any other early English kingdom.[24] The most outstanding Scandinavian feature of East Anglian archaeology is the rite of royal ship-funeral,[25] which, on the present evidence, appears in early Anglo-Saxon England to have been practiced *only* by the Wuffings.[26] The

---

18 J. Campbell, *The Anglo-Saxons*, p. 67.
19 W. Russell and C. Russell, "The Social Biology of Werewolves", pp. 174–175.
20 For an eccentric discussion of these ideas, see Hauck, "Zum zweiten Band der Sutton Hoo-edition", pp. 356–359.
21 Winterbottom (ed.), *Three Lives of English Saints*, pp. 67–87.
22 Gransden, "The Legends and Traditions concerning the Origins of the Abbey of Bury St Edmunds", p. 6.
23 Gransden, *ibid.*, p. 7.
24 See Bruce-Mitford, "The Sutton Hoo Ship-Burial: Some Foreign Connections"; Carver, "Kingship and Material Culture in Early Anglo-Saxon East Anglia; "Pre-Viking Traffic in the North Sea"; and more generally, Hines, *The Scandinavian Character of Anglian England in the pre-Viking Period*.
25 Müller-Wille, "Boat-Graves in Northern Europe".
26 See my arguments on this point in Chapter Two.

best example of this rite, which is seen as signalling dynastic allegiance with Scandinavia, is the early seventh-century burial from Mound One at Sutton Hoo in Suffolk.[27] Among the exhumed contents of this burial, moreover, are several instances of specific parallels with objects found in the sixth- and seventh-century boat-graves at Vendel and at nearby Valsgärde in Uppland, Sweden, the old heartland of the Swedish kingdom.[28] Of particular note are the similarities between the Sutton Hoo shield and that from Vendel, Grave Twelve,[29] as well as between the Sutton Hoo helmet and those from Vendel, Graves Twelve and Fourteen,[30] and from Valsgärde, Grave Seven.[31] The great gold buckle from Sutton Hoo, furthermore, is adorned with niello ornament closely paralleled by that on a harness mount from Vendel, Grave Twelve.[32] Although these individual parallels may seem impressive in themselves, it is their concentration within the overall context of the Anglo-Scandinavian rite of ship- and boat-burial which suggests a significant connection between the archaeologies of East Anglia and this part of Sweden. As Bruce-Mitford has written,

> it is the accumulation of points of relevance, in the context of a single grave, and a royal one, that needs to be considered. . . . That so distinctive a rite, not found in England outside East Anglia, should be shared between two areas is, for a start, something that puts the case beyond talk of a diplomatic gift or accident of trade.[33]

There are also close parallels between items from Mound One at Sutton Hoo and some fragmentary objects from the old Swedish royal cremation-burials which have been excavated from beneath two of the three great mounds at Gamla Uppsala, a few miles south of Vendel and Valsgärde. The easternmost of these appears to date from *ca* 500 and could be

[27] On the regal status of this burial, see Bruce-Mitford, *SHSB*, vol. 1, pp. 685–690; for discussion of the ideological implications of the rite, see Carver, "Pre-Viking Traffic in the North Sea"; and "Ideology and Allegiance in Early East Anglia".
[28] On possible sixth or seventh-century dating of these Swedish boat-graves, see Arrhenius, "The Chronology of the Vendel Graves"; but note Bruce-Mitford's cautionary comments in his 1985 review of this paper.
[29] See Bruce-Mitford, *SHSB*, vol. 2, pp. 11–99, and figs 34, 53, 70 & 71; and "The Sutton Hoo Ship-Burial: some Foreign Connections", pp. 167–172.
[30] See Bruce-Mitford, *SHSB*, vol. 2, pp. 150–225, and figs 103, 158 & 182a; and "The Sutton Hoo Ship-Burial: some Foreign Connections", pp. 173–175.
[31] See Lindqvist, *Uppsala Högar och Ottarshögen*, fig. 89a; Bruce-Mitford, *SHSB*, vol. 2, figs 159–165. The Valsgärde 7 grave has been dated by Arrhenius to the first decade of the seventh century ("The Chronology of the Vendel Graves", p. 44).
[32] On this buckle and its parallels, see Bruce-Mitford, *SHSB*, vol. 2, pp. 536–564; "The Sutton Hoo Ship-Burial: some Foreign Connections", pp. 176–187; and Speake, *Anglo-Saxon Animal Art*, p. 94; figs 3j, 16h.
[33] Bruce-Mitford, "The Sutton Hoo Ship-Burial: some Foreign Connections", pp. 196–197.

Figure 8
Fragment of 'dancing
warriors' design from
the East Mound, Old
Uppsala, Sweden
(scale 1 to 1)

Figure 9
The 'dancing warriors' design from the front
of the helm from Mound 1 at Sutton Hoo
(scale 1 to 1)

the last resting-place of Ongenþeow, the Scylfing king whose fall is described in *Beowulf* (ll.2484–2489, 2922–2998).[34] Among the burnt finds
from this mound is a fragment of stamped bronze foil, probably from a
helmet, showing part of a 'dancing warriors' design (Fig. 8). The fragment is so close, in every surviving detail, to the corresponding 'dancing
warriors' design on the helmet from Mound One at Sutton Hoo (Fig. 9)
that the two designs may have come from dies which had been either cut
by the same craftsman or had been made in the same workshop.[35] The
westernmost of the three mounds at Gamla Uppsala, which appears to
date from the second half of the sixth century, has been identified as the
burial-place of Eadgils, another Swedish king mentioned in *Beowulf*.[36] It
was found to contain a fragment of a gold cloisonné panel, probably
from a pyramid mount, which appears to employ the technical device of
the 'beaded cell', a thickening or looping of the gold cell-wall between

[34] See Lindqvist, *Uppsala Högar och Ottarshögen*, pp. 343–353, especially p. 352; and
Chambers, *Introduction*, pp. 411–419.
[35] See Lindqvist, *Uppsala Högar och Ottarshögen*, p. 341 and fig. 89a; Bruce-Mitford,
Aspects of Anglo-Saxon Archaeology, p. 40 and plates 14b–d; *SHSB*, vol. 2, p. 208 and fig.
155). Variants of this design appear on (a) a gold belt-buckle from Finglesham, Kent
(Bruce-Mitford, *Aspects*, pp. 207–208 and plates 53 and 54; *SHSB*, vol. 2, p. 189); and (b) a
silver foil fragment from a seventh-century mound at Caenby, Lincolnshire (Bruce-
Mitford, *Aspects*, pl. 54b; *SHSB*, vol. 2, pp. 189, 207 and plate 153).
[36] See Lindqvist, *Uppsala Högar och Ottarshögen*, pp. 343–353, especially p. 352; and
Chambers, *Introduction*, pp. 411–419.

inlays to permit a greater fluidity of design. The 'beaded cell' device is also a feature of the exquisite gold cloisonné jewellery from Mound One at Sutton Hoo.[37] The westernmost mound at Gamla Uppsala also contained three classical cameos and a plaque bearing a figural scene, which are comparable to the late Roman intaglio set in an Anglo-Saxon gold ring from the probably late sixth-century ship-burial at Snape, as well as to the cameo fragment showing a classical figure of Winged Victory from Mound Three at Sutton Hoo.[38]

These parallels imply that there was some sort of relation between the Wuffings of East Anglia and the Scylfings of Uppland. This could have involved kinship, as Dr Bruce-Mitford once suggested,

> the concentration of close parallels in Uppland ... strongly suggest that if the Wuffingas came from Sweden, they were an off-shoot of the Royal House of Uppsala, the Scylfings.[39]

Lindqvist went further and advanced the theory that the name *Wehha*, which is listed in seventh position in King Ælfwald's pedigree, could be identified with the name *Wīhstān*, which is borne by the father of Wiglaf (*lēod Scylfinga*, 1.2603ᵇ) in *Beowulf*.[40] Such a theory is certainly philologically tenable, for the form *Wehha* could be explained as a hypocoristic variant of the name *Wīhstān*.[41]

Yet the archaeological parallels between East Anglia and Uppland need not necessarily stem from kindred relations between the Wuffings and the Scylfings, as instances of other close archaeological parallels outside Uppland suggest. For example, as Bruce-Mitford has also pointed out, the discovery of four bronze helmet-plate stamping dies from Torslunda (one of which was mentioned above) implies that helmets of the type found at Sutton Hoo and at Vendel were not made only in Uppland.[42] Furthermore, a gold cloisonné sword-pommel from Hög Edsten in the western Swedish province of Bohuslän has emerged as the closest parallel yet to the splendid gold cloisonné jewellery from Sutton Hoo. This pommel has facetted garnets on its outer edges, a detail which is only found elsewhere on the cloisonné pyramid-mounts from the Sutton Hoo sword-harness.[43] An examination of the chemical

[37] See Lindqvist, *Uppsala Högar och Ottarshögen*, p. 341 and fig. 101; Bruce-Mitford, *Aspects of Anglo-Saxon Archaeology*, p. 41 and plate 10d; *SHSB*, vol. 2, p. 598).
[38] Lindqvist, *Uppsala Högar och Ottarshögen*, p. 341 and figs 106–107; Bruce-Mitford, *Aspects of Anglo-Saxon Archaeology*, pp. 122, 123–124 and fig. 21; *SHSB*, vol. 1, pp. 100–136, especially at pp. 112–113 and pp. 125–126.
[39] Bruce-Mitford, *Aspects of Anglo-Saxon Archaeology*, p. 57.
[40] Lindqvist, "Sutton Hoo and *Beowulf*, p. 139, note 19.
[41] See also the discussion of this point by O'Loughlin, "Sutton Hoo ...", pp. 10–11.
[42] Bruce-Mitford, *Aspects of Anglo-Saxon Archaeology*, pp. 214–222; and "The Sutton Hoo Ship-Burial: Reflections after Thirty Years", pp. 34–35.
[43] Bruce-Mitford, *Aspects of Anglo-Saxon Archaeology*, pp. 42 and plate 11c; *SHSB*, vol. 2,

constitution of the garnets used in the Hög Edsten pommel, moreover, has revealed a remarkable closeness to that of some of the Sutton Hoo garnets, especially those in the magnificent shoulder clasps.[44] Two independent details of this pommel, therefore, show close parallels with some of the Sutton Hoo regalia.

Viewed thus in a wider context, the parallels between the archaeologies of East Anglia and Sweden do not necessarily imply that the Wuffings were descended from the Scylfings. As Professor Martin Carver has pointed out, "the link with Swedish Uppland *appears* strong because that is where the principal and most affluent Scandinavian power centre had emerged at the time of East Anglia's own period of demonstrative wealth".[45] Nevertheless, the parallels do permit the possibility of Wuffing kinship with, or descent from, one or more aristocracy in the broader context of sixth-century southern Scandinavia.

I have dwelt on this archaeological point because both *Beowulf* and *Widsith* may also suggest that the Wulfings were thought to dwell in southern Scandinavia. They are listed in *Widsith* as follows:

> "Sigehere lengest   Sǣ-Denum wēold,
> Hnæf Hōcingum,   Helm Wulfingum ..."

> ' "Sigehere ruled the Sea-Danes for a long time, Hnæf the Hocings and Helm the Wulfings" ' (ll.28–29).

The *Wulfingas* (l.29[b]) are grouped here with *Sǣ-Dene* (l.28[b]) and *Hōcingas* (l.29[a]). The latter appear to have been closely associated with the Scylding dynasty in *Beowulf*, as is clear from the *Frēswæl* episode (ll.1071–1159). Hnæf, the brother of *Hōces dohtor* (l.1076[b]) is described there as *hæleð Healf-Dena, Hnæf Scyldinga*, 'the hero of the Half-Danes, Hnæf of the Scyldings' (l.1069).[46] The Wulfings thus have been grouped with two Danish clans in *Widsith*, a grouping which suggests that they were thought to be located within a Danish sphere of influence.

Although the geography is uncertain, a relationship between Danes and Wulfings is also implied by *Beowulf*. They are named once in the poem as *Wylfingas* (l.461[a]) and once as *Wilfingas* (l.471[a]), both of which are close variants of OE *Wulfingas*.[47] They are mentioned by King

p. 303 and plate 230; and "The Sutton Hoo Ship-Burial: Some Foreign Connections", p. 193).

[44] Bimson and Leese, "The Characterization of Mounted Garnets and its Value as Archaeological Evidence"; Bruce-Mitford, "The Sutton Hoo Ship-Burial: some Foreign Connections", pp. 194–195.

[45] Carver, "Kingship and Material Culture in Early Anglo-Saxon East Anglia", p. 149.

[46] See Malone, *Widsith*, 2nd edition, pp. 172–173; and Tolkien, *Finn and Hengest*, pp. 40–45, 50–52.

[47] Leake once sought to show that the *Wylfingas* of *Beowulf* were entirely fictional (*The*

Hroðgar in his response to Beowulf's offer of help against the terror of Grendel. He recounts how, once long before, he had settled a feud incurred by Ecgþeow, the hero's father, *"mid Wilfingum"*, ' "among the Wulfings" ' (ll.459–472). It is probable that he regards the young hero's offer as reciprocating the aid he had formerly given Ecgþeow, as lines 457–458 seem to imply.

Hrōðgār maþelode,   helm Scyldinga:
"For [g]ewy[r]htum þū,   wine mīn Bēowulf,
7 for ārstafum   ūsic sōhtest.
Geslōh þīn fæder   fæhðe mǣste
wearþ hē Heaþolāfe   tō handbonan
mid Wilfingu*m*;   ðā hine <   >gara cyn
for herebrōgan   habban ne mihte.
Þanon hē gesōhte   Sūð-Dena folc
ofer ȳða gewealc,   Ār-Scyldinga;
ðā ic furþum wēold   folce Den*i*ga
7 on geogoðe hēold   gin*n*e rice,
hordburh hæleþa;   ðā wæs Heregār dēad
mīn yldra mæg   unlifigende,
bearn Healfdenes;   sē wæs betera ðonne ic!
Siððan þā fæhðe   fēo þingode;
sende ic Wylfingum   ofer wæteres hrycg
ealde mādmas;   hē mē āþas swōr."

'Hroðgar spoke, the lord of the Scyldings: "My dear Beowulf, you have sought us because of a sense of duty and of honour. Your father kindled the greatest of feuds among the Wulfings when he became the killer of Heaðolaf. Because of fear of strife, < >*gara cyn* were unable to keep him. Then he sought the *Sūð-Dena* folk, the Honour-Scyldings, over the surging waves. It was then that I first ruled the Danish folk, and in youth held the precious realm and the citadel of heroes; Heorogar, Healfdene's boy, my elder brother, was dead by then and living no longer – he was better than I! So I settled the feud with riches; I sent ancient treasures over the waters' wave to the Wulfings – he [Ecgþeow] swore oaths to me" ' (ll.456–472).

It appears clear that, because of Ecgþeow's killing of Heaðolaf *"mid Wilfingum"* ' "among the Wulfings" ' (ll.460–461[a]), Beowulf's father was obliged to seek *"Sūð-Dena folc"* (l.463[b]). The compound *Sūð-Dene* is used only once elsewhere in the poem (l.1996[a]). In both instances, the choice of the first element *sūð*, as opposed to *ēst*, *west* or *norð*, may have been preferred because of alliterative considerations, so may be void of any

---

Geats of Beowulf, p. 86), but her position was demolished comprehensively by Smithers, "The Geats in *Beowulf*", especially pp. 90–94.

geographical significance.[48] Yet alliterative requirements do not necessarily mean that that the compound is void of significance, as Godfrid Storms has argued, for *Sūð-Dene* in *Beowulf* appears to refer to the Danes from a *northern* point of view.[49] This also seems to be the case with the use of the compound in *Widsith*:

> "Ic wæs mid Hūnum   7 mid Hrēð-Gotum,
> mid Swēom 7 mid Gēatum   7 mid Sūþ-Denum."

> ' "I was with with the Huns and with the Victory-Goths, with the Swedes and with the Geats and with *Sūð-Denum*" ' (ll.57–58).

That the *Sūð-Dene* are grouped here *mid Swēom 7 mid Gēatum* (1.58) suggests that Danish homeland was thought to be to the south of the Swedes and Geats.[50] The same implication arises from the second instance of the compound *Sūð-Dene* in *Beowulf* (l.1996[a]), when the Geatish king, Hygelac, voices the doubts he had harboured about Beowulf's decision to cross the sea to Denmark and fight Grendel.

> "ic ðē lange bæd,
> þæt ðū þone wælgǣst   wihte ne grētte,
> lēte Sūð-Dene   sylfe geweorðan
> gūðe wið Grendel."

> ' "I long entreated you not to confront the slaughterous ghost at all, to let the *Sūð-Dene* themselves settle the war with Grendel" ' (ll.1994[b]–1997[a]).

As the *Gēatas* appear to have been located in the vicinity of what are now the Swedish provinces of Västergötland and Bohuslän,[51] the indications are that the compound *Sūð-Dene* is used to refer to the Danes relative to their northern neighbours.[52]

The reference to Ecgþeow's journey from "*mid Wilfingum*" (ll.460–461[a]) to "*Sūð-Dena folc*" (l.463[b]) thus may also suggest the Danish homeland was thought to be to the south of that of the Wulfings. Moreover,

[48] Magoun, "Danes, North, South, East, and West, in *Beowulf*".

[49] Storms, *Studies in Compounded Names of Peoples in Beowulf*, pp. 12–13.

[50] It was Tolkien's opinion that the context of the *Widsith* reference to *Sūþ-Dene* (l.58) is "purely Scandinavian or 'Scedelandic', in which *Sūþ* is probably an ancient affix, referring to their original location with regard to their northern neighbours, which enabled this ancient triad to be fitted into an alliterative line" (*Finn and Hengest*, p. 163).

[51] See Klaeber, pp. xlvi–xlviii; Farrell, *Beowulf, Swedes and Geats*, pp. 34–36, 38; Overing, "Reinventing Beowulf's Voyage to Denmark"; and Osborn, "Beowulf's Landfall in *Finna Land*".

[52] Bryan agreed, maintaining that "on the only occasion when any clear geographical notion may be read [*i.e.* ll.1994[b]–1997[a]] . . . , the direction implied in the compound is accurate" ("Epithetic Compound Folk-Names in *Beowulf*", p. 125); see also Niles, *Beowulf: The Poem and Its Tradition*, pp. 145–146.

just as the Geats are said to have been separated from the Danes by sea (ll.210–224ª; 1903ᵇ–1913), so are the Wulfings, for Ecgþeow *"gesōhte Sūð-Dena folc | ofer ȳða gewealc"*, ' "sought the *Sūð-Dena* folk over the surging waves" ' (ll.463–464ª). Similarly, King Hroðgar was able to settle Ecgþeow's feud by sending treasure back across the sea to the Wulfings: *"sende ic Wylfingum ofer wæteres hrycg | ealde mādmas,"* ' "I sent ancient treasures over the waters' wave to the Wulfings" ' (ll.471–472ª). *Beowulf* seems then to imply that the Wulfings were deemed to dwell in the proximity of the Geats, with the Danes across the sea to the south. If so, it would appear that the Wulfing home was believed to be along the western coastlands of the south Scandinavia, in what is now south-western Sweden and south-eastern Norway, during the time with which the poem appears to be concerned, that is, between the late fifth and mid-sixth centuries.[53]

A southern Scandinavian location for the Wulfings has also been deduced by other scholars,[54] though some have favoured a homeland on the southern shores of the Baltic. On the basis that the OE *Wylfingas* are identifiable with the *Wölfinge* of Middle High German legend (ON *Ylfingar*),[55] for example, where the *Wölfinge* appear as the supporters of the famous Ostro-Gothic king Þeodric (Dietrich von Bern), Chambers reckoned that the home of the Wulfings was in northern Germany.[56] This German association of Wulfings and Goths, however, could have derived from a common Scandinavian background, a situation perhaps reflected in *Beowulf*, where the *Wylfingas* seem to be represented as dwelling in the same general area as the Gothic *Gēatas*.

Kemp Malone once located them in south-western Sweden,[57] but later argued that they may have been neighbours of the Langobards, whom he located in what is now Holstein, suggesting the Wulfings lived around Micklenburg or Nether Pomerania.[58] His suggestion was based on the Langobardic tradition, recorded by Paulus Diaconus,[59] which told of a conflict with a people named as *Vulgares*, whom Malone identified as the Wulfings. Despite making a good case for this identification (see the discussion below on Ecgþeow and the Wulfings), it is not clear what period or area this tradition stems from; again, it could derive from a common Scandinavian background.

[53] See Map 1 and the discusion of the poem's historical horizon in Chapter Two.
[54] See, for example, Björkman, *Studien über Eigennamen im Beowulf*, pp. 121–122; Nerman, *Det Svenske Rikets Uppkomst*, p. 116; and O'Loughlin, "Sutton Hoo: the Evidence of the Documents", pp. 3–4.
[55] Gillespie, *Catalogue of Persons Named in German Heroic Literature*, p. 153.
[56] See, for example, the discussion by Chambers, *Widsith*, p. 198.
[57] Malone, *The Literary History of Hamlet*, pp. 35, 37.
[58] Malone, "Agelmund and Lamicho", pp. 86–107, pp. 96, 101; see also the discussion in his second edition of *Widsið*, pp. 213–214.
[59] Bethmann and Waitz (ed.) *Scriptores Rerum Langobardicarum*, I.

There thus appear to be no arguments which compel us to ignore the indications gleaned from *Beowulf* and *Widsith* which suggest that the Wulfings were thought to live in what is now south-western Sweden and south-eastern Norway during the late fifth and early sixth centuries.

The main points considered so far in this section are as follows:

(1) the name of the East Anglian royal family, *Wuffingas*, is etymologically identical to that of the *Wylfingas* of *Beowulf* and the *Wulfingas* of *Widsith*;

(2) there are archaeological indications that the East Anglian Wuffings may have had kindred relations with southern Scandinavia in the sixth century; and

(3) *Beowulf* and *Widsith* suggest that the Wulfings were thought to have dwelt in southern Scandinavia.

Each one of these points has been deduced independently of the others. Taken together, they lead to the hypothesis that the East Anglian Wuffings may have considered themselves to be related to, or descended from, the Wulfings of Old English poetry.

Let us now return to the *Beowulf* passage concerning Ecgþeow and the Wulfings (ll.456–472) cited above. As I pointed out, because Ecgþeow was held responsible for the killing of Heaðolaf *"mid Wilfingum"*, ' "among the Wulfings" ' (ll.460–461ª), he was obliged to seek *"Sūð-Dena folc"* (l.463ᵇ). Although Hroðgar was eventually able to settle the matter by sending compensation across the sea to the Wulfings, it is not clear why Ecgþeow should have gone to the Scylding court in the first place. We are told that

> "... ðā hine <   >gara cyn
> for herebrōgan   habban ne mihte"

' "Because of fear of strife, <   >*gara cyn* were unable to keep him" ' (ll.461ᵇ–462).

The situation is then that *"for herebrōgan"*, ' "out fear of strife" ' (l.462ª), Ecgþeow was unable to remain with a folk whose name is spelt in the manuscript as *gara cyn* (l.461ᵇ).[60] This form must be the consequence of scribal error, as nearly all editors and commentators of the poem agree.[61] It appears to be a characteristic type of error, based on the scribe's

---

[60] Folio 140ʳ (new foliation 143ʳ), line 18; Zupitza's facsimile of the *Beowulf* manuscript, p. 22.

[61] Kelly, "The Formative Stages of *Beowulf* Textual Scholarship: part II", p. 242.

misunderstanding of a personal name.[62] The question is, therefore, how should this error be emended?

Kiernan actually proposed the acceptance of the scribal *gāra cyn*, which he translated as 'spear-troop' or *comitatus*.[63] This proposal may be rejected, however, not only because it is metrically difficult, but also because it implies that Ecgþeow's *comitatus* was reprehensibly unheroic, *"for herebrōgan"*, ' "for fear of strife" ' (l.462ᵃ). Such behaviour would have invited the same rebuke which Wiglaf delivered to the late hero's troop after their failure to aid their lord against the dragon: *"dēað bið sēlla / eorla gehwylcum þonne edwītlīf"*, ' "death is better for each man than a life of disgrace" ' (ll.2890ᵇ–2891). Byers emended the phrase to *wine-gāra cyn*, arguing that it refers to the *Gēatas*.[64] Similarly, the emendation which has been favoured by most scholars, *Wedera cyn*,[65] would also refer to the *Gēatas*, for *Wederas* is synonymous with *Gēatas* in *Beowulf*.[66] Yet there is no necessary palaeographical connection between *Wedera* and *gāra* for there is nothing in the preceding lines which might have misled the scribe. Both *Wedera cyn* and *wine-gāra cyn*, moreover, create contextual problems, for they imply that the *Gūð-Gēatas* were unwilling to assist the hero's father *"for herebrōgan"*, ' "for fear of strife" ' (l.462ᵃ). Ecgþeow was certainly related to the Geatish royal family, the *Hrēðlingas*, through his marriage to the daughter of Hreðel (ll.374–375ᵃ). In almost every other instance in *Beowulf* where a princess is given in marriage, the father's intention appears primarily political, and the daughter becomes the bride of a leading member of another clan.[67] The marriage of Hreðel's daughter thus probably realised an allegiance between the *Gēatas* and Ecgþeow's clan. Assuming that Ecgþeow's trouble *mid Wilfingum*, which must have occurred some time before Beowulf's visit to Heorot (ll.465–469), took place after his marriage to the Geatish princess, the proposed emendation *wara cyn* might be semantically plausible,[68] if *wara* is understood as the genitive plural of *wǣr*, 'treaty' or 'pledge'. Again, however, as well as being metrically difficult, this emendation is palaeographically difficult to substantiate, as there is no reason to suppose scribal

[62] As Sisam noted, *Studies*, p. 37.
[63] Kiernan, *Beowulf and the Beowulf Manuscript*, pp. 182, 185.
[64] Byers, "A Possible Emendation of *Beowulf* 461ᵇ".
[65] First proposed by Grundtvig, *Beowulfes Beorh eller* (1861), and since followed by a majority of scholars – see Kelly, "The Formative Stages of *Beowulf* Textual Scholarship: part II", p. 242.
[66] Lines 225ᵃ, 423ᵃ, 498ᵇ, 697ᵇ, 1894ᵇ, 2120ᵃ, 2186ᵃ, 2462ᵃ, 2656ᵃ, 2705ᵃ, 2786ᵇ, 2900ᵇ, 3037ᵃ and 3156ᵇ.
[67] See my discussion of other examples of this kind of marriage in *Beowulf* later in this chapter.
[68] First proposed by Thorpe, *The Anglo-Saxon Poems of Beowulf, the Scop or Gleeman's Tale, and the Fight at Finnesburg* (1855).

confusion between the insular g of *gara* and the w (runic *wynn*) of *wara*.[69] It also seems unlikely that Hroðgar would be so tactless as point out to Beowulf, who has just offered Geatish help to the Scylding king, that Hreðel had acted dishonourably in this affair by refusing to help his own son-in-law *"for herebrōgan"*, ' "for fear of strife" ' (l.462ᵃ).

The proposed emendations for line 461ᵇ, *wine-gāra cyn*, *Wedera cyn* and *wara cyn*, therefore appear inadequate. It seems clear that the emendation of *gara cyn* requires either a personal name or a kenning for a name which, following *Wilfingum* in the *a*-verse, begins with *wynn*; which explains palaeographically the presence of *gara*; and which makes contextual sense. On these criteria, Malone's proposal to emend the half-line to <*Wul*>*gara cyn* seems a most satisfactory solution.[70] It supplies the necessary alliteration without compromising metrical requirements. It also accounts for the manuscript reading <   >*gara cyn*, for the omission of the first syllable may be partly explained by the type of scribal error known as haplography, whereby the scribe has been confused by the similarity of two forms in his master-copy, with the result that he has written only one of them. Here, the scribe could have written <   >*gara* in error for <*Wul*>*gara* in the *b*-verse because he had only just penned *Wilfingum* in the *a*-verse. Malone supported his emendation by drawing attention to another case of the same scribe's confusion over a personal name, also apparently involving the omission of its first syllable, when he copied *elan* (l.62ᵇ) in probable error for <*On*>*elan*.[71] The emendation <*Wul*>*gara cyn* thus avoids the palaeographical, metrical problems inherent in accepting *Wedera cyn*, *wara cyn* or *wine-gāra cyn*. Its implications, however, have caused some scholars to hesitate to accept it,[72] for <*Wul*>*gara* is the genitive form of *Wulgaras*, which, according to Malone, is a synonym for *Wylfingas*. He argued that *Vulgares*, used by Paulus Diaconus to refer to the enemies of the Langobards, is a Latinised form of the Langobardish *Wulg(w)aras*, which he identified plausibly as a name for the Wulfings.[73] The second element, *-(w)aras* is found in another of the folk-names in *Beowulf*, *Hetware*, 'helmeted inhabitants' (ll.2363ᵃ, 2916ᵃ). The acceptance of <*Wul*>*gara cyn* thus implies that the feud was initially an internal affair *mid Wilfingum* and that Ecgþeow himself was a

---

69 Tuso has also argued for the reading *wāra cyn*, proposing a possible alternative meaning for *wara* as the genitive plural of the neuter noun *wār*, 'seaweed', 'sand' or 'shore' (*"Beowulf* 461ᵇ and Thorpe's *wara"*, p. 261). As such, according to Tuso, the phrase could refer to the Wulfings, a possibility considered below.

70 Malone, "Ecgtheow", pp. 39–40.

71 "Ecgtheow", p. 40; though haplography does not appear to have been the cause of this error.

72 For example, Holthausen, "Zur Textkritik des *Beowulf*"; Byers, "A Possible Emendation of *Beowulf* 461b", pp. 125–6, and Kiernan, *Beowulf and the Beowulf Manuscript*, p. 182.

73 Malone, "Ecgtheow", p. 40; "Agelmund and Lamicho", p. 92, and his second edition of *Widsith*, p. 213.

Wulfing. Certainly, this does seem to clarify the context of the matter. As a Wulfing, Ecgþeow would have been obliged to go into exile to avoid further strife (*"for herebrōgan"* [l.462ª]) amongst the Wulfings themselves, perhaps until such a time as he would have been able to pay compensation (*wergild*) to the relatives of Heaðolaf. Malone's proposed emendation appears thus to be more satisfying in its palaeographical, metrical and narrative contexts than any of the alternatives.

If Ecgþeow was understood to be a Wulfing, the corollary is that Beowulf himself would have been regarded as being of half-Wulfing blood. Yet we cannot be sufficiently sure that Ecgþeow really was known to be a Wulfing, not least because the claim depends largely on the question of how we emend line 461ᵇ. Ecgþeow's tribal identity is not actually specified anywhere in the poem, but that it was implicit knowledge is indicated by Beowulf's reference to his father's reputation during his address to the Danish coastguard:

> "Wæs mīn fæder   folcum gecȳþed,
> æþele ordfruma,   Ecgþēow hāten;
> gebād wintra worn,   ǣr hē on weg hwurfe,
> gamol of geardum;   hine gearwe geman
> witena wēlhwylc   wīde geond eorþan"

> ' "My father was well-known among folk – he was a noble battle-leader, called Ecgþeow; he knew many winters before, in old age, he wended his way from this world; every wise man on this wide earth readily recalls him" ' (ll.262–266).

We are told that Ecgþeow was widely known (l.262ᵇ) before he died in old age (ll.264ᵇ–265ª). His fame, moreover, continues after his death: *"hine gearwe geman / witena wēlhwylc wīde geond eorþan"*, ' "every wise man on this wide earth readily recalls him" ' (ll.265ᵇ–266). The continuity of that fame is particularly emphasised by the use of the present tense in this clause, which suggests that Ecgþeow's kindred identity was unstated background knowledge.

There have been a number of attempts at deducing Ecgþeow's ancestry. Edith Wardale once suggested that he was a Swede on rather questionable contextual grounds.[74] She might have added that his name fits into the alliterative pattern characteristic of the Swedish dynasty, the Scylfings, whose kings and princes in *Beowulf* all bear names beginning with a vowel. It is also linked to that of the Scylfing king, Ongenþeow, by front-variation, which may prompt the possibility of some affinity between the two.[75] It has also been suggested that Ecgþeow may have been of Wægmunding kin, a claim which rests on the explicit reference which

---

[74] Wardale, "*Beowulf*: The Nationality of *Ecgðeow*".
[75] As Gordon argued, "Wealhþeow and Related Names".

Beowulf makes in his dying speech to his lone supporter against the dragon, the young Wiglaf.

"Þū eart endelāf ūsses cynnes,
Wǣgmundinga; ealle wyrd forswēop
mīne māgas tō metodsceafte,
eorlas on elne; ic him æfter sceal"

' "You are the last of our clan, the Wægmundings; *wyrd* has swept away all my kinsmen to their appointed destinies, those courageous warriors; I shall now follow them" ' (ll.2813–2816).

The exact kindred relationship between the hero and the Wægmundings is not specified, but the possibility that he may have been connected with the clan through his father cannot be ruled out.[76] The Wægmundings themselves appear to have had close relations with both Scylfings and Hreðlings, who themselves were often in conflict. Wiglaf's father, Wihstan Wægmunding, is referred to as fighting in the service of King Onela in his battle with his nephews, who were supported by King Heardred Hreðling (ll.2612b–2619). Wiglaf himself is described as *lēod Scylfinga*, 'a member of the Scylfing clan' (l.2603b), and yet he is also a relative and retainer of Beowulf of the Hreðlings. Glosecki's suggestion, that Scylfings and Hreðlings were alienated branches of the same race, and that the Wægmundings, caught between the two, were obliged to ally themselves first with the former and then with the latter, perhaps comes closest to making the references to the clan intelligible.[77]

Yet whatever the tribal identity of Ecgþeow, the immediately ensuing consequence of his troubles *mid Wilfingum* (ll.460–462) is clear – "*Þanon hē gesōhte Sūð-Dena folc / ofer ȳða gewealc*", ' "then he sought the *Sūð-Dena* folk over the surging waves" ' (ll.463–464b). He appears not to have been of Danish blood, nor yet bound to Hroðgar by *āþas*, 'oaths' (l.472b), so it remains unclear as to why he goes straight to the court of the Scylding king. Once there, however, King Hroðgar is able to reconcile the contending parties successfully:

"Siððan þā fæhðe feo þingode;
sende ic Wylfingum ofer wæteres hrycg
ealde mādmas; hē mē āþas swōr."

' "So I settled the feud with riches; I sent ancient treasures over the waters' wave to the Wulfings – he [Ecgþeow] swore oaths to me" ' (ll.470–472).

---

[76] See, for example, Byers, "The Last of the Wægmundings and a Possible Emendation of *Beowulf*".
[77] Glosecki, "The Boar's Helmet in *Beowulf*", pp. 290–291.

The outcome of the affair thus shows that the Wulfings had relations with – and were mutually respected by – the mighty Scyldings. That King Hroðgar was acceptable as arbiter to the contending parties, moreover, may imply that there was some sort of unstated special relationship between Scyldings and Wulfings. This point is also suggested independently by the indications that Hroðgar's queen, Wealhþeow, may have been regarded as a Wulfing.

QUEEN WEALHÞEOW AND THE WULFINGS

Apart perhaps from Grendel's monstrous mother, Queen Wealhþeow can be said to be *Beowulf*'s leading lady. We have already seen how prominent a part she plays in the episode of the victory-feast in Heorot (ll.991–1250). She is described earlier in the poem as *ides Helminga*, 'the Helming lady' (l.620b). *Helmingas* must be her family name, the eponym of which is listed in *Widsith*: "*Helm (weold) Wulfingum*", ' "Helm (ruled) the Wulfings" ' (l.29b). *Helm* is an element which occurs in many Old English compound personal names, but is rare in uncompounded form. Some scholars have supposed it to be an "imaginary name for an epic king",[78] or as some sort of neutral "heraldic" emblem.[79] Yet the use of the patronymic form in *Beowulf* implies a genealogical function, in that, as *ides Helminga*, Wealhþeow was regarded as the daughter of *Helm*, who may have been understood to be either her father or her family's eponymous founder. If the former, he may be also referred to as *þeoden* in line 2174a of *Beowulf*, when Wealhþeow is described as *ðeod(nes) dohtor*.

Professor Fred Robinson, however, once cast doubt on her royal status in *Beowulf* by arguing that the phrase *ðeod(nes) dohtor* does not refer to Wealhþeow.[80] The phrase in question occurs in the passage concerned with the special neck-ring which Wealhþeow had given to Beowulf (ll.1192–1217a), and which he presents later to Hygd on his return to the kingdom of the Hreðlings:

> hȳrde ic þæt hē ðone healsbēah   Hygde gesealde,
> wrǣtlicne wundurmāððum,   ðone þe him Wealhðēo geaf,
> ðēod(nes) dohtor . . .

> 'I heard that he presented to Hygd the neck-ring which Wealhþeow had given him, the folk-king's daughter' (ll.2172–2174a)

[78] J. Hill, *Old English Minor Heroic Poems*, p. 89.
[79] As Bliss suggested in one of his annotations to Tolkien's *Finn and Hengest*, p. 41, note 19.
[80] Robinson, "Is Wealhþeow a Prince's Daughter?" (1964).

The question is, is it *Hygde* (1.2172^b) or *Wealhðeo* (1.2173^b) which precedes the appositional epithet *ðeod(nes) dohtor*, 'the folk-king's daughter' (1.2174^a)? Arguably, there is an alliterative collocation, linked by the ð-syllables, between ll.2173^b and 2174^a, which may suggest that it is Wealhþeow, rather than Hygd, who is the one referred to as *ðeod(nes) dohtor*. This possibility was not mentioned by Robinson, who argued for Hygd. His case depended on two points.

First, he had to explain why *dohtor* was not, as it appears to be in the manuscript, a nominative singular form in agreement with *Wealhðeo*, the original giver of the ring. He argued that *dohtor* could be an unumlauted dative singular form, which would then be in grammatical agreement with the dative singular *Hygde*. Second, he had to account for the syntactic separation of the appositive epithet from its antecedent. This he did by examining the seven comparable occurrences of the form *-es dohtor* in Old English verse, concluding that "in every instance of such apposition in Old English poetry the patronymic epithet is separated from its antecedent by at least a full half-line" and, therefore, "that such separation is not only possible but is stylistically more probable".[81] His example from *Widsith* similarly concerns the presentation of a ring by a queen:

> ... 7 mē þā Ealhhild   ōþerne forgeaf,
> dryhtcwēn duguþe,   dohtor Eadwines.

> 'and Ealhhild gave me another [ring], noble queen of excellence, Edwin's daughter' (ll.97–98).

The appositive *dohtor Eadwines* (1.98^b), the giver of the ring, is indeed, as Robinson noted, separated from its antecedent *Ealhhild* (1.97^a) by at least a full half-line; but it also immediately follows the half-line *dryhtcwēn duguþe* (1.98^a), which also refers appositively to Ealhhild. Robinson only cited one other example, besides *ðeod(nes) dohtor* (1.2174^a), of an instance of the patronymic appositive *-es dohtor* from *Beowulf* – 1.1929^a. As the well-separated antecedent of this is also *Hygd* (1.1926^b), it might just confirm his point. Yet why should examples of the syntactic relation of the patronymic appositive to its antecedent be selected only from instances of the epithet *-es dohtor*? Examination of the occurrences of the same syntactic relation involving the directly analogous patronymic epithet *-es sunu* in *Beowulf* reveals a very high frequency of the juxtaposition of the appositive to its antecedent in adjacent half-lines.[82] It is the same high frequency in the case of *-es bearn*.[83] It would appear thus that the separation of the patronymic appositive epithet from its antecedent

81 Robinson, *ibid.*, p. 38.
82 For example, ll.268, 590, 1485, 1652, 1699, 1808, 2147, 2602, 2612, 2862, 3076.
83 For example, ll.499, 529, 631, 888, 957, 1383, 1483, 1651, 1817, 1999, 2425.

by at least a full half-line is not necessarily stylistically probable. There is, therefore, no compelling reason why the epithet *ðeod(nes) dohtor* (l.2174ª) cannot stand in appositive relation to *Wealhðeo* in the preceding half-line (l.2173ᵇ). That Professor Robinson has not attempted to sustain his 1964 argument in his recent book on the uses of apposition in *Beowulf* suggests to me that he would concede that the phrase *ðeod(nes) dohtor* may indeed refer to Wealhþeow.[84] If so, the *þeoden* of *Beowulf*, line 2074ª, is identifiable as the *Helm* of *Widsith*, line 29ª.

Yet whether Wealhþeow was *Helmes dohtor* or the descendant of a more remote eponymous figure called *Helm*, the implication arising from *Widsith* is that *Helmingas* was an alternative name for *Wulfingas* in Old English poetic tradition. The epithet *ides Helminga* thus can be interpreted as being synonymous with *ides Wulfinga* and Wealhþeow thus can be identified as a Wulfing princess.[85] If so, her marriage to Hroðgar can be seen to have realised a close allegiance, through royal kinship, between Wulfings and Scyldings.

As I mentioned briefly above, in almost every instance in *Beowulf* where a princess is given in marriage, the motive appears primarily political, and the princess becomes the bride of leading member of another clan.[86] Two of these fail with tragic consequences: that of the Danish princess, Hildeburh, to Finn Folcwalding, king of the Frisians (ll.1071–1159), whose marriage appears to represent an attempt at an alliance between Frisians and Danes;[87] and that of Hroðgar's daughter, Freawaru, to the Heaðobard prince, Ingeld (ll.2024ª–2069ª), through which Hroðgar hopes to secure a peaceful end to the old feud between Scyldings and Heaðobards. The failure of the latter is foretold by Beowulf with gnomic wisdom.

> "Oft seldan hwær
> æfter lēodhryre   lȳtle hwīle
> bongār būgeð,   þeah sēo brȳd duge."

' "Seldom anywhere after the fall of a folk-prince does the spear of death lie still for long, however excellant the bride be" ' (ll.2029ᵇ–2031).

---

[84] Robinson, *Beowulf and the Appositive Style* (1985).

[85] As other scholars have noted – Sarrazin, "Neue *Beowulf*-Studien" (1897), pp. 228–230; Arnold, *Notes on Beowulf* (1898), p. 43; Gordon, "Wealhðeow and Related Names" (1935), p. 169; Malone, "Ēcgþeow" (1940), p. 40; 2nd edition of *Widsith* (1959), p. 169; O'Loughlin, "Sutton Hoo: the Evidence of the Documents (1964), p. 5; and Farrell, *Beowulf, Swedes and Geats* (1972), p. 19.

[86] The widespread occurrence and function of such marriages in tribal societies has been discussed by Glosecki in his unpublished dissertation, "The Boar's Helmet in *Beowulf*: Reflexes of Totemism and Exogamy in Early Germanic Literature", pp. 180–203.

[87] This tragic episode in *Beowulf* was discussed earlier in this chapter.

We seem to have here an allusion to the killing of Ingeld's father, Froda. Beowulf's words imply that Ingeld's thirst for vengeance will not be quenched by oaths of marriage.[88] Wealhþeow's marriage to Hroðgar is depicted as a more enduring example of this kind of union, and so may be regarded as successfully constituting, through interdynastic kinship, a political allegiance and affinity between Wulfings and Scyldings. Wealhþeow is thus referred to as both *ides Helminga* (l.620[b]) and *ides Scyldinga* (l.1168[b]). Of special importance in this context is the reference to her as *friðusibb folca*, 'the kindred pledge of peace between peoples' (l.2017[a]), a phrase which seems to describe succinctly her matrimonial function.[89] She herself can thus be seen as the very personification of peaceful relations between Wulfings and Scyldings.

All of this offers an excellent reason for Ecgþeow to seek the aid of the Danish king in settling his dispute *mid Wilfingum*.[90] As husband of the *friðusibb folca*, Hroðgar would have had the authority to act as an effective reconciler of the opposing factions. He was thus able to settle the affair by sending compensation across the sea to the Wulfings in return for Ecgþeow's *āþas* (ll.470–472). In alluding to the help he had given formerly to Ecgþeow, Hroðgar is able to accept with undiminished dignity the offer of help against Grendel from Ecgþeow's son.

Now, when the indications for the identification of Wealhþeow as a Wulfing princess are linked to the hypothesis advanced earlier in this chapter – that the East Anglian Wuffings may have considered themselves to have been related to, or descended from, the Wulfings of *Beowulf* and *Widsith* – the conclusion is that Wealhþeow may have been regarded as an East Anglian dynastic ancestor. Klaeber himself noted that "the name of Wealhþeow's family, *Helmingas*, possibly points to East Anglia".[91] He appears to have based this view on the hypothesis of Gregor Sarrazin, who drew attention to the likely synonymity of *Helmingas* and *Wulfingas* and the latter's equivalence with *Wuffingas* as early as 1897.[92] Sarrazin's hypothesis depended partly on the references in two Northern sources concerned with the Scyldings which explicitly associate the wife of King Hroðgar with England. These are:

(1) Arngrímur Jónsson's late sixteenth-century Latin abstract of the lost, probably twelfth-century, *Skjǫldunga saga*, which states simply

---

[88] See Klaeber, pp. xxxiv–xxxvi. For a detailed discussion of these and other references to this conflict, see Malone, "The Tale of Ingeld".

[89] The significance of this phrase has been similarly noted by Malone, "The Daughter of Healfdene", p. 140; see also Sklute, "*Freoðuwebbe* in Old English Poetry", pp. 538–540.

[90] Assuming (not unreasonably) that Weahlþeow and Hroðgar were understood to have already been in wedlock at this time.

[91] Klaeber, p. xxxiii, n. 2.

[92] Sarrazin, "Neue *Beowulf*-Studien", pp. 228–230.

that *Roas* (Hroðgar) married the daughter of an English king (ch. 11);[93] and

(2) the probably fourteenth-century Old Icelandic *Hrólfs saga kraka*, which states that *Hróarr* (Hroðgar) married the daughter of a king of *Norðhymbraland* called *Norðri* (ch. 5).[94]

Professor Gwyn Jones has warned since that, "to find significance in such fortuitous references for the presence of a Danish king in the English poem *Beowulf* is surely perilous and probably absurd".[95] Nevertheless, out of all the figures involved in Northern sources concerned with the Danish royal family, it may be significant that Hroðgar's queen is the only one who is directly associated with England, especially if that association was derived from an old genealogical tradition.

Sarrazin may have overstated his case, however, when he construed the name *Norðri* in *Hrólfs saga kraka* as a consequence of a misunderstanding of *Norðfolc* (Norfolk) on the basis that the Norfolk place-name *Helmingham* could be based on Wealhþeow's family-name in *Beowulf*.[96] Although we need not agree with the conjectural construal of the suspicious looking name *Norðri*, we cannot deny that the Old English clanname *Helmingas* is indeed identifiable as the first element of the East Anglian place-name *Helmingham*.[97] There are in fact two such placenames in East Anglia, one in Norfolk and the other in Suffolk.[98] The former is the name of a lost village located in the upper valley of the River Wensum, at a site now contained within the extant parish of Morton-on-the-Hill.[99] Archaeologically, the site is close to a sizeable barrow cemetery, unfortunately undated.[100] Considerable early Anglo-Saxon activity in the vicinity is indicated, however, by the large cemetery just upstream at Spong Hill, which dates from the fifth century.[101] Another cemetery, also dating from the fifth century, has been found just downstream at Drayton.[102] These sites imply that there was Anglo-Saxon settlement in this part of Norfolk from the fifth century onwards.

93 Benediktsson (ed.), *Arngrimi Jonae*, vol. 9.
94 Slay (ed.), *Hrólfs saga kraka*.
95 Jones, *Kings, Beasts and Heroes* (1972), pp. 132–134, at p. 134; see also generally Olson, *The Relation of the Hrólfs Saga Kraka and the Bjarkarímur to Beowulf* (1916).
96 Sarrazin, "Neue *Beowulf*-Studien", p. 229.
97 Ekwall, *The Concise Oxford Dictionary of English Place-Names*, *s.v. Helmingham*. The earliest surviving spelling appears in the Domesday Book.
98 Sarrazin made no reference to Suffolk example, as O'Loughlin noted ("Sutton Hoo . . .", p. 5).
99 Allison, "The Lost Villages of Norfolk", p. 149.
100 Lawson *et al.*, *The Barrows of East Anglia*, figs 5 and 22.
101 C. Hills, *et al.*, *The Anglo-Saxon Cemetery at Spong Hill, North Elmham*.
102 Myres and Green, *The Anglo-Saxon Cemeteries of Caistor-by-Norwich and Markshall, Norfolk*, p. 259 and Map 3.

Helmingham in Suffolk is situated on a tributary of the upper River Deben. Archaeologically, the parish once contained several barrows, of which one survives, of possibly Bronze Age date but with later, apparently Romano-British, secondary cremation burials within them.[103] The River Deben below Helmingham flows through what appears to have been the old heartland of the Wuffing kingdom, a territory corresponding to the group of hundreds administered by the Abbey of Ely from the tenth century, if not earlier, and known as the Wicklaw or the Liberty of St Etheldreda.[104] Helmingham's location just outside this territory could be significant in relation to the sixth- and seventh-century cemeteries downstream at Wickham Market, Rendlesham and Sutton Hoo.[105] Rendlesham was also a royal centre in the second half of the seventh century, if not earlier, as it is described by Bede as being an East Anglian *vicus regius* around the year 660.[106] At the mouth of the Deben, moreover, stood the Roman Saxon Shore fortress of Walton Castle, one of the possible sites of *Dommoc*, named by Bede as the seat of the first East Anglian bishop, St Felix.[107] Although both instances of the place-name *Helmingham* appear to be based on the clan-name *Helmingas*, we cannot be sure that the *Helmingas* of the East Anglian place-names are identifiable with the *Helmingas* of *Beowulf*. Nevertheless, these appear to be the only place-names in England based on *Helmingas*, and the geographical location of the Suffolk example does seem significant in relation to the known East Anglian royal sites.[108]

Sarrazin's hypothesis, therefore, need not be rejected, although we need not accept some of its more conjectural aspects. As such, we may have some grounds for regarding the Scylding queen in *Beowulf* as an East Anglian dynastic forebear. Wealhþeow may represent, therefore, a vital genealogical link between its past Scandinavian world and its Old English audience. Such a link would point to the genealogical traditions of the pre-Viking kingdom of East Anglia as the original context in which

---

103 Lawson *et al.*, *The Barrows of East Anglia*, pp. 70–71 and fig. 25.
104 Scarfe, *The Suffolk Landscape*, pp. 40–42, 88–91; and Warner, "Pre-Conquest Territorial and Administrative Organisation in East Suffolk". St Etheldreda (Æþelþryð) was the daughter of the East Anglian king Onna and founder-abbess of the Abbey of Ely.
105 Myres and Green, *The Anglo-Saxon Cemeteries of Caistor-by-Norwich and Markshall, Norfolk*, p. 262 and Map 3.
106 Bede, *HE*, III, 22; Bruce-Mitford, *Aspects of Anglo-Saxon Archaeology*, pp. 73–113.
107 Bede, *HE*, II, 15; see Rigold, "The Supposed See of Dunwich"; and "Further Evidence about the Site of *Dommoc*".
108 The place-name *Hemley*, if based on the personal name *Helm*, as Arnott suggested (*Place-Names of the Deben Valley*, p. 30), is also worth noting here. It is sited on the western side of the Deben estuary just four miles south of Sutton Hoo, at the point where the river is joined by the tributary of Kirton Creek. Early OE activity has been detected here by Newman ("East Anglian Kingdom Survey – Final Interim Report", fig. 10).

Beowulf's ubiquitous concerns with Northern, especially Danish, dynastic affairs were fostered. Klaeber himself thought possible

> that there may have existed close relations, perhaps through marriage, between an Anglian court and the kingdom of Denmark, whereby a special interest in Scandinavian traditions was fostered among the English nobility.[109]

The Scylding queen's suggested East Anglian connection would not only be highly conducive to such Anglo-Danish relations, it would also account for her prominence in the episode of the victory-feast in Heorot (ll.991–1250) and for the poem's marked interest in Hroðgar's side of the Danish royal family. True, Wealhþeow's name is not listed on the pedigree of King Ælfwald of East Anglia, yet nor should we expect it to be, for that document is only concerned with the line of Ælfwald's forefathers. It may be significant, however, that her name alliterates with the *Wilhelm – Wehha – Wuffa* sequence. The name of one of her sons in *Beowulf*, moreover, *Hrōðmund*, is listed in exactly the same form as we find it in the poem.

This point brings us back to the question of the identifiability of Hroðmund the Scylding with his namesake in the pedigree of King Ælfwald. At the end of the previous chapter, I advanced the supposition that Hroðmund the Scylding could have been understood to have followed the exile's path in the aftermath of the dynastic feud which appears to have divided the Scylding house. I also argued that Hroðmund the ancestor of King Ælfwald was perhaps associated with an East Anglian royal origin-myth. We now have some grounds for identifying the two, for if Queen Wealhþeow was regarded as an East Anglian dynastic forebear, then her son would have been similarly viewed, and hence perhaps his listing in the pedigree of a Wuffing king. Indeed, as the son of *friðusibb folca*, 'the kindred pledge of peace between peoples' (l.2017a), the blood of his parents' two peoples would have been mingled in his veins. He would thus have been seen as the living proof of the special relationship between the Wulfings and Scyldings.

Yet it is not clear as to how the two Hroðmunds might be identifiable, if at all, and we cannot rule out the possibility that there could have been two distinct figures bearing the same name. On one hand, we have Hroðmund the Scylding *æþeling*, whose mother may have been regarded as a possible East Anglian dynastic forebear, in hypothetical exile; on the other, we have a genealogical figure from Wuffing origin-legend. The situation is not unlike the case of the famous Hengest, analogy with whom may suggest how the two Hroðmunds might be identified.[110]

---

[109] Klaeber, p. cxv.
[110] I am indebted to Professor Evison for pointing out this analogy.

Hengest appears in *Beowulf* as a leading figure in the tragedy of the *Frēswæl* (ll.1071–1159),[111] where he is described as a *wrecca*, 'exile' (l.1137[b]).[112] The name *Hengest* is also listed in the pedigree of King Æþelberht II of Kent (725–762).[113] Surviving narrative material concerned with the legendary deeds of Hengest shows that he was seen as an important early English founding figure.[114] The case for the likely identification of the bearer of the name *Hengest* in these sources with his namesake in the *Frēswæl* has been established by Tolkien.[115] He summarised it as follows:

> it is not forcing the evidence, but following its most obvious leading, to identify the two Hengests, and believe that we have preserved two traditions of different adventures in the life-history of one famous adventurer – and each where we should expect it, were the two Hengests one: the story of the gallant defence in the heroic traditions mainly concerned with *Germania*, not Britain; [and] the story of the landing in Britain and the foundation of a new kingdom in the embryonic history of that new kingdom.[116]

The *wrecca* Hengest's adventure across the North Sea in the wake of dynastic strife in the fifth century provides an analogy to that suggested of the putative *wrecca* Hroðmund in not dissimilar circumstances in the sixth century. These dates are of course hypothetical, being inferred from the one datable event referred to in *Beowulf*, namely, the fall of King

---

[111] The same tragedy is also the subject for the heroic fragment, *The Fight at Finnsburh*, where *Hengest sylf* (l.17[a]) is similarly prominent. See Tolkien, *Finn and Hengest* (ed. Bliss), pp. 63–76, 159–162, 168–180. That the *Frēswæl* in *Beowulf* may have been intended to anticipate the tragic fate of the Scyldings, as was argued in the previous chapter, could strengthen the suggested analogy between Hroðmund and Hengest.

[112] As Tolkien argued, Hengest may be understood as a *wrecca* here in the sense of one who is an exiled or dispossessed adventurer in the service of Hnæf (*Finn and Hengest* pp. 64–65). Another of Hnæf's men, Sigeferþ of the *Finnsburh* fragment, who claims to be "*wreccea wīde cūð*", ' "a widely known adventurer" ' (ll.25–26), provides a comparable example. The term *wrecca* may also be used with negative connotations, as was noted above in the case of the compound *wræcmæcg* (l.2379[b]).

[113] This pedigree is also preserved in the Anglian Collection. Like King Ælfwald's, it appears to have been compiled in 725 or 726, as Dumville noted ("The Anglian Collection", p. 40, note 2. Hengest is also named by Bede as an ancestor of King Æþelberht I of Kent, who died on 24th February, 616 (*HE*, II, 5).

[114] *Historia Brittonum*, §§ 31, 36–38, 43–46, 56; the deeds of Hengest are also referred to in the *A* and *E* manuscripts of the *Anglo-Saxon Chronicle*, s.a. 449, 455; and by Bede, *HE*, I, 15, and II, 5. See the discussion by Moisl, "Anglo-Saxon Royal Genealogies and Germanic Oral Tradition", pp. 232–233.

[115] Tolkien, *Finn and Hengest* (ed. Bliss), pp. 66–76. Although at one point in his Appendix on the nationality of Hengest, Bliss attempted (unnecessarily) to impose a chronological sequence onto a version of the Kentish royal pedigree (*ibid.*, p. 176), Tolkien's converging arguments remain sound.

[116] Tolkien, *ibid.*, pp. 67–68.

Hygelac, *ca* 523.[117] Accordingly, the Scylding feud can be estimated to have taken place perhaps around the end of the first quarter of the sixth century, as Klaeber observed.[118] Hroðmund's hypothetical exile may then be provisionally dated to around the beginning of the second quarter of the sixth century. Concomitantly, the *Frēswæl*, which *Beowulf* implies happened a generation or two prior to the main events of the poem, is datable to the previous century, perhaps *ca* 450.[119] Therefore, just as Hengest was to become associated with the legendary origins of the Kentish Oiscings and thus be listed in King Æþelberht's pedigree,[120] so perhaps Hroðmund could have become associated with the legendary origins of the East Anglian Wuffings, and hence his listing in King Ælfwald's ancestral tally.[121]

Again, as in the case of Hengest in Oiscing tradition, it is not certain whether Hroðmund in Wuffing tradition should be regarded as a purely legendary hero who came to be associated retrospectively with dynastic origin-myth or as a proto-historical figure whose deeds helped to establish the Wuffing kingdom during the sixth century.[122] As I noted above, the *Beowulf* Hroðmund's hypothetical exile may be approximately dated to around the beginning of the second quarter of the sixth century. Such a date would not be inconsistent with the foundation of the East Anglian kingdom, which is generally held to have taken place in the course of the sixth century.[123] Archaeological evidence would certainly permit the supposition that a prince of Denmark could have migrated to the proto-East Anglian kingdom in the second quarter of the sixth century.[124] It was once maintained that the distribution of late fifth- and sixth-century square-headed brooches and scutiform pendants indicated that southeastern Suffolk showed a strong Danish connection.[125] The more recent

---

[117] See the discussion on the historical horizon of the poem in Chapter Two.

[118] Klaeber, p. xxxvi.

[119] On the dating of the *Frēswæl*, see also Tolkien, *Finn and Hengest* (ed. Bliss), pp. 165–167.

[120] As was noted above Æþelberht's pedigree appears to have been compiled during the third decade of the eighth century. Bede was writing his great work of English ecclesiastical history, completed in 731, during the same decade. Both of these documentary sources agree that Hengest was the father of the eponymous *Oisc*.

[121] That the names *Hrōðmund* and *Hengest* are both listed in the tenth position within their respective pedigrees may prompt a further parallel between the two.

[122] Sims-Williams noted the possibility that the presence of Hengest in the pedigree of a Kentish king might reflect no more than an eighth-century retrospective claim ("The Settlement of England", p. 21), but he did advance a plausible view of Hengest as a fifth-century historical figure (*ibid.*, p. 23). For J. Turville-Petre, Hengest's name derives from "the cult-image venerated by the warriors of early Kent" ("Hengest and Horsa", p. 286).

[123] Stenton, *Anglo-Saxon England*, p. 50; and J. Campbell, *The Anglo-Saxons*, pp. 32–34.

[124] See generally Carver, "Pre-Viking Traffic in the North Sea", *Maritime Celts, Frisians and Saxons*.

[125] Leeds, "Denmark and early England"; and C. Green, *Sutton Hoo* (1963), p. 138.

work of John Hines, however, has suggested that the distribution of square-headed brooches reflects a more general relationship between eastern England and southern Scandinavia, although East Anglia is still to be regarded as a primary focus of Northern influence.[126] The distribution of Hines's 'Anglian English' scutiform pendants, moreover, which appear to have been intended to function as amuletic shields,[127] may imply a direct sixth-century connection between East Anglia and Denmark.[128] If then a Danish influence on the early Wuffing kingdom may be inferred archaeologically, the name *Hrōðmund* in the pedigree of an eighth-century East Anglian king may well represent the memory of such an influence, whether its bearer was a legendary or proto-historical figure.

[126] Hines, *The Scandinavian Character of Anglian England in the Pre-Viking Period*, pp. 197, 241–242, 277.
[127] Hines, *ibid.*, p. 238.
[128] Hines, *ibid.*, pp. 235, 241.

CHAPTER SIX

EAST ANGLIA AND THE MAKING OF *BEOWULF*

WE SHALL NOW REVIEW the matters discussed in previous chapters in relation to the overall question of the origin of *Beowulf*. I began with the unique manuscript of the poem, which appears to be a copy dating from around the year 1000. I argued that although palaeographic and linguistic considerations provide no clear proof as to its origin, independent orthographic, lexical, and phonological indications permit the hypothesis that *Beowulf* may have been composed in an Anglian kingdom as early as the eighth century. In Chapter Two, I sought to demonstrate that independent comparative, historical, and archaeological considerations provide some degree of corroboration for this hypothesis, insofar as they point to the greater likelihood of composition before, rather than after, the establishment of Viking settlement in England in the latter part of the ninth century. In Chapter Three, I suggested that the poem's ubiquitous Northern, especially Danish (Scylding), dynastic concerns seem curious if *Beowulf* were pre-Viking in origin. I argued that these concerns may have derived from the genealogical traditions of an Old English royal family which claimed descent from the Scyldings, and that a clue as to the identity of that family might be found in some of the surviving Old English royal genealogies. Following a consideration of the pedigree genre and its relation to pre-literary genealogical verse, I compared the eulogy in *Beowulf* for Offa of Angel with the claim to descent from this hero made in the late eighth-century Mercian royal pedigree. I concluded that this claim does not point exclusively to Mercia as the source of the poem's Northern dynastic concerns. Next, I examined the claim to Scylding ancestry made in the version of the West Saxon pedigree preserved in the *Anglo-Saxon Chronicle*. Although it seems probable that some of the names in this pedigree ultimately stem from the same genealogical source as the upper part of the Scylding pedigree in *Beowulf*, I argued that the considerable differences between the two suggest that poem was composed independently of any influence of West Saxon royal genealogy.

In Chapter Four, I considered the pedigree of Ælfwald, king of East Anglia during the first half of the eighth century, which lists the name *Hrōðmund* in its upper reaches. Because this name is one of an alliterative pair, I advanced the view that its bearer may have been associated with an East Anglian dynastic foundation-legend. I then turned to examine the status of Hroðmund the Scylding prince in *Beowulf*, and sought to demonstrate that both he and his brother, Hreðric, the sons of King Hroðgar, are central figures in one of the poem's major episodes, the victory-feast in Heorot after the defeat of Grendel (ll.991–1250). I argued that the use of irony in this episode, so sharply brought into focus by Hroðmund's mother, Queen Wealhþeow, reveals within the Scylding dynasty a latent rivalry between cousins contesting the question of King Hroðgar's successor. I concluded that, as Wealhþeow herself seems to forebode in *Beowulf*, and as Northern comparative material – especially Saxo's paraphrase of the lost *Bjarkamál* – also implies, Hreðric is destined to be killed by his cousin Hroþulf in the course of a struggle for the Danish throne. As to the fate of Hroðmund in all of this, I reasoned that he could have escaped his brother's fate by following the *wrecca*'s path into exile.

In Chapter Five, I attempted to show that there are independent indications that Hroðmund's mother may have been understood to be an East Anglian dynastic ancestor. I argued, on the basis of the probable etymology of the East Anglian dynastic eponym, *Wuffa*, that the Wuffings may have been regarded as descendants of the Wulfings of *Beowulf*. Examining the references to the latter, I contended that Queen Wealhþeow may have been a Wulfing princess prior to her marriage to King Hroðgar and thus a possible Wuffing family forebear. I also argued that her matrimonial function as *friþusibb folca*, 'the kindred pledge of peace between peoples' (1.2017ª), would have constituted an implicitly understood allegiance, realised through royal marriage, between Scyldings and Wulfings, and that Wealhþeow may therefore represent a vital genealogical link between the sixth-century Northern world of *Beowulf* and its Old English audience. Although Wealhþeow's name is not listed in King Ælfwald's patrilineal pedigree, I argued that the presence of the name of one of her sons there may be significant; for the suggested genealogical importance of Wealhþeow's marriage in *Beowulf* would have been only enhanced by her children, who would have been seen as the living proof of the kindred allegiance of Scyldings and Wulfings. I concluded that the name *Hroðmund* in King Ælfwald's pedigree may thus signal an explicit Wuffing claim to descent from the legendary Danish royal family.

The proposal is then as follows: through a consideration of the relation of *Beowulf* to surviving Anglo-Saxon royal pedigrees, East Anglia emerges as the kingdom most likely to have fostered the poem's prominent Danish dynastic concerns, insofar as a Scylding genealogical affinity is identifiable through *two* names listed in the ancestral tally of King Ælfwald. If this proposal is acceptable, we would have grounds for a claim that *Beowulf* could have been composed in East Anglia during King Ælfwald's reign (*ca* 713–749).

As far as we can tell, Ælfwald's kingdom possessed the means for the composition and preservation of the poem. One of the earliest schools of English literacy had been established in East Anglia several generations before by King Sigeberht (*ca* 630–635).[1] In 673, the East Anglian church was divided into two sees, *Dommoc* and *Helmham*,[2] both of whose episcopal name-lists have been preserved.[3] We also know from a reference in a surviving letter of King Ælfwald to St Boniface that there were at least seven minsters in the kingdom by the latter part of his reign.[4] Besides the two episcopal seats of *Dommoc* and *Helmham*,[5] these seven may have included the monastery founded by King Sigeberht, where he later retired and may have been buried;[6] St Botwulf's minster at *Icanho*;[7] a

---

[1] Bede, *HE*, III, 18; P.F.Jones, "The Gregorian Mission and English Education"; for a discussion of the dates of the East Anglian kings of the first half of the seventh century, see Bruce-Mitford, *SHSB*, vol. 1, pp. 696–698.

[2] Bede, *HE*, IV, 5; *Dommoc* has been identified as either Dunwich or the Roman Saxon Shore fortress at Walton Castle, Felixstowe (Rigold, "The Supposed See of Dunwich", and "Further Evidence about the Site of *Dommoc*; and "Whitelock, "The pre-Viking Age Church in East Anglia", p. 4), both of which have since been destroyed by coastal erosion.

Helmham is usually identified with ruined minster complex at North Elmham, Norfolk (*e.g.*, by Rainbird Clarke, *East Anglia*, p. 148; and Whitelock, "The pre-Viking Church", p. 8, note 5), though a site in the vicinity of the curious ruin at South Elmham, Suffolk, is also a possibility (Scarfe, *The Suffolk Landscape*, pp. 110–111, 116–128; Ridgard, "References to South Elmham Minster in the Medieval Account Rolls of South Elmham Manor"; and Hardy and Martin, "South Elmham St Margaret"). Early spellings of this see show an intial *H*, as in the profession of its early ninth-century bishop, Hunferð (Birch, *Cartularium Saxonicum*, no. 375; Whitelock, "The pre-Viking Age Church", pp. 19, 22). If these represent its original form, it might be another East Anglian place-name based on personal name *Helm* (for the possible royal significance of which, see Chapter Five). The usual interpretation is, however, '*hām* where elms grow' (Ekwall, *The Concise Oxford Dictionary of Place-Names*, p. 164; Gelling, *Place-Names in the Landscape*, pp. 220, 278).

[3] Page (ed.), "Anglo-Saxon Episcopal Lists", parts 1, 2 & 3; and Whitelock, "The Pre-Viking Age Church", pp. 19–22. It may be worth noting that three of the listed bishops bear names which also appear in *Beowulf*: Hunferð, Ecglāf and Heardrēd. No other surviving Anglo-Saxon episcopal list appears to show as many as three names common to the poem: that for Wessex shows two (Hunfrið and Wulfgār), while that for Northumbria shows one (Heardrēd).

[4] Tangl (ed.), *Die Briefe des heiligen Bonifatius und Lullus*, pp. 181–182. The letter is dated between 742 and 749 (Whitelock, "The Pre-Viking Church", p. 16).

[5] St Fursey's foundation at the Roman fortress site of *Cnobheresburg*, also dating from the reign of King Sigeberht, may be discounted from the list as it appears to have been destroyed around about the year 651 (Bede *HE*, III, 19; Whitelock, "The pre-Viking Church", pp. 5–6).

[6] Bede, *HE*, III, 18; according to a note in the twelfth-century *Liber Eliensis*, this was located at *Betrichesworde*, the old name for Bury St Edmunds (E.O. Blake, p. 11). If so, the burial of Sigeberht, East Anglia's first martyr-king, would be a precedent for the later burial there of East Anglia's last martyr-king, St Edmund (Whitelock, "The pre-Viking Church", p. 4, note 4).

[7] The founding of St Botwulf's minster at Iken, Suffolk is referred to in the *A* version of the *Chronicle*, *s.a.* 654 (Whitelock, "The pre-Viking Church in East Anglia", pp. 10–11;

possible minster at Blythburgh, where Sigeberht's successor, Onna (*ca* 635–654), was buried;[8] the double minster of Ely, originally founded by St Æþelðryþ, daughter of King Onna;[9] and the nunnery at East Dereham, Norfolk, founded by St Wihtburh, who may have been the youngest of Onna's daughters.[10]

Because all of these minsters were founded by, or were closely associated with, the East Anglian royal family, any one of them could have provided the kind of clerical context described by historian Patrick Wormald as likely to have permitted the maintenance of Old English heroic verse, especially if such verse was concerned with the noble ancestry of the Wuffings themselves.[11] As one of them probably housed the scriptorium where the original version of King Ælfwald's ancestral tally was compiled,[12] we can see that there would have been at least one East Anglian minster in which Wuffing dynastic traditions could have come into contact with the new literacy.

Certainly, the claim that *Beowulf* could have been composed in Ælfwald's East Anglia would be consistent with the hypothesis, advanced in Chapters One and Two, that the poem may have been composed in an Anglian kingdom in the eighth century. It would also be reinforced by two other arguments that certain passages within the poem may reflect an East Anglian perspective: (1), its account of the royal rite of ship-funeral; and (2), its representation of Grendel and his monstrous kin.

1. THE ROYAL RITE OF SHIP-FUNERAL

It will be recalled that in Chapter Two, prior to my consideration of *Beowulf* and the Old English royal pedigrees, I discussed the value of

West, Scarfe, and Cramp, "Iken, St Botolph, and the Coming of East Anglian Christianity"). The same entry records the slaying of King Onna (by the hand of Penda of Mercia according to Bede, *HE*, III, 18), which could imply that the two events were not unrelated, as Bruce Mitford suggested (*SHSB*, vol. 1, p. 707. note 2).

[8] E.O.Blake (ed.), *Liber Eliensis*, p. 18; according to a local tradition, the battle where Onna fell was at Bulcamp, just across the river from Blythburgh. Archaeological evidence that Blythburgh may have been an early minster site exists in the form of a carved whale-bone writing tablet, found before 1902, which dates from the eighth century (Webster and Backhouse, *The Making of England*, p. 81).

[9] Bede *HE*, IV, 19; Barbara Yorke has suggested that Abbess Ecgburh, King Ælfwald's sister according to the author of *Vita Sancti Guthlaci* (ed. Colgrave, pp. 146–147), could have been Abbess of Ely (Yorke, *Kings and Kingdoms in Early Anglo-Saxon England*, p. 70).

[10] Yorke, *ibid.*, p. 70. Other possible sites include Burrow Hill, Butley (Fenwick, "*Insula de Burgh*: Excavations at Burrow Hill, Butley, Suffolk, 1978–1981"), and the similarly insular site at Brandon (Carr, *et al.*, "The Middle Saxon Settlement at Staunch Meadow, Brandon").

[11] See the summary of Patrick Wormald's arguments at the beginning of Chapter Two.

[12] As was argued in Chapter Four, there are indications that the original compilation date of the version of King Ælfwald's pedigree in the Anglian Collection was 725 or 726.

archaeology to the question of the poem's origin. I pointed out there that there is a case, on current Anglo-Saxon archaeological evidence, for regarding East Anglia as the possible source of its ship-funeral account (ll.26–52). As *Beowulf* attributes the rite to the eponymous founding-father of the Scyldings, Scyld Scefing, this point can now be seen to complement my genealogically-based proposal that other aspects of Scylding legend in *Beowulf* might have been fostered in Wuffing dynastic traditions.

I argued in Chapter Two that, by analogy with the archaeology of the ninth-century Norse kingdom of Vestfold, it is not at all improbable that information on royal burials in sixth- or seventh-century East Anglia could have been preserved in Wuffing genealogical verse, just as information on the similar royal burial-rites in Vestfold appears to have been preserved in *Ynglingatal*.[13] From an archaeological point of view, the royal rite of ship-funeral in East Anglia is seen as signalling dynastic allegiance with Scandinavia.[14] Such allegiance could have been realised in the correlative medium of Wuffing genealogical verse by attributing the mythic precedent for the rite to a legendary Northern forebear. Again, Yngling traditions seem to provide an analogy, for according to Snorri Sturluson, the establishment of the rite of mound-inhumation was attributed to the dynasty's eponymous founder, the divine figure *Yngvi-Freyr*:

> after Freyr had been buried in a mound at Uppsala, many chiefs made mounds no less than standing-stones to the memory of their kinsmen (preface to *Heimskringla*).[15]

In other words, the enactment of this particular burial rite was understood by those who believed themselves to be his descendants to be a *re*enactment of Freyr's mythic precedent, so reaffirming their allegiance to him. Snorri also provides a Danish version of the story, where again we have attribution to an eponyous ancestor:

> The Age of Mounds began properly in Denmark after Dan the Magnificent had a burial-mound raised for himself, and ordered that he should be buried in it on his death, with his royal ornaments and armour, his horse and saddle-furniture, and other valuable goods; and many of his descendants followed his example (preface to *Heimskringla*).

[13] As J.E. Turville-Petre put it, the "social correlative of this literary genre is a grave-cult" ("On *Ynglingatal*", p. 51).
[14] Professor Carver has described the rite as "a major exercise in legitimation [of dynastic authority] inspired by a Scandinavian or at least non-Roman ideology" ("Kingship and Material Culture", p. 152).
[15] Snorri tells the story of the mound-burial of Yngvi-Freyr in more detail in *Ynglinga saga* (ch. 10).

The rite of mound-burial in the Northlands would seem thus to have entailed, in the words of Mircea Eliade, the

> repetition of an archetypal action performed *in illo tempore* by ancestors or by gods.... By its repetition, the act coincides with its archetype, and time is abolished.[16]

In *Beowulf*, the rite of ship-funeral is attributed to the eponymous figure Scyld Scefing in similarly mythic conditions. The account of the rite forms the climax of the poem's version of his legend, which introduces the genealogy of the Scyldings through the story of their founding-father (ll.1–52).[17] This Scylding origin-myth is set *in geardagum*, 'in days of yore' (l.1b), and *æt frumsceafte*, 'at the beginning' (l.45a). As with Snorri's eponymous *Dan*, moreover, we are told that it was the founder himself who had ordered that he be given the rite of ship-funeral.

> hī hyne þā ætbǣron   tō brimes faroðe,
> swǣse gesīþas,   swā hē selfa bæd,
> þenden wordum wēold

> 'His dear companions then carried him out to the water's side, as he himself had bidden while he still could (ll.28–30a).

The implication is that the legend of Scyld Scefing in *Beowulf* represents a version of a story told to explain the mythic origin and purpose of the Old English royal rite of ship-funeral.[18]

Now, as I have argued, we can infer the existence of such a legend in Wuffing genealogical verse from archaeology. The noted Scandinavian orientation of the rite in East Anglia also complements its attribution to Scyld Scefing in *Beowulf*; so although a form equivalent to the name of the hero appears not to have been included in the selection of fourteen ancestral-names listed in King Ælfwald's surviving pedigree, it is quite possible that the rite was similarly attributed in Wuffing genealogical verse.

One name in Ælfwald's pedigree which could be related to the legend of the boat-borne hero is *Trygil*, to which the name *Hrōðmund* is filiated. *Trygil* is unparalleled in Old English.[19] If regarded as a personal name with a diminutive suffix *-il*, it may be based on a variant of OE *trog* (*trēg*

16 Eliade, *Patterns in Comparative Religion*, p. 32.
17 As I argued in Chapter Three, the genealogy of the Scyldings is used to structure the poem's introduction.
18 Dr Ellis Davidson has noted similarly that the account "reads like a myth to account for a funeral-rite" (*Gods and Myths of Northern Europe*, p. 136).
19 O'Loughlin ("Sutton Hoo: the Evidence of the Documents", pp. 2–3) did note that a similar diminutive of ON *trog*, *trygill*, is recorded as a nickname, *Haraldr Trygill*, which

or *trīg*), 'trough', 'tray', or '(dug-out) boat',[20] and so be construed to mean something like 'Little Trough'. That *trog* also includes '(dug-out) boat' within its range of semantic potential, as is implied particularly by the compound *trogscip*,[21] suggests also that the personal name *Trygil* may be construed as meaning 'Little Boat'. Certainly it would appear to have derived from the name of some sort of hollowed-out wooden vessel, a derivation which may seem curious for a royal ancestral appelative. Personal names based on the names of wooden objects are not unknown, however, in early Germanic origin-legends. According to Dio Cassius, the Vandal Hasding dynasty was led by two brothers, *Raos* and *Raptos*, names which may be understood to mean 'reed' (or 'pole') and 'rafter' respectively.[22] If *Trygil* may be construed as 'Little Boat', perhaps its bearer should be regarded as an emblematic figure derived from the symbolic function of boats in East Anglian origin-legend. This possibility is strengthened by the prominent use of the boat in East Anglian burial-rites, which indicates clearly the symbolic power with which the vessel was imbued by early East Anglians.[23]

The suggestion is that *Trygil*, if construed as 'Little Boat', could have derived from an East Anglian origin-legend in which the symbolic function of the boat was the same as the legendary vessel which bore the royal founding-hero Scyld in and out of the world of men in *Beowulf*. This suggestion is only reinforced by the observation that *Trygil* can be seen to stand as a metonym for the name of the hero of the Scylding origin-legend, a metonym being an alternative name for another with which it is closely associated, as, for example, in the use of 'Vatican' for 'Pope'. The listing of the name *Trygil* in King Ælfwald's ancestral tally could imply, therefore, that a version of the legend of the boat-borne royal founding hero was current in East Anglian dynastic tradition. If so, the filiation of the Scylding name *Hrōðmund* to *Trygil* in Ælfwald's pedigree would seem not inappropriate, even though it would involve the

---

appears in the lists of Norwegian jarls preserved in *Háleygjatal* (Vigfússon and Powell, *Corpus Poeticum Boreale*, vol. 1, pp. 251–253; vol. 2, pp. 522–523).

[20] Bosworth and Northcote Toller (ed.), *An Anglo-Saxon Dictionary*, pp. 1012, 1015; and supplement, p. 725. The word is used to refer to a boat in King Ælfred's translation of *Orosius*, II, v (ed. Bately, p. 48, l.17).

[21] On the compound *trogscip*, see Meritt, "Studies in Old English Vocabulary", p. 426; and *Fact and Lore about Old English Words*, p. 116.

[22] Cary (ed.), *Dio Cassius: Historia Romanorum*, lxxii, p. 14; for a discussion of these and other such names, see J.E. Turville-Petre, "Hengest and Horsa", pp. 276–277; and G. Dumézil, *From Myth to Fiction*, pp. 116–118.

[23] It may be significant that either one of the two dug-out boats discovered in recent excavations (1987 and 1991) at the Anglo-Saxon cemetery at Snape could be aptly described as a *trygil*. On the first, see Filmer-Sankey, "A New Boat from the Snape Anglo-Saxon Cemetery, Suffolk"; we await eagerly the publication of the report on the second.

conflation of several generations relative to the Scylding genealogy in *Beowulf*.[24]

Another possible East Anglian alternative for the name *Scyld* may be contained in the important Wuffing place-name *Rendlesham*. Located some four miles upriver from Sutton Hoo, it is described by Bede as an East Anglian *vicus regius*, 'royal township', in the reign of King Æþelwald (*ca* 655–664).[25] The site of this *vicus regius* has yet to be pinpointed on the ground with certainty, but there is no reason to doubt the validity of this reference.[26] Bede also explains to us that the place-name *Rendlesham* is based on the personal name *Rendil*. If he is right, *Rendil* would appear to be a diminutive form of a close variant of OE *rand*, a term designating either the round metal rim of the Germanic shield or the flange of its metal boss, or even the boss itself.[27] Exactly like *Trygil*, therefore, *Rendil* would seem to be a personal name in diminutive form which is based on the name of an object. It may be thus construed as 'Little Shield-Rim' or 'Little Shield-Boss'.[28] If so, the personal name *Rendil* could be seen to represent a particular type of metonym for *Scyld* known as a synecdoche. Like a metonym, a synecdoche is an alternative name for another with which it is closely associated, but specifically it is the name of a part of something which is used to refer to the whole, as in the use of 'keel' for 'ship' in line 38[b] of *Beowulf*. As such, the suggested etymology of the place-name *Rendlesham* may also imply that a version of the legend of Scyld was current in pre-Viking East Anglia.

Taken together, these suggestions provide some degree of corroboration for the current archaeological indications that the legend of the boat-borne royal foundling may have been maintained in the pre-Viking kingdom of East Anglia. The corollary of this claim is that East Anglia may also have been the source of the West Saxon version of the legend, which, as I argued in Chapter Two, appears to be a retrospective genealogical elaboration dating from the late ninth century and probably derived from an earlier English dynastic source. Yet if that source was East Anglian, it is not clear how such putatively Wuffing dynastic lore should have come to be incorporated in West Saxon genealogical tradition in the course of the ninth century.

[24] Such conflation of generations is a not uncommon feature of early genealogies; see the discussion by Dumville, "Kingship, Genealogies and Regnal Lists", pp. 87–88.
[25] Bede, *HE*, III, 22.
[26] Bruce-Mitford, *Aspects of Anglo-Saxon Archaeology*, pp. 73–113; for recent work, see Newman, "East Anglian Kingdom Survey – Final Interim Report on the South East Suffolk Pilot Field Survey", especially figs. 9 and 10.
[27] Brady, " 'Weapons' in *Beowulf*" pp. 126–128.
[28] As O'Loughlin noted ("Sutton Hoo", p. 3). Gelling has preferred a toponymic interpretation, whereby 'little shield-rim' may be construed as 'little shore' (*Signposts to the Past*, p. 189).

Close relations between the two kingdoms during the middle years of the seventh century may be inferred from Bede's report that King Coenwalh of Wessex, when forced into exile by King Penda of Mercia, found refuge at the court of King Onna of East Anglia.[29] Whilst there, according to the *Liber Eliensis*, Coenwalh was baptised by Bishop Felix, with Onna acting as his godfather.[30] This spiritual relation between kings suggests a political allegiance, perhaps in common cause against Mercia. The *Anglo-Saxon Chronicle*'s record of events during the third decade of the ninth century also points to a close allegiance between East Anglia and Wessex, again against the common Mercian foe. The *A* manuscript of the *Chronicle, s.a.* 823, states that

Þy ilcan gēare East Engla cyning 7 sēo þēod gesōhte Ecgbryht cyning him to friþe 7 mund boran for Miercna ege, 7 þy gēare slōgon East Engle Beornwulf Miercna cyning.

'that same year the king of the East Angles and his folk sought King Ecgberht as their protector and guardian against Mercian terror, and that same year the East Angles slew Beornwulf, the king of the Mercians'.[31]

The successful military alliance between Ecgberht of Wessex and the unnamed king of East Anglia referred to here also implies a political allegiance. As there are some indications that there may have been kinship between the West Saxon dynasty and the East Anglian royal house, at least from the late 820s until the latter's extinction in the winter of 869–870, it is not impossible that this allegiance could have been sealed by marriage. The two families appear to have employed the same patterns of vocalically alliterating name-giving, with certain names, such as *Æþelstān*, *Æþelweard*, and *Eadmund*, being in common to both.[32] It was also once argued that St Edmund, the last English king of East Anglia, who ruled *ca* 855 until his martyrdom on 20th November, 869, may have been of West Saxon stock.[33]

Furthermore, if it could be shown that the early twelfth-century Anglo-Norman poet Geffrei Gaimar used a reliable version of the *Anglo-*

[29] Bede, *HE*, III, 7.
[30] E.O. Blake (ed.), *Liber Eliensis*, pp. 17–18.
[31] On this phase of Anglo-Saxon history, see Stenton, *Anglo-Saxon England*, 3rd edition, pp. 231–232.
[32] The names of these three ninth-century East Anglian kings are known from numismatic evidence; see Pagan, "The Coinage of the East Anglian Kingdom from 825 to 870". K. Werner has argued that the occurrence of the same names and name-elements among the leading figures of noble families can indicate kinship ("Important Noble Families in the Kingdom of Charlemagne", pp. 149–152).
[33] Hervey (ed.), *The Garland of Saint Edmund*, p. xxxviii.

Saxon Chronicle to inform his metrical *L'Estoire des Engleis*,[34] there could be significance in his statement that Æþelstan, the brother of King Æþelwulf of Wessex, was king of East Anglia (ll.2478–2480) around the year 850. The same Æþelstan appears in surviving manuscripts of the *Chronicle*, where, in the entry for the year 836 (839), he is named as king of Kent, Surrey, Sussex and Essex.

> Hēr Ecgbryht cyning forþférde. . . . 7 sē Ecgbryht rīcsode xxxvii winter 7 vii mōnaþ. 7 fēng Eþelwulf Ecgbrehting tō Wesseaxna rīce, 7 hē salde his suna Æþelstāne Cantwara rīce 7 East Seaxna 7 Sūþrigea 7 Sūþ Seaxna.

> 'In this year Ecgberht passed away. . . . And that Ecgberht had reigned thirty-seven winters and seven months; and Æþelwulf, Ecgberht's son, succeeded to the West Saxon throne, and he gave his son Æþelstan the thrones of Kent, Essex, Surrey and Sussex'.

The identity of the subject of the clause *hē salde*, 'he gave', in this passage (l.3) is ambiguous. As it stands, the subject of the clause – and thus the father of Æþelstan – can be read as either Æþelwulf or Ecgberht. Æþelweard's late tenth-century Latin *Chronicon* states that this Æþelstan was the son of Æþelwulf, though Æþelweard's source may have contained the same ambiguity as the *A* manuscript of the *Chronicle*. Yet as this entry is concerned primarily the death and legacy of King Ecgberht, he is the one more likely to have been the original intended subject of the clause in question. In other words, I agree with Plummer that Æþelstan should be regarded as the son of Ecgberht rather than of Æþelwulf,[35] just as the same entry in the twelfth-century *E* manuscript unambiguously states:

> Hēr Ecgbriht cining forðférde. . . . 7 sē Ecgbriht rīxade xxxvii winter 7 vii mōnðas. 7 fēng Æþelwulf his sunu tō WestSeaxna rīce. and Æðelstān his ōðer sunu fēng tō Cantwara rīce. 7 tō Sūðrigan. 7 tō Sūðseaxna rīce.

> 'In this year Ecgberht passed away. . . . And this Ecgberht had reigned thirty-seven winters and seven months; and Æþelwulf, his son, succeeded to the throne of Wessex; and Æþelstan, *his other son*, succeeded to the thrones of Kent, Surrey and Sussex'.

Although none of the surviving *Chronicle* manuscripts refer to the possible lordship of Æþelstan over East Anglia, numismatic evidence reveals that there was an East Anglian king named Æþelstan ruling from around the late 820s to the late 840s.[36] The chronology and find spots of King Æþelstan's coinage, moreover, suggest that he could be identifiable

[34] Bell (ed.), Geffrei Gaimar, *L'Estoire des Engleis*.

[35] Plummer, *Two of the Saxon Chronicles Parallel*, vol. 2, pp. 75–76; see also Hodgkin, *A History of the Anglo-Saxons*, vol. 2, p. 767).

[36] Pagan, "The Coinage of the East Anglian Kingdom from 825 to 870".

as Æþelstan the son of Ecgberht of Wessex.[37] A recently discovered silver penny of East Anglia's King Æþelstan, moreover, bears on its obverse a design depicting a ship of a type unprecedented in Anglo-Saxon coinage.[38] Although the design appears to influenced by classically inspired Frankish examples, it is no mere imitation, and it may have historical and political implications as a possible emblem of East Anglian independence from Mercia, as Fenwick has suggested.[39] If so, it could have been regarded as being of more than mercantile significance, in that the design may have been motivated by a more traditional association of the boat with East Anglian kingship.

There are, therefore, some indications that there may have been dynastic kinship between East Anglia and Wessex during the second quarter of the ninth century. Insofar as such putative royal kinship could have been registered genealogically through a conjunction of retrospective ancestral claims,[40] we would have thus a context for the West Saxon acquisition of Wuffing ancestral traditions. As such, the presence of a version of the legend of the boat-borne hero in a late ninth-century West Saxon royal pedigree can be seen to be reconcilable with the indications that the legend itself may originally have been fostered by the Wuffings.

2. GRENDEL AND EAST ANGLIA

A final point suggesting that *Beowulf* could have originated in East Anglia concerns the pedigree of another of the poem's major figures, namely, the monster Grendel.

Earlier in this chapter, I suggested that one of the seven East Anglian royal minsters mentioned in King Ælfwald's letter to St Boniface would have provided an appropriate context for the composition and preservation of *Beowulf*. Another literary work which was written in East Anglia at this time is *Vita Sancti Guthlaci*, 'The Life of St Guthlac, a work which was commissioned by King Ælfwald and which its author, Felix, dedicated to him.[41] Besides revealing Ælfwald's willingness to promote literary endeavours, Felix's depiction of Guthlac's demonic opponents shows notable similarities in some respects to the depiction of Grendel and his mother in *Beowulf*. In both works, the heroes exorcise specific

---

[37] Pagan, *ibid.*, pp. 57–67.
[38] Archibald, "A Ship-Type of Athelstan I of East Anglia"; and Fenwick, "A New Anglo-Saxon Ship".
[39] Fenwick, *ibid.*, p. 175.
[40] Possible examples of this kind of genealogical conjunction have been identified in the Anglian Collection of OE royal pedigrees by David Dumville ("Kingship, Genealogies and Regnal Lists", pp. 79–80).
[41] Colgrave (ed.), *Felix's Life of St Guthlac*; as was noted at the beginning of Chapter Four.

places haunted by fen-dwelling demons who are angered initially by a particular type of song. Grendel, who is *eald-gewinna*, 'the old enemy' (1.1776ª), and *feond moncynnes*, 'the enemy of mankind' (1.164ᵇ), begins his haunting of the newly-built hall of Heorot after he hears there the sound of the song of Creation (ll.86–101). Similarly, Felix refers to the *antiquus hostis prolis humanae*, 'ancient foe of the human race', beginning to trouble Guthlac as he sings psalms and hymns at his newly-built hermitage in a burial-mound on the island of Crowland (ch. 29).[42] Furthermore, the fiends who subsequently attack Guthlac are addressed by the saint as the 'seed of Cain' (ch. 31). This reference to fiends as descendants of Cain does not appear in any of the later Old English poetic versions of *Vita Sancti Guthlaci* and yet exactly the same monstrous pedigree is attributed to Grendel and his kind in *Beowulf* (ll.102–114, 1261ᵇ–1265ª).[43] This point has led some scholars to suggest that the poem could have been composed in East Anglia,[44] although in this Fenland context the possibility of composition in Middle Anglia or Mercia cannot be ruled out. At the very least, the parallels between the poem and *Vita Sancti Guthlaci* show that some early eighth-century East Anglians, like the audience of *Beowulf*, believed that fens and marshes were haunted by the evil seed of Cain.

Finally, although more research is needed in this area, it is worth noting that Grendel's suggested East Anglian connections appear to be corroborated by the evidence of folklore, for there are indications that a belief that his monstrous ilk haunt estuaries and fenlands has endured in the region for centuries. Of particular interest in this context is the apparition known in the East Anglian dialect as *Shuck*,[45] a version of the spectral hound or Black Dog, a well-known phenomenon in English folklore.[46] The East Anglian name *Shuck* derives from OE *scucca*, meaning 'devil' or 'demon',[47] a word used in *Beowulf* by Hroðgar to refer to

---

[42] Colgrave, *ibid.*, pp. 94–95; Whitelock, *The Audience of Beowulf*, p. 81.

[43] Colgrave, *Life of St Guthlac*, pp. 106–107, and note, p. 185; Whitelock *The Audience of Beowulf*, p. 80.

[44] Whitelock, *ibid.*, pp. 29, 80–81, 104–105; and Mayr-Harting, *The Coming of Christianity to Anglo-Saxon England*, pp. 229–239. The latter concluded that "there is a chance that East Anglia was the home of the poem" (*ibid*, p. 235). More cautiously, Niles argued that "the poet . . ., more likely, drew on vernacular accounts of Guthlac's life for some of his inspiration concerning fenland demons" (*Beowulf: the Poem and Its Tradition*, p. 89).

[45] Forby (ed.), *The Vocabulary of East Anglia*, vol. 2, p. 238, s.v. 'Old-Shock'; J. Wright (ed.), *The English Dialect Dictionary*, vol. 5, p. 415, s.v. 'Shuck'.

[46] For studies, see Brown, "The Black Dog" (1958); and "The Black Dog in English Folklore" (1978). The 'Shuck' appears to be the East Anglian name for Brown's more widespread 'Barguest' type of Black Dog (Brown, "The Black Dog", p. 176). See Forby, *The Vocabulary of East Anglia*, s.v. 'Old-Shock'; Serjeantson, "The Vocabulary of Folklore in Old and Middle English", p. 50; *The Oxford English Dictionary, s.v.* 'Shuck'; and Reeve, *A Straunge & Terrible Wonder: the Story of the Black Dog of Bungay*, p. 42.

[47] Bosworth and Northcote Toller (ed.), *An Anglo-Saxon Dictionary*, p. 843, and Supple-

Grendel and his kind (1.939ᵃ).[48] Shuck also seems to have several characteristics in common with Grendel and his mother. Reports of both seem correspondingly inexact as to their appearance and ontological status. The 'Barguest' type of Black Dog, Brown concluded, "is not essentially a dog, but a shapeless monster . . . it is a subconscious, partly chthonic entity".[49] Some East Anglian sightings attribute a humanoid form to the creature,[50] as does Hroðgar of Grendel (*Beowulf*, l.1352ᵃ). The Shuck's canine characteristics are comparable with the lupine traits of Grendel and his mother, implied by the use of such terms to describe them as *brimwylf* (ll.1506ᵃ, 1599ᵃ), *heorowearh* (l.1267ᵃ), *grundwyrgenne* (l.1518ᵇ), *werhðo* (l.589) and the adjective *werga* (l.133ᵃ, 1747ᵇ).[51] Shuck and his kind are also noted for the prominence of their shining eyes, which are characteristically described as 'saucer-shaped' and 'burning like coals'.[52] Grendel's are comparable: *him of ēagum stōd ligge gelīcost lēoht unfæger*, 'from his eyes shone a fire-like, baleful light' (ll.726ᵇ–727). Like Grendel, moreover, Shuck is associated with the Devil and with death;[53] and again like Grendel, he usually dwells in and around fens and marshlands, whence he emerges, generally only at night, to walk alone, haunting specific places.[54] Finally, it may also be significant the Grendel's association with low-lying, watery places seems to be echoed in the cognate East Anglian dialect word *grindle*, 'drain' or 'ditch'.[55] This word is preserved in the names of several Suffolk watercourses, such as the Grundles of Wattisfield and Stanton, or Grindle Lane, Sproughton.

Although these apparent parallels between Grendel and East Anglia may stem from a wider Anglian interest in monster lore, they do provide some degree of corroboration for the suggestion that East Anglians, like the audience of *Beowulf*, believed in the reality of marsh-haunting *scuccan*.

We appear thus to have folk, literary, and archaeological points complementing my principal, genealogically-based, claim that *Beowulf* could

ment, p. 699; variants include *scocca* and *sceocca* – see Meritt, *Some of the Hardest Glosses in Old English*, pp. 94–95.

48 The term also appears in some Old English religious prose, this is the only instance of the use of *scucca* in the poetry; see Wiersma, "A Linguistic Analysis of Words Referring to Monsters in *Beowulf*", pp. 323–330, 335.

49 Brown, "The Black Dog", p. 189.

50 Brown, *ibid.*, p. 178

51 Gerstein, "Germanic Warg: the Outlaw as Werwolf", pp. 141–142, 145–146.

52 Brown, "The Black Dog", p. 187; and Reeve, *A Straunge & Terrible Wonder*, p. 42.

53 Brown, "The Black Dog", pp. 185–187.

54 Brown, *ibid.*, pp. 179–184; Reeve, *A Straunge & Terrible Wonder*, pp. 42–43.

55 E.Moor (ed.), *Suffolk Words and Phrases*, pp. 114 (*s.v* its variant, *drindle*) and 155–156 (*s.v. grip*); Wright (ed.), *The English Dialect Dictionary*, vol. 2, p. 730; and *The Oxford English Dictionary*, p. 427 (*s.v. grindle*).

have been composed in eighth-century East Anglia. As such, until we have more positive evidence, this claim may perhaps be accepted as a hypothesis for the origin of the poem.

It would entail a model of textual history which may be only loosely sketched: the poem's putative first manuscript could have been written in the scriptorium of one of the seven East Anglian minsters mentioned above, and preserved in its library at least until the winter of 869–870. At that time, according to the *A* version of the *Anglo-Saxon Chronicle* (*s.a.* 870), a Danish army invaded East Anglia and took winter-quarters in Thetford (*Þeodford*);

> 7 þȳ wintre Eadmund cyning him wiþ feaht, 7 þā Deniscan sige namon, 7 þone cyning ofslōgon, 7 þæt lond all ge-ēoden,

> 'and that winter, King Edmund fought against them, and the Danes had the victory, and they killed the king and overran the whole kingdom'.

The *E* version adds 7 *fordiden ealle þā mynstre þā hī to cōmen*, 'and they destroyed all the minsters that they came to'. The destruction of the East Anglian minsters, along with their libraries, during the winter of 869–870 would explain the apparent loss of pre-Viking East Anglian manuscripts. A copy of *Beowulf* could have escaped destruction, however, if it was preserved somewhere in southern England – perhaps London, as Sisam suggested,[56] or Wessex, so enabling our only surviving manuscript to be copied.

We return thus, albeit by a long and sometimes tenuous path, to our starting point, the manuscript of *Beowulf*. Although we cannot be certain exactly when and where the words written on these vellum leaves were first woven into verse, Tolkien was surely close to the truth when he wrote that

> When new *Beowulf* was already antiquarian . . . Its maker was telling of things already old and weighted with regret . . . If the funeral of Beowulf moved once like the echo of an ancient dirge, far-off and hopeless, it is to us as a memory brought over the hills, an echo of an echo. . . . *Beowulf* . . . would still have power had it been written in some time or place unknown and without posterity, if it contained no name that could now be recognised or identified by research. Yet it is in fact written in a language that after many centuries has still essential kinship with our own, it was made in this land, and moves in our northern world beneath our northern sky, and for those who are native to that tongue and land, it must ever call with a profound appeal – until the dragon comes.[57]

---

[56] Sisam, *Studies in the History of Old English Literature*, p. 95.
[57] Tolkien, "*Beowulf*: the Monsters and the Critics", pp. 277–278.

BIBLIOGRAPHY

ÅKERLAND, W., *Studier över Ynglingatal* (Lund, 1939).

ALLISON, J., "The Lost Villages of Norfolk," *Norfolk Archaeology*, 31, (1955), pp. 116–162.

AMOS, A., *Linguistic Means of Determining the Dates of Old English Literary Texts* (Cambridge, Mass., 1980).

ANDERSON, E.R., "A Submerged Metaphor in the Scyld Episode", *Yearbook of English Studies*, 2 (1972), pp. 1–4.

ANDERSON, L.F., *The Anglo-Saxon Scop* (Toronto, 1903).

ANDERSSON, T.M., "The Dating of *Beowulf*", *University of Toronto Quarterly*, 52 (1983), pp. 288–301.

ANDREW, S.O., *Postscript on Beowulf* (Cambridge, 1948).

ARCHIBALD, M.M., "A Ship-Type of Athelstan I of East Anglia", *The British Numismatic Journal*, 52 (1982), pp. 34–40.

ARENT, A.M., "The Heroic Pattern: Old Germanic Helmets, *Beowulf* and *Grettis saga*", *Old Norse Literature and Mythology: A Symposium*, ed. E.C. Polomé (Austin, Texas, 1969), pp. 130–199.

ARNOLD, T., (ed.), *Abbonis Floriacensis Passio Sancti Eadmundi*, Memorials of St Edmund's Abbey, 1 (London, 1890), pp. 1–25.

———, *Notes on Beowulf* (London, 1898).

ARNOTT, W.G. (ed.), *The Place-Names of the Deben Valley Parishes* (Ipswich 1946).

———, *Suffolk Estuary* (Ipswich, 1950).

ARRHENIUS, B., "The Chronology of the Vendal Graves", *Vendel Period Studies*, ed. J.P. Lamm & H-Å. Nordström (Stockholm, 1983), pp. 39–70.

AÐALBJARNASON, B., (ed.), *Heimskringla* (incorporating *Ynglinga saga*), Íslenzk Fornrit, 26 (Reykjavík, 1941).

BAIRD, J.L., "Unferth the Þyle", *Medium Ævum*. 39 (1970), pp. 1–12.

BANDY, S.C., "*Beowulf*: The Defense of Heorot", *Neophilologus*, 56 (1972), pp. 85–92.

BASSETT, S. (ed.), *The Origins of the Anglo-Saxon Kingdoms* (Leicester, 1989).

BATELY, J. (ed.), *The Old English Orosius*, Early English Text Society, supplementary series, 6 (Oxford, 1980).

——— , "Linguistic Evidence as a Guide to the Authorship of Old English Verse: a Reappraisal, with Special Reference to *Beowulf*", *Learning and Literature in Anglo-Saxon England: Studies Presented to Peter Clemoes on the Occasion of His Sixty-Fifth Birthday*, ed. M. Lapidge and H. Gneuss (Cambridge, 1985), pp. 409–431.

——— (ed.), *The Anglo-Saxon Chronicle: MS A* (Cambridge, 1986).

BAUSCHATZ, P., *The Well and the Tree: World and Time in Early Germanic Culture* (Massachusetts, 1982).

BELDEN, H.M., "Onela the Scylfing and Áli the Bold", *Modern Language Notes*, 28 (1913), pp. 149–153.

BELL, A. (ed.), *Geffrei Gaimar: L'Estoire des Engleis*, Anglo-Norman Text Society, 14–16 (Oxford, 1960).

BENEDIKTSSON, J. (ed.), *Arngrimi Jonae: Opera Latine Conscripta*, Bibliotheca Arnamagnæana, vols 9–12 (Copenhagen, 1950–1957): vol. 9 (*Rerum Danicarum Fragmenta*) contains the extant version of *Skjǫldunga saga*; vol. 12, discussion and notes.

———, "Icelandic Traditions of the Scyldings," *Saga Book*, 15, (1957–1959), pp. 48–66.

BENSON, L.D., "The Literary Character of Anglo-Saxon Formulaic Poetry", *Publications of the Modern Language Association*, 81 (1966), pp. 334–341.

BERTELSEN, H. (ed.), *Þiðrekssaga*, 2 vols, Samfund til udgivelse ag gammel nordisk Litteratur (Copenhagen, 1911).

BESSINGER, J.B., Jr (ed.), *A Concordance of the Anglo-Saxon Poetic Records* (Ithaca, 1978).

BETHMANN, L., and G. WAITZ (ed.), *Scriptores Rerum Langobardicarum et Italicarum*, Monumenta Germaniae Historica, vol 6–9 (Hanover, 1878).

BIDDLE, M., and B. KJØLBYE-BIDDLE, "The Repton Stone", *Anglo-Saxon England*, 14 (1985), pp. 233–292.

BIMSON, M., and M.N. LEESE, "The Characterization of Mounted Garnets and its Value as Archaeological Evidence", *Vendel Period Studies*, ed. J. Lamm & H-Å. Nordström (Stockholm, 1983), pp. 83–90.

BIRCH, W. de G. (ed.), *Cartularium Saxonicum*, 3 vols and Index (London, 1885–1899).

BJÖRKMAN, E., "Bēow, Bēaw und Bēowulf", *English Studies*, 52 (1918), pp. 145–193.

———, "Scedeland, Scedenig", *Namn och Bygd*, 6 (1918), pp. 162–168.

———, *Studien über die Eigennamen im Beowulf* (Halle, 1920).

BLAKE, E.O. (ed.), *Liber Eliensis*, Royal Historical Society, Camden Third Series, 92 (London, 1962).

BLAKE, N.F., "The Dating of Old English Poetry", *An English Miscellany presented to W.S. Mackie*, ed. B.S. Lee (Cape Town, 1977), pp. 14–27.

BLISS, A.J., *The Metre of Beowulf* (Oxford, 1958).

BLUNT, C.E., "The Anglo-Saxon Coinage and the Historian", *Medieval Archaeology*, 4 (1960), pp. 1–15.

———, "The Coinage of Offa", *Anglo-Saxon Coins*, ed. R.H.M. Dolley (London, 1961), pp. 39–62.

BONJOUR, A., *The Digressions in Beowulf*, (Oxford, 1950; rpt. 1970).

BOSWORTH, J., and T. NORTHCOTE TOLLER (ed.), *An Anglo-Saxon Dictionary*, with Supplement (Oxford, 1921).

BOYLE, L.E., "The Nowell Codex and the Poem of *Beowulf*", *The Dating of Beowulf*, C. Chase (Toronto, 1981). pp. 23–32.

BRADY, C., *The Legends of Ermanaric* (Berkeley, 1943).

———, " 'Weapons in *Beowulf*: an Analysis of the Nominal Compounds and an Evaluation of the Poet's Use of Them", *Anglo-Saxon England*, 8 (1978), pp. 79–141.

BRODEUR, A.G., "The Structure and Unity of *Beowulf*", *Publications of the Modern Language Association*, 68 (1953), pp. 1183–1195.

———, *The Art of Beowulf* (Berkeley, 1959).

BRØGGER, A.W., H. FALK, and H. SHETELIG, *Osebergfundet*, vols 1–3 & 5 (Oslo, 1917–1927).

BROWN, T., "The Black Dog", *Folklore*, 69 (1958), pp. 175–192.

———, "The Black Dog in English Folklore", *Animals in Folklore*, ed. J.R. Porter and W. Russell (Ipswich, 1978), pp. 45–58.

BRUCE-MITFORD, R., *Aspects of Anglo-Saxon Archaeology* (London, 1974).

———— (ed.), *The Sutton Hoo Ship-Burial*, 3 vols (London, 1975, 1978, 1982).

————, "The Sutton Hoo Ship-Burial: Reflections after Thirty Years", *University of York Medieval Monograph Series*, 2 (1979).

————, "Review of *Vendel Period Studies*", *Medieval Archaeology*, 29 (1985), pp. 231–233.

————, "The Sutton Hoo Ship-Burial: Some Foreign Connections", *Settimane di studio del centro italiano di studi sull'alto medioevo*, 32 (1986 for 1984), pp. 143–218.

BRYAN W.F., "Epithetic Compound Folk-Names in *Beowulf*", *Studies in English Philology: a Miscellany in Honour of Frederick Klaeber*, ed. K. Malone and M.B. Ruud (Minneapolis, 1929), pp. 120–134.

BYERS, J.R., Jr., "A Possible Emendation of *Beowulf* 461^{b}", *Philological Quarterly*, 46 (1967), pp. 125–128.

————, "The Last of the Wægmundings and a Possible Emendation of *Beowulf*", *Modern Philology*, 66 (1968), pp. 45–47.

CABLE, T., *The Meter and Melody of Beowulf*, Illinois Studies in Language and Literature, 64 (Urbana, 1974).

————, "Metrical Style as Evidence for the Date of *Beowulf*", *The Dating of Beowulf*, ed. C. Chase (Toronto, 1981), pp. 77–82.

CAMERON, A., *et al.*, "A Reconsideration of the Language of *Beowulf*", *The Dating of Beowulf*, ed. C. Chase (Toronto, 1981), pp. 33–75.

CAMERON, K.H. (ed.), *The Place-Names of Derbyshire*, English Place-Names Society, 3 vols (Cambridge, 1959).

CAMPBELL, A. (ed.), *The Battle of Brunanburh* (London, 1938).

————, *Old English Grammar* (Oxford, 1959).

————, *The Chronicle of Æthelweard* (London, 1962).

————, "The Old English Epic Style", *English and Medieval Studies Presented to J.R.R. Tolkien on the Occasion of his Seventieth Birthday*, ed. N. Davis and C.L. Wrenn (London, 1962), pp. 13–26.

————, "The Use in *Beowulf* of Earlier Heroic Verse", *England before the Conquest: Studies in Primary Sources presented to Dorothy Whitelock*, ed. P. Clemoes and K. Hughes (Cambridge, 1971).

CAMPBELL, A.P., "The Decline and Fall of Hrothgar and His Danes", *Revue de l'Université d'Ottawa*, 45 (1975), pp. 417–429.

CAMPBELL, J. (ed.), *The Anglo-Saxons* (Oxford, 1982).

CARR, C.T., *Nominal Compounds in Germanic* (Oxford, 1939).

CARR, R.D., A. TESTER, and P. MURPHY, "The Middle Saxon Settlement at Staunch Meadow, Brandon", *Antiquity*, 62 (1988), pp. 371–377.

CARVER, M.O.H., "Sutton Hoo in Contest", *Settimane di studio del centro italiano di studi sull'alto medioevo*, 32 (1986 for 1984), pp. 77–123.

————, "Kingship and Material Culture in Early Anglo-Saxon East Anglia," *The Origins of the Anglo-Saxon Kingdoms*, ed. S. Bassett (Leicester, 1989), pp. 141–158, 270–275.

————, "Pre-Viking Traffic in the North Sea," *Maritime Celts, Frisians and Saxons*, ed. S. Macgrail (forthcoming).

————, "Ideology and Allegiance in Early East Anglia", ed. R.T. Farrell (forthcoming).

———— (ed.), *The Age of Sutton Hoo* (Woodbridge, 1992).

————, and A.C. EVANS, "Anglo-Saxon Discoveries at Sutton Hoo, 1987–8", *Bulletin of the Sutton Hoo Research Committee*, 6 (1989), pp. 4–15.

CARY, E. (ed. and tr.), *Dio Cassius: Historia Romanorum*, Loeb Classical Library, vol. 9 (London, 1914–1927).

CHADWICK, H.M., *The Origin of the English Nation* (Cambridge, 1907).

———, *The Heroic Age* (Cambridge, 1912).

———, and N.K. CHADWICK, *The Growth of Literature*, vol. 1 (Cambridge, 1932).

CHAMBERS, J.K., and P. TRUDGILL, *Dialectology* (Cambridge, 1980).

CHAMBERS, R.W. (ed.), *Widsith* (Cambridge, 1912).

———, *Beowulf: An Introduction to the Study of the Poem*, 3rd edition, with supplement by C.L. Wrenn (Cambridge, 1959).

CHANEY, W.A., *The Cult of Kingship in Anglo-Saxon England* (Manchester, 1970).

CHASE, C. (ed.), *The Dating of Beowulf* (Toronto, 1981).

———, "Opinions on the Date of *Beowulf*, 1815–1980", *The Dating of Beowulf*, ed., C. Chase (Toronto, 1981), pp. 3–8.

CLANCHY, M.T., *From Memory to Written Record: England 1066–1307* (London, 1979).

CLARK, M.G., *Sidelights on Teutonic History during the Migration Period: Studies from Beowulf and Other Old English Poems* (Cambridge, 1911).

CLARK HALL, J.R., *A Concise Anglo-Sacon Dictionary*, 4th edition, with supplement by H.D. Meritt (Cambridge, 1962).

CLARKE, D.E.M., "The Office of Þyle in *Beowulf*", *Review of English Studies*, 12 (1936), pp. 61–66.

CLEMENT, R.W., "Codicological Consideration in the *Beowulf* Manuscript", *Proceedings of the Illinois Medieval Association*, ed. R.B. Bosse *et al.* (Illinois, 1984), pp. 13–27.

CLEMOES, P., "Style as a Criterion for the Dating of the Composition of *Beowulf*", *The Dating of Beowulf*, ed. C. Chase (Toronto, 1918), pp. 173–185.

CLOVER, C.J., "The Germanic Context of the Unferþ Episode", *Speculum*, 55 (1980), pp. 444–468.

COLGRAVE, B. (ed. and tr.), *Felix's Life of Saint Guthlac* (Cambridge, 1956).

——— and R.A.B. MYNORS (ed. and tr.), *Bede's Ecclesiastical History of the English People* (Oxford, 1969).

CRAMP, R.J., "*Beowulf* and Archaeology", *Medieval Archaeology*, 1 (1957), pp. 57–77.

CROWLEY, J.P., "The Study of Old English Dialects", *English Studies*, 67 (1986), pp. 97–112.

DAMICO, H., "*Sǫrlapáttr* and the Hama Episode in *Beowulf*", *Scandinavian Studies*, 55 (1983), pp. 222–235.

DAVIES, W., "Annals and the Origin of Mercia", *Mercian Studies*, ed. A. Dornier (Leicester, 1977), pp. 17–29.

———, and H. VIERCK, "The Contexts of the Tribal Hidage", *Frühmittelalterliche studien*, 8 (1974), pp. 223–293.

DENHOLM-YOUNG, N., *Handwriting in England and Wales* (Cardiff, 1954).

DEUTSCHBEIN, M., "Beowulf der Gautenkönig", in *Festschrift für L. Morsbach*, Studien zur Englischen Philologie, 50 (Halle, 1913), pp. 291–297.

DOBBIE, E.V.K. (ed.), *The Anglo-Saxon Minor Poems* (New York, 1942).

DRONKE, U. (ed.), *The Poetic Edda*, vol. 1 (Oxford, 1969).

———, "*Beowulf*, and Ragnarǫk", *Saga Book*, 17 (1969), pp. 302–325.

DUMMLER, E. (ed.), *Alcuini Epistolae*, Monumenta Germaniae Historica, Epistolae Aevi Carolini, vol. 2 (Berlin, 1895).

DUMVILLE, D.N., "Some Aspects of the Chronology of the *Historia Brittonum*", *Bulletin of the Board of Celtic Studies*, 25 (1972–1974), pp. 439–445.

———,"A New Chronicle-Fragment of Early British History," *English Historical Review*, 88, (1973), pp. 312–314.

———, " 'Nennius' and the *Historia Brittonum*", *Studia Celtica*, 10–11 (1975–1976), pp. 78–95.

——— (ed.), "The Anglian Collection of Royal Genealogies and Regnal Lists," *Anglo-Saxon England*, 5, pp. 23–50.

———, "Kingship, Genealogies and Regnal Lists," *Early Medieval Kingship*, ed. P.H. Sawyer and I.N. Wood (Leeds), pp. 72–104.

———, "The Ætheling", *Anglo-Saxon England*, 8 (1979), pp. 1–33.

———, "*Beowulf* and the Celtic World: The Uses of Evidence", *Traditio*, 37 (1981), pp. 109–160.

———, "*Beowulf* come lately: some Notes on the Palaeography of the Nowell Codex", *Archiv für das Studium der neueren Sprachen und Literaturen*, 225, (1988), pp. 49–63.

EARL, J.W., "The Role of the Men's Hall in the Development of the Anglo-Saxon Superego", *Psychiatry*, 46 (1983), pp. 139–160.

———, "*Beowulf* and the Sparrow" (abstract), *Old English Newsletter*, 14, 2 (1986), pp. A/38–39.

EARLE, J. (ed.), *A Handbook of Land-Charters and other Saxonic Documents* (Oxford, 1888).

———, *The Deeds of Beowulf* (Oxford, 1892).

EKWALL, E. (ed.), *The Concise Oxford Dictionary of English Place-Names*, 4th edition (Oxford, 1960).

ELIADE, M., *Patterns in Comparative Religion*, tr. R. Sheed (New York, 1958).

———, *A History of Religious Ideas*, vol. 2, tr. W.R. Trask (Chicago, 1982).

ELIASON, N.E., "The 'Thryth-Offa Digression' in *Beowulf*", *Franciplegius: Medieval and Linguistic Studies in Honour of Francis Peabody Magoun, Jr.*, ed. J.B. Bessinger, Jr., and R.P. Creed (New York, 1965), pp. 124–138.

———, "Beowulf, Wiglaf and the Wægmundings", *Anglo-Saxon England*, 11 (1982), pp. 95–105.

ELLIS DAVIDSON, H.R., *Gods and Myths of Northern Europe* (Harmonsworth, 1964).

———, "Archaeology and *Beowulf*", *Beowulf and Its Analogues*, ed. G.N. Garmonsway and J. Simpson, 2nd edition (London, 1980), pp. 351–364.

——— (ed.), *Saxo Grammaticus: The History of the Danes*, 2 vols, tr. P. Fisher (Cambridge, 1979).

EVISON, V., "Anglo-Saxon Glass Claw-beakers", *Archaeologia* 107 (1982), pp. 43–76.

FARRELL, R.T., *Beowulf, Swedes and Geats* (London, 1972).

———, "*Beowulf* and the Northern Heroic Age", *The Vikings*, ed. R.T. Farrell (Chichester, 1982), pp. 180–216.

FAULKES, A., "Descent from the Gods," *Medieval Scandinavia*, 11, (1979), pp. 92–125.

FELL, C., "Old English *Wiking*: A Question of Semantics", *Proceedings of the British Academy*, 72 (1987), pp. 295–316.

FENWICK, V., "A New Anglo-Saxon Ship", *The International Journal of Nautical Archaeology and Underwater Exploration*, 12 (1983), pp. 174–175.

————, "*Insula de Burgh*: Excavations at Burrow Hill, Butley, Suffolk, 1978–81", *Anglo-Saxon Studies in Archaeology and History*, 3 (1989), pp. 35–54.

FILMER-SANKEY W., "The Snape Anglo-Saxon Cemetery and Ship Burial: Current State of Knowledge", *Bulletin of the Sutton Hoo Research Committee*, 2 (1984), pp. 13–15.

————, "A New Boat from the Snape Anglo-Saxon Cemetery, Suffolk", *Maritime Celts, Frisians and Saxons*, ed. S. McGrail (forthcoming).

FLECK, J., "*Konr – Óttarr – Geirroðr*: A Knowledge Criterion for Succession to the Germanic Sacred Kingship", *Scandinavian Studies*, 42 (1970), pp. 39–49.

FLOM, G.T., "Alliteration and Variation in Old Germanic Name-Giving", *Modern Language Notes*, 32 (1917), pp. 7–17.

FOOTE, P.G., and D.M. WILSON, *The Viking Achievement* (London, 1970).

FORBY, R. (ed.), *The Vocabulary of East Anglia*, 2 vols (London, 1830).

FOULKE, W.D. (ed. and tr.), *Paulus Diaconus: The History of the Lombards* (Philadelphia, 1974).

FOX, D., and H. PÁLSSON (ed. and tr.), *Grettir's Saga* (Toronto, 1974).

FRANK, R., "Skaldic Verse and the Date of *Beowulf*", *The Dating of Beowulf*, ed. C. Chase (Toronto), pp. 123–139.

FRY, D.K. (ed.), *Finnsburh: Fragment and Episode* (London, 1974).

FULK, R.D., "Dating *Beowulf* to the Viking Age". *Philological Quarterly*, 61, (1982), pp. 341–359.

————, "Unferth and His Name", *Modern Philology*, 85 (1987), pp. 113–127.

————, "An Eddic Analogue to the Scyld Scefing Story", *Review of English Studies*, 40 (1989), pp. 313–322.

————, "West Germanic Parasiting, Siever's Law, and the Dating of Old Engish Verse", *Studies in Philology*, 86 (1989), pp. 117–138.

————, "Contraction as a Criterion for Dating Old English Verse", *Journal of English and Germanic Philology*, 89 (1990), pp. 1–16.

GALBRAITH, K.J., "Early Sculpture at St Nicholas's Church, Ipswich", *Proceedings of the Suffolk Institute of Archaeology and History*, 31 (1969–1970), pp. 172–187.

————, "Further Thoughts on the Boar at St Nicholas's Church, Ipswich", *Proceedings of the Suffolk Institute of Archaeology and History*, 33 (1973–1974), pp. 68–74.

GARMONSWAY, G.N., and J. Simpson, (ed. and tr.), *Beowulf and Its Analogues* (London, 1968; 2nd edition, 1980).

GELLING, M., *Signposts to the Past: Place-Names and the History of England* (London, 1982).

————, *Place-Names in the Landscape* (London, 1984).

GERRITSEN, J., "British Library Cotton Vitellius A.xv – A Supplementary Description", *English Studies*, 69 (1988), pp. 293–302.

————, "Have with you to Lexington! The *Beowulf* Manuscript and *Beowulf*", *In Other Words: Transcultural Studies in Philology, Translation and Lexicography Presented to Prof. dr. H.H. Meier on the Occasion of his Sixty-fifth Birthday* (Dordrecht, 1989).

GERSTEIN, M., "Germanic Warg: the Outlaw as Werwolf", *Myth in Indo-European Antiquity*, ed. G.J. Larson (Berkeley, 1974), pp. 131–156.

GERTZ, M.C.L. (ed.), *Sven Aggesøns Værker* (Copenhagen, 1916).

————, *Scriptores Minores Historiæ Danicæ*, vol. 1 (Copenhagen, 1970).

GILLESPIE, G.T., *Catalogue of Persons Named in German Heroic Literature* (Oxford, 1973).

GIRVAN, R., *Beowulf and the Seventh Century*, 2nd edition (London, 1971).

GLASS, S., "The Sutton Hoo Ship Burial", *Antiquity*, 36 (1962), pp. 179–183.

GLOB, P.V., *Denmark: An Archaeological History from the Stone Age to the Vikings*, tr. J. Bulman (Ithaca, 1967).

GLOSECKI, S.O., "The Boar's Helmet in *Beowulf*: Reflexes of Totemism and Exogamy in Early Germanic Literature", unpub. Ph.D. diss., (University of California, Davis, 1980).

GOFFART, W., "*Hetware* and *Hugas*: Datable Anachronisms in *Beowulf*", *The Dating of Beowulf*, ed. C. Chase (Toronto, 1981), pp. 83–100.

GOLDSMITH, M.E., "The Christian Perspective in *Beowulf*", *Comparative Literature*, 14 (1962), pp. 71–90.

GOODY, J., and I. WATT, "The Consequences of Literacy", *Language and Social Context*, ed. P.P. Giglioli (Harmondsworth, 1972), pp. 311–357.

GORDON, E.V., "Wealhðeow and Related Names," *Medium Ævum*, 4 (1935), pp. 169–175.

———, *An Introduction to Old Norse* (Oxford, 1957).

GRADON, P.O.E. (ed.), *Cynewulf's Elene* (London, 1958).

GRANSDEN, A., "The Legends and Traditions concerning the Origins of the Abbey of Bury St Edmunds", *English Historical Review*, 100 (1985), pp. 1–24.

GREEN, B., "An Anglo-Saxon Bone Plaque from Larling, Norfolk", *The Antiquaries' Journal*, 51 (1971), pp. 321–323.

GREEN, C., *Sutton Hoo* (London, 1963).

GREENFIELD, S.B., "The Authenticating Voice in *Beowulf*", *Anglo-Saxon England*, 5 (1976), pp. 51–62.

GRUNDTVIG, N.F.S. (ed.), *Beowulfes Beorh eller Bjovulfs-Drapen, det Old-Angelske Heltedigt, paa Grund-Sproget* (Copenhagen, 1861).

GUREVICH, A.Ya., "Wealth and Gift-Bestowal among the Ancient Scandinavians", *Scandinavica*, 17 (1968), pp. 126–138.

GUÐNASSON, B. *Um Skjöldungasögu* (Reykjavík, 1963).

HADDEN, A.W., and W. STUBBS (ed.), *Councils and Ecclesiastical Documents Relating to Great Britain and Ireland*, vol. 3 (Oxford, 1871).

HALLIDAY, M.A.K., *Language as a Social Semiotic* (London, 1978).

HALSALL, M. (ed.), *The Old English Rune Poem: A Critical Edition* (Toronto, 1981).

HARDY, M.J., and E.A. MARTIN, "South Elmham St Margaret (Field Survey)", *Proceedings of the Suffolk Institute of Archaeology and History*, 36 (1987), pp. 232–234.

HATTO, A.T., "Snake-swords and Boar-helms in *Beowulf*", *English Studies*, 38 (1957), pp. 145–160, 257–259.

HAUCK, K., "Halsring und Ahnenstab als herrscherliche Wurdezeichen", *Herschaftzeichen und Staatssymbolik*, ed. P.E. Schramm *et al.*, *Schriften der Monumenta Germaniae Historica*, 13/1 (Stuttgart, 1954), pp. 145–212.

———, "Herrschaftszeichen eines Wodanistischen Königtums", *Jahrbuch für fränkische Landesforschung*, 14 (Kallmunz-Opf., 1954), pp. 9–66.

———, "Zum ersten Band der Sutton Hoo-Edition", *Frühmittelalterliche Studien*, 12 (1978), pp. 438–456.

———, "Zum zweiten Band der Sutton Hoo-Edition", *Frühmittelalterliche Studien*, 16 (1982), pp. 319–362.

HAUGEN, E., "The *Edda* as Ritual: Odin and his Masks", *Edda: A Collection of Essays*, ed. R.J. Glendinning and H. Bessason (Manitoba, 1983), pp. 3–24.

HEDEAGER, L., "Processes towards State Formation in Early Iron Age Denmark", *Studies in Scandinavian Prehistory and Early History*, 1 (1978), pp. 217–223.

HELDER, W., "The Song of Creation in *Beowulf* and the Interpretation of Heorot", *English Studies in Canada*, 13 (1987), pp. 243–255.

HENIGE, D.P., "Oral Tradition and Chronology", *Journal of African History*, 12 (1971), pp. 371–389.

HERBEN, S.J., Jr., "Heorot", *Publications of the Modern Language Association*, 50 (1935), pp. 933–945.

HERVEY, F. (ed.), *The Garland of Saint Edmund King and Martyr*, (London, 1907).

HICKS, C., "A Note on the Provenance of the Sutton Hoo Stag", *The Sutton Hoo Ship Burial*, vol. 2, ed. R. Bruce-Mitford (London, 1978), pp. 378–382.

HILL, J. (ed.), *The Old English Minor Poems* (Durham, 1983).

——, Widsið and the Tenth Century", *Neuphilologische Mitteilungen*, 85 (1984), pp. 305–315.

HILL, J.M., "*Beowulf* and the Danish Succession: Gift Giving as an Occasion for Complex Gesture", *Medievalia at Humanistica*, new series, 11 (1982), pp. 177–197.

HILL, T.D., "Scyld Scefing and the *Stirps Regia*: Pagan Myth and Christian Kingship in *Beowulf*", *Magister Regis*, ed. A. Groos *et al.* (Fordham 1986), pp. 37–47.

——, "The Myth of the Ark-Born Son of Noe and the West-Saxon Royal Genealogical Tables", *Harvard Theological Review*, 80 (1987), pp. 379–383.

——, "Woden as 'Ninth Father': Numerical Patterning in some Old English Royal Genealogies", *Germania: Studies in Old Germanic Languages and Literature*, ed. D.G. Calder and T.C. Christy (Woodbridge, 1987), pp. 161–174.

HILLS, C., et al., *The Anglo-Saxon Cemetery at Spong Hill, North Elmham: Part 1, Catalogue of Cremations*, East Anglian Archaeology, 6 (Norwich, 1977); *Part 2, Catalogue of Cremations*, East Anglian Archaeology, 11 (1981); *Part 3, Catalogue of Inhumations*, East Anglian Archaeology, 21 (1984); *Part 4, Catalogue of Cremations*, East Anglian Archaeology, 34 (1987).

——, "The Gold Bracteate from Undley, Suffolk: some Further Thoughts", *Studien zur Sachsen-forschung* (forthcoming).

HINES, J., *The Scandinavian Character of Anglian England in the pre-Viking Period*, British Archaeological Reports, British Series, 124 (Oxford, 1984).

HODGKIN, R.H., *A History of the Anglo-Saxons*, 2 vols (Oxford, 1952).

HOLLOWELL, I.M., "Unferð the Þyle in *Beowulf*", *Studies in Philology*, 73 (1976), pp. 239–265.

HOLTHAUSEN, F., "Zur Textkritik des *Beowulf*", *Studia Neophilologica*, 14 (1942), p. 160.

HOPE-TAYLOR, B., *Yeavering: An Anglo-British Centre of Early Northumbria* (London, 1977).

HOPPITT, R., "Sutton Hoo 1860", *Proceedings of the Suffolk Institute of Archaeology and History*, 36 (1985), pp. 41–42.

HÜBENER, G., "*Beowulf* and Germanic Exorcism", *Review of English Studies*, 11 (1935), pp. 163–181.

HUDSON, R.A., *Sociolinguistics* (Cambridge, 1980).

HUGHES, G., "Beowulf, Unferð and Hrunting: an Interpretation", *English Studies*, 58 (1977), pp. 385–395.

HUME, K., "The Concept of the Hall in Old English Poetry", *Anglo-Saxon England*, 3 (1974), pp. 63–74.

HUNTER, M., "Germanic and Roman Antiquity and the Sense of the Past in Anglo-Saxon England", *Anglo-Saxon England*, 3 (1974), pp. 29–50.

IRVING, E.B., Jr., *A Reading of Beowulf* (New Haven and London, 1968).
———, "The Nature of the Christianity in *Beowulf*", *Anglo-Saxon England*, 13 (1984), pp. 7–21.

JACKSON, K.H., *The Oldest Irish Tradition: A Window on the Iron Age* (Cambridge, 1964).
JACOBS, N., "Anglo-Danish Relations, Poetic Archaism and the Date of *Beowulf*", *Poetica* (Tokyo), 8 (1978), pp. 23–43.
JAKOBSON, R., "Closing Statement: Linguistics and Poetics", *Style in Language*, ed. T.A. Sebeok (Cambridge, Mass., 1960), pp. 350–377.
JAMES, M.R. (ed.), "Two Lives of St Ethelbert, King and Martyr," *English Historical Review*, 32 (1917), pp. 214–244.
JANKUHN, H., "The Continental Home of the English, *Antiquity*, 26 (1952), pp. 14–24.
JESPERSON, O., *Growth and Structure of the English Language* (Leipzig, 1905).
JOHN, E., "*Beowulf* and the Margins of Literacy", *Bulletin of the John Rylands Library*, 56 (1974), pp. 38–422.
JONES, G., *Kings, Beasts and Heroes* (Oxford, 1972).
———, *A History of the Vikings*, 2nd edition (Oxford, 1984).
JONES, P.F., "The Gregorian Mission and English Education" *Speculum*, 3 (1928), pp. 335–348.
JÓNSSON, Finnur (ed.), *Njáls saga*, Altnordische sagabibliothek (Halle, 1908).
———, *Edda Snorra Sturlusonar* (Copenhagen, 1931).
JÓNSSON, Guðni (ed.), *Fornaldar sogur Norðurlanda*, 4 vols (Reykjavík, 1950).

KÅLUND, K. (ed.), *Alfræði Íslenzk*, vol. 3, Samfund til udgivelse af gammel nordisk litteratur, 45 (Copenhagen, 1918).
KASKE, R.E., "*Sapientia et Fortitudo* as the Controlling Theme of *Beowulf*", *Studies in Philology*, 55 (1958), pp. 423–457.
KELLY, B., "The Formative Stages of *Beowulf* Textual Scholarship": part 1, *Anglo-Saxon England*, 11 (1982), pp. 247–274; part 2, *Anglo-Saxon England*, 12 (1983), pp. 239–275.
KER, N.R. (ed.), *Catalogue of Manuscripts Containing Anglo-Saxon* (Oxford, 1957).
KEYNES, S., and M. LAPIDGE (ed. & tr.), *Alfred the Great* (Harmondsworth, 1983).
KIERNAN, K., *Beowulf and the Beowulf Manuscript* (New Jersey, 1981).
———, "The Eleventh-Century Origin of *Beowulf* and the *Beowulf* Manuscript", *The Dating of Beowulf*, ed. C. Chase (Toronto, 1981), pp. 9–22.
KINSELLA ,T. (ed.), *Táin Bó Cúailnge* (Oxford, 1970).
KIRBY, D.P., "Bede's Native Sources for the *Historia Ecclesiastica*", *Bulletin of the John Rylands Library*, 48 (1966), pp. 341–371.
KLAEBER, F. (ed.), *Beowulf and the Fight at Finnsburg*, 3rd edition (Boston, 1950).
KOTZOR, G. (ed.), *Das Altenglische Martyrologium*, 2 vols, Bayerische Academie der Wissenschaften Philologisch-historische Klasse, new series, 88 (Munich, 1981).
KRAG, C., *Ynglingatal og Ynglingesaga: En Studie i Historiske Kilder*, Studia Humaniora, 2 (Oslo, 1991).
KRAPPE, G.P. (ed.), *The Junius Manuscript* (New York and London, 1931).

————, and E. van K. DOBBIE (ed.), *The Exeter Book* (New York and London 1936).

KROMAN, E. (ed.), *Danmarks middelalderlige annaler*, vol. 1 (Copenhagen, 1980).

KRUSCH, B., and W. LEVISON (ed.), *Gregorii Episcopi Turonensis Libri Historiarum X*, Monumenta Germaniae Historica, Scriptores Rerum Merovingicarum, vol. 1, 2nd edition (Hanover, 1951).

LAMM, J.P., and H-Å. NORDSTROM (ed.), *Vendel Period Studies* (Stockholm, 1983).

LAPIDGE, M., "Aldhelm's Latin Poetry and Old English Verse", *Comparative Literature*, 31 (1979), pp. 209–231.

————, "*Beowulf*, Aldhelm, the *Liber Monstrorum* and Wessex", *Studi Medievali*, 23 (1982), pp. 151–192.

LAWRENCE, W.W., *Beowulf and Epic Tradition* (Cambridge, Mass., 1928).

LAWSON, A.J., E.A. MARTIN, and D. PRIDDY, *The Barrows of East Anglia*, East Anglian Archaeology, 12 (Norwich, 1981).

LEAKE, J.E., *The Geats of Beowulf* (Wisconsin, 1967).

LEE, A.A., *The Guest-Hall of Eden* (New Haven, 1972).

LEEDS, E.T., "Denmark and Early England", *The Antiquaries' Journal*, 26 (1946), pp. 22–37.

———— (ed.), *A Corpus of Early Anglo-Saxon Square-Headed Brooches* (Oxford, 1949).

LEHMANN, W.P., "Post-consonantal *l m n r* and Metrical Practice in *Beowulf*", *Nordica et Anglica*, ed. A.H. Orrick (The Hague, 1968), pp. 148–167.

LIND, E., *Norsk-isländska dopnamn och fingerade namn från meideltiden* (Uppsala, 1905–1915).

LINDQVIST, S., *Uppsala Högar och Ottershögen* (Stockholm, 1936).

————, "Sutton Hoo and *Beowulf*" (ed. and tr. R. Bruce-Mitford), *Antiquity*, 22 (1948), pp. 131–140.

LUCE, J.V., *Homer and the Heroic Age* (London, 1975).

MACRAE-GIBSON, O.D., "The Metrical Entities of Old English", *Neuphilologische Mitteilungen*, 87 (1986), pp. 59–91.

MAGOUN, F.P., Jr., "Fifeldore and the Name of the Eider", *Namn och Bygd*, 26 (1940), pp. 94–114.

————, "Danes, North, South, East, and West, in *Beowulf*", *Philologica: The Malone Anniversary Studies*, T.A. Kirby and H.B. Woolf (Baltimore, 1949), pp. 20–24.

————, "The Geography of Hygelac's Raid on the Lands of the West Frisians and the Hætt-ware, *ca* 530 A.D.", *English Studies*, 34 (1953), pp. 160–163.

————, "Beowulf and King Hygelac in the Netherlands", *English Studies*, 35 (1954), pp. 193–204.

————, "*Beowulf A*: A Folk Variant", *Arv: Journal of Scandinavian Folklore*, 14 (1958), pp. 95–101.

————, "*Beowulf B*: A Folk-Poem on Beowulf's Death", *Early English and Norse Studies Presented to Hugh Smith in Honour of His Sixtieth Birthday*, ed. A. Brown and P. Foote (London, 1963), pp. 127–140.

MAJOR, A.F., "Ship-Burials in Scandinavian Lands and the Beliefs that Underlie them" *Folklore*, 35 (1924), pp. 113–150.

MALONE, K., *The Literary History of Hamlet: The Early Tradition* (New York, 1923).

——, "Hrethric", *Publications of the Modern Language Association*, 42 (1927), pp. 268–313.

——, untitled review, *Speculum*, 6 (1931), pp. 149–150.

—— (ed.), *Widsith*, 1st edition (London, 1936).

——, "Swerting", *Germanic Review*, 14 (1939), pp. 235–257.

——, "Humblus and Lotherus, *Acta Philologica Scandinavica*, 13 (1939), pp. 201–214.

——, "Ecgtheow", *Modern Language Quarterly* (1940), pp. 37–44.

——, "Agelmund and Lamicho", *Studies in Heroic Legend and in Current Speech*, ed. S. Einarsson and N.E. Eliason (Copenhagen, 1959), pp. 86–107.

——, "The Daughter of Healfdene", *Studies . . .*, ed. S. Einarsson and N.E. Eliason (Copenhagen, 1959), pp. 124–141.

——, "Epithet and Eponym", *Studies . . .*, ed. S. Einarsson and N.E. Eliason (Copenhagen, 1959), pp. 189–192.

——, "The Tale of Ingeld", *Studies . . .*, ed. S. Einarsson and N.E. Eliason (Copenhagen, 1959), pp. 1–62.

—— (ed.), *Widsith*, 2nd edition (Copenhagen, 1962).

——, *The Nowell Codex*, Early English Manuscripts in Facsimile, 12 (Copenhagen, 1963).

MARTIN, E., "The *Iclingas*", *East Anglian Archaeology*, 3 (1976), pp. 132–134.

MATTHES, H.C., "Hygd", *Gestschrift zum 75. Geburtstag von Theodor Spira*, ed. H. Viebrock and W. Erzgräber (Heidelberg, 1961), pp. 14–31.

MAYR-HARTING, H., *The Coming of Christianity to Anglo-Saxon England* (London, 1972).

MEANEY, A.L., "St Neots, Æthelweard, and the *Anglo-Saxon Chronicle*", *Studies in Earlier Old English Prose*, ed. P.E. Szarmach (Albany, New York, 1986), pp. 193–245.

——, "Scyld Scefing and the Dating of *Beowulf* – Again", *Bulletin of the John Rylands Library*, 71 (1989), pp. 7–40.

MERITT, H.D., "Studies in Old English Vocabulary", *Journal of English and Germanic Philology*, 46 (1947), pp. 413–427.

——, *Fact and Lore about Old English Words* (Stanford, 1954).

——, *Some of the Hardest Glosses in Old English* (Stanford, 1968).

METCALF, D.M., "Monetary Circulation in Southern England in the First Half of the Eighth Century", *Sceattas in England and on the Continent*, ed. D. Hill and D.M. Metcalf, British Archaeological Reports, British Series, 128 (Oxford, 1984), pp. 27–69.

MILLER, M., "Date-Guessing and Pedigrees", *Studia Celtica*, 10–11 (1975–1976), pp. 96–109.

——, "Bede's Use of Gildas", *English Historical Review*, 90 (1975), pp. 241–261.

MITCHELL, B., *Old English Syntax* (Oxford, 1985).

MOISL, H., "Anglo-Saxon Royal Genealogies and Germanic Oral Tradition," *Journal of Medieval History*, 7 (1981), pp. 215–248.

MOLTKE, E., *Runes and their Origin: Denmark and Elsewhere*, tr. P. Foote (Copenhagen, 1985).

MOMMSEN, T., *Historia Brittonum*, Monumenta Germaniae Historica, Auctores Antiquissimi, vol. 13 (Berlin, 1894).

MOOR, E. (ed.), *Suffolk Words and Phrases* (London, 1823; repr. New York, 1970).

MOORE, B., "*Eacen* in *Beowulf* and other OE Poetry", *English Language Notes*, 13 (1976), pp. 161–165.

MOORMAN, F.W., "English Place-Names and Teutonic Sagas", *Essays and Studies*, 5 (1914), pp. 75–103.

MORGAN, G., "The Treachery of Hrothulf", *English Studies*, 53 (1972), pp. 23–39.
MORSBACH, L., "Zur Datierung des *Beowulf* Epos", *Nachrichten der K. Gesellschaft der Wissenschaften zu Göttingen*, Philologisch-historische Klasse (Munich, 1906), pp. 251–277.
MÜLLENHOFF, K., *Beowulf: Untersuchungen über das angelsächsische Epos und die älteste Geschichte der germanischen Seevölker* (Berlin, 1889).
MÜLLER-WILLE, M., "Boat-Graves in Northern Europe", *The International Journal of Nautical Archaeology and Underwater Exploration*, 3 (1974), pp. 187–204.
MURRAY, A.C., "*Beowulf*, the Danish Invasions, and Royal Genealogy", *The Dating of Beowulf*, ed. C. Chase (Toronto, 1981), pp. 101–112.
MYRES, J.L.N., *The English Settlements* (Oxford, 1986).
———, and B. GREEN, *The Anglo-Saxon Cemeteries of Caistor-by-Norwich and Markshall, Norfolk* (London, 1973).
MYHRE, B., "The Royal Cemetery at Borre, Vestfold: A Norwegian Centre in a European Periphery", *The Age of Sutton Hoo*, ed. M. Carver (Woodbridge, 1992).

NÄSMAN, U., "Vendel Period Glass", *Acta Archaeologica*, 55 (1984), pp. 55–116.
NECKEL, H. von G., "Sigminds Drachenkampf" *Edda*, 13 (1920), pp. 122–140, 204–229.
———, *Edda: die Lieder des Codex Regius*, rev. H. Kuhn (Heidelberg, 1962).
NERMAN, B., *Det Svenska Rikets Uppkomst* (Stockholm, 1925).
NEWMAN, J., "East Anglian Kingdom Survey – Final Interim Report on the South East Suffolk Pilot Field Survey", *Bulletin of the Sutton Hoo Research Committee*, 6 (1989), pp. 17–20.
———, "The Boss Hall Anglo-Saxon Cemetery, Ipswich", *Saxon: The Newletter of the Sutton Hoo Society*, 14 (1991).
NEUMANN, E., *The Origins and History of Consciousness*, tr. R. Hull (Princeton, 1970).
NICHOLSON, L.E., "*Beowulf* and the Pagan Cult of the Stag", *Studi Medievali*, 27 (1986), pp. 637–669.
NILES, J.D., "Ring-Composition and the Structure of *Beowulf*" *Publications of the Modern Language Association*, 94 (1979), pp. 924–935.
——— (ed.), *Old English Literature in Context: Ten Essays* (Woodbridge, 1980).
———, *Beowulf: the Poem and its Tradition* (Harvard, 1983).
NIST, J.A., *The Structure and Texture of Beowulf* (São Paulo, 1959).
NOREEN, A., *Altisländische und Altnorwegische Grammatik*, 4th edition (Halle, 1923).

O'LOUGHLIN, J.L.N., 1964: "Sutton Hoo: the Evidence of the Documents," *Medieval Archaeology*, 8 (1964), pp. 1–19.
OLRIK, A., The Heroic Legends of Denmark, tr. L.M. Hollander (New York, 1919).
OLRIK, J., and H. Raeder, (ed.), *Saxonis Gesta Danorum* (Copenhagen, 1931).
OLSEN, B.M., *Volsunga saga*, Samfund til Udgivelse af gammel nordisk litteratur (Copenhagen, 1906–1908).
OLSON, O., *The Relation of the Hrólfs Saga Kraka and the Bjarkarímur to Beowulf*, Publications of the Society for the Advancement of Scandinavian Study (Urbana, Illinois, 1916).
OPLAND, J., *Anglo-Saxon Oral Poetry: A Study of Traditions* (Yale, 1980).

————, "From Horseback to Monastic Cell: The Impact on English Literature of the Introduction of Writing", *Old English Literature in Context: Ten Essays*, ed. J.D. Niles (Woodbridge, 1980), pp. 30–41.

OSBORN, M., "*Beowulf*'s Landfall in *Finna Land*", *Neuphilologische Mitteilungen*, 90 (1989), pp. 137–142.

OVERING, G., "Reinventing Beowulf's Voyage to Denmark", *Old English Newsletter*, 21, 2 (1988), pp. 30–39.

OWEN, G.R., *Rites and Religions of the Anglo-Saxons* (London, 1981).

PAGAN, H.E., "The Coinage of the East Anglian Kingdom from 825 to 870", *British Numismatic Journal*, 52 (1982), pp. 41–83.

PAGE, R.I. (ed.), "Anglo-Saxon Episcopal Lists", parts 1 and 2, *Nottingham Medieval Studies*, 9 (1965), pp. 71–95; part 3, *Nottingham Medieval Studies*, 10 (1966), pp. 2–7.

————, *An Introduction to English Runes* (London, 1973).

————, "The Audience of *Beowulf* and the Vikings", *The Dating of Beowulf*, ed. C. Chase (Toronto, 1981), pp. 114–122.

PARKS, W., "The Traditional Narrator and the 'I heard' Formulas in Old English Poetry", *Anglo-Saxon England*, 16 (1987), pp. 45–66.

PARKER PEARSON, M., R. van de NOORT, and A. WOOLF, "Three Men and a Boat: Sutton Hoo and the Saxon Kingdom" (forthcoming).

PLUMMER, C. (ed.), *Two of the Saxon Chronicles Parallel*, 2 vols (Oxford, 1899).

POPE, J.C., *The Rhythm of Beowulf* (New Haven, 1942).

————, "On the Date of Composition of *Beowulf*", *The Dating of Beowulf*, ed. C. Chase (Toronto, 1981), pp. 187–195.

PORSIA, F. (ed.), *Liber Monstrorum* (Bari, 1976).

POUSSA, P., "The Date of *Beowulf* Reconsidered: the Tenth Century?", *Neuphilologische Mitteilungen*, 82 (1981), pp. 276–288.

QUIRK, R., "Poetic Language and Old English Metre", *Early English and Norse Studies Presented to Hugh Smith*, ed. A. Brown and P. Foote (London, 1963), pp. 150–171.

RAINBIRD CLARKE, R., *East Anglia* (London, 1960).

RAUSING, Gad, "*Beowulf, Ynglingatal* and the *Ynglinga saga*", *Fornvännen*, 80 (1985), pp. 163–178.

REEVE, C., *A Straunge & Terrible Wonder: the Story of the Black Dog of Bungay* (Bungay, 1988).

REDIN, M., *Studies in Uncompounded Personal Names in Old English* (Uppsala, 1919).

REINHARD, M., *On the Semantic Relevance of the Alliterative Collocations in Beowulf* (Bern, 1976).

RENOIR, A., and A. HERNÁNDEZ (ed.), *Approaches to Beowulfian Scansion: Four Essays*, Old English Colloquium Series, 1 (Berkeley, 1982).

RICCI, A., "The Chronology of Anglo-Saxon Poetry", *Review of English Studies*, 5 (1929), pp. 257–266.

RICKERT, R., "The Old English Offa Saga", *Modern Philology*, 2 (1905), pp. 29–76, 321–376.

RIDGARD, J., "References to South Elmham Minster in the Medieval Account Rolls of South Elmham Manor", *Proceedings of the Suffolk Institute of Archaeology and History*, 36 (1987), pp. 196–201.

RIGOLD, S.E., "The Supposed See of Dunwich", *Journal of the British Archaeological Association*, 24 (1961), pp. 55–59.
——, "Further Evidence about the Site of *Dommoc*", *Journal of the British Archaeological Association*, 37 (1974), pp. 97–102.
ROBINSON, F.C., "Is Wealhtheow a Prince's Daughter?", *English Studies*, 45 (1964), pp. 36–39.
——, "History, Religion and Culture", *Approaches to Teaching Beowulf*, ed. J.B. Bessinger, Jr, and R.F. Yeager (New York, 1984), pp. 107–122.
——, *Beowulf and the Appositive Style* (Knoxville, 1985).
ROBINSON, R.P., *The Germania of Tacitus* (Middletown, 1935).
ROSIER, J.L., "Design for Treachery: the Unferð Intrigue", *Publications of the Modern Language Association*, 77 (1962), pp. 1–7.
RUMBLE, A., " 'Hrepingas' Reconsidered", *Mercian Studies*, ed. A. Dornier (Leicester, 1977), pp. 169–172.
RUSSELL, W.M.S., and C. RUSSELL, "The Social Biology of Werewolves", *Animals in Folklore*, ed. J.R. Porter and W.M.S. Russell (Cambridge, 1978), pp. 143–182.
RYPINS, S. (ed.), *Three Old English Prose Texts in MS Cotton Vitellius A.XV*, Early English Text Society, original series, 161 (London, 1924).

SARLVIK, I., *Paths towards a Stratified Society: A Study of Economic, Cultural and Social Patterns in South-West Sweden during the Roman Iron Age and the Migration Period*, Stockholm Studies in Archaeology, 3 (Stockholm, 1982).
SARRAZIN, G., "Neue *Beowulf*-Studien: I. König Hrodgeirr und seine Familie. II. Das Skjöldungen-Epos. III. Das Drachenlied. IV. Das Beowulflied und Kynewulfs *Andreas*", *Englishche Studien*, 23, pp. 221–267.
SAVILLE, H., *Rerum Anglicarum Scriptores post Bedam Praecipui* (London, 1596).
SAWYER, P. (ed.), *Anglo-Saxon Charters: An Annotated List and Bibliography*, Royal Historical Society Guides and Handbooks, 8 (London, 1968).
SCARFE, N., *The Suffolk Landscape* (London, 1972).
——, *Suffolk in the Middle Ages* (Woodbridge, 1986).
SCHABRAM, H., *Superbia: Studien zum Altenglische Wortschatz*, part 1 (Munich, 1965).
SCHÖNBÄCK, B., "The Custom of Burial in Boats", *Vendel Period Studies*, ed. J.P. Lamm and H.-Å. Nordström (Stockholm, 1983), pp. 123–132.
SCHÜCKING, L.L., *Beowulfs Rückkehr* (Halle, 1905).
——, "Wann entstand der *Beowulf*? Glossen, Zweifel und Fragen", *Beitrage zur Geschichte der deutschen Sprache und Literatur*, 42 (1917), pp. 347–410.
——, "Die Beowulfdatierung: Eine Replik", *Beiträge zur Geschichte der deutschen Sprache und Literatur*, 47 (1923), pp. 292–311.
——, "Heldenstolz und Würde im Angel-Sächsischen, mit einem Anhang: Zur Charakterisierungstechnik im Beowulfepos", *Abhandlungen der Philologisch-historischen Klasse der sächsischen Akademie der Wissenschaften*, 42, no. 5 (Leipzig 1933).
SCHÜTTE, G., *Our Forefathers: the Gothonic Nations*, 2 vols, tr. J. Young (Cambridge, 1933).
SCRAGG, D.G., "Initial H in Old English", *Anglia*, 88 (1970), pp. 165–196.
——, (ed.), *The Battle of Maldon* (Manchester, 1981).
SEARLE, W.G., (ed.), *Onomasticum Anglo-Saxonicum. A List of Anglo-Saxon Proper Names from the Time of Beda to that of King John* (Cambridge, 1897).

SERJEANTSON, M.S., "The Vocabulary of Folklore in Old and Middle English", *Folklore*, 47 (1936), pp. 42–73.

SHETELIG, H., and H. FALK, *Scandinavian Archaeology*, tr. E.V. Gordon (Oxford, 1937).

SHIPPEY, T.A., *Old English Verse* (London, 1972).

——, *Poems of Wisdom and Learning in Old English* (Cambridge, 1976).

——, *Beowulf* (London, 1978).

SIEVERS, E., "Zur Rhythmik des germanischen Alliterations-verses: I. Vorbemerkungen: Die Metrik des *Beowulf*" *Beiträge zur Geschichte der deutschen Sprache und Literatur*, 10 (1885), pp. 209–314.

——, *Altgermanische Metrik* (Halle, 1893).

SIMS-WILLIAMS, P., "The Settlement of England in Bede and the *Chronicle*", *Anglo-Saxon England*, 12 (1983), pp. 1–41.

SISAM, K., *Studies in the History of Old English Literature* (Oxford, 1953).

——, "Anglo-Saxon Royal Genealogies", *Proceedings of the British Academy*, 39 (1953), pp. 287–348.

——, *The Structure of Beowulf* (Oxford, 1956).

SJØVOLD, T., *The Viking Ships in Olso* (Oslo, 1979).

SKEAT, W.W. (ed.), *Ælfric's Lives of Saints*, vol. 2 (Oxford, 1890).

SKLUTE, L.M., "*Freoðuwebbe* in Old English Poetry", *Neuphilologische Mitteilungen*, 71 (1971), pp. 534–541.

SLAY, D. (ed.), *Hrólfs saga kraka* (Copenhagen, 1960).

SMITH, A.H. (ed.), *The Place-Names of the West Riding of Yorkshire*, 8 vols (Cambridge, 1961–1963).

SMITHERS, G.V., *The Making of Beowulf* (Durham, 1961).

——, "Destiny and the Heroic Warrior in *Beowulf*", *Philological Essays: Studies in Old and Middle English in Honour of H.D. Meritt*, ed. J.L. Rosier (The Hague, 1970), pp. 65–81.

——, "The Geats of *Beowulf*," *Durham University Journal*, 63 (1971), pp. 87–103.

SMYTH, A.P., *Scandinavian Kings in the British Isles, 850–880* (Oxford, 1977).

SPEAKE, G., *Anglo-Saxon Animal Art* (Oxford, 1980).

STANLEY, E.G., "The Date of *Beowulf*: some Doubts and no Conclusions," *The Dating of Beowulf*, ed. C. Chase (Toronto, 1981), pp. 197–211.

STENTON, F., "The East Anglian Kings of the Seventh Century," *The Anglo-Saxons: Studies presented to Bruce Dickins*, ed. P. Clemoes (London, 1959), pp. 43–52.

——, *Anglo-Saxon England*, 3rd edition (Oxford, 1971).

STEVENSON, W.H. (ed.), *Asser's Life of King Alfred*, rev. D. Whitelock (Oxford, 1959).

STEWART, I., "The London Mint and the Coinage of Offa", *Anglo-Saxon Monetary History* (Leicester, 1986), pp. 27–43.

STJERNA, K., *Essays on Questions Connected with the Old English Poem of Beowulf*, ed. and tr. J.R. Clark Hall (Coventry, 1912).

STORMS, G., *Compounded Names of Peoples in Beowulf* (Utrecht and Nijmegen, 1957).

——, "The Significance of Hygelac's Raid", *Nottingham Medieval Studies*, 14 (1970), pp. 3–26.

——, "The Sutton Hoo Ship Burial: An Interpretation", *Proceedings of the State Service for Archaeological Investigation in the Netherlands*, 28 (1978), pp. 309–345.

STRÖM, H., *Old English Personal Names in Bede's History: An Etymological-Phonological Investigation*, Lund Studies in English, 8 (Lund, 1939).

SVENNUNG, J., *Scadinavia und Scandia*, Lateinisch-Nordische Namenstudien (Uppsala and Wiesbaden, 1963).

SWEET, H. (ed.), *King Alfred's Orosius*, part I, Early English Text Society, original series, 79 (London, 1883).

TANGL, M. (ed.), *Die Briefe des heiligen Bonifatius und Lullus*, Monumenta Germaniae Historica, Epistolae Selectae, vol. 1 (Berlin, 1916).

TAYLOR, P.B., "Heorot, Earth and Asgard: Christian Poetry and Pagan Myth", *Tennessee Studies in Literature*, 11 (1966), pp. 119–130.

———, "The Traditional Language of Treasure in *Beowulf*", *Journal of English and Germanic Philology*, 85 (1986), pp. 191–205.

TAYLOR, S. (ed.), *The Anglo-Saxon Chronicle : MS B* (Cambridge, 1983).

THOMAS, P.G., "Notes on the Language of *Beowulf*", *Modern Language Review*, 1 (1906), pp. 202–207.

THORPE, B. (ed.), *The Anglo-Saxon Poems of Beowulf, the Scop or Gleeman's Tale, and the Fight at Finnesburg* (Oxford, 1855).

THRANE, H., "Das Gudme-Problem und die Gudme-Untersuchung. Fragen der Besiedlung in der Völkerwanderungs und der Merowingerzeit auf Fünen", *Frühmittelalterliche Studien*, 21 (1987), pp. 1–48.

TIMMER, B.J. (ed.), *Judith* (London, 1961).

TOLKIEN, J.R.R., "*Beowulf*: The Monsters and the Critics", *Proceedings of the British Academy*, 22 (1936), pp. 245–295.

———, "Prefatory Remarks on Prose Translation of *Beowulf*", in J. Clark Hall's edition of *Beowulf and the Finnsburg Fragment* (London, 1940).

———, *The Old English Exodus: Text, Translation, and Commentary*, ed. J. Turville-Petre (Oxford, 1981).

———, *Finn and Hengest: The Fragment and the Episode*, ed. A.J. Bliss (London, 1982).

TOON, T.E., *The Politics of Early Old English Sound Change* (New York, 1983).

TRIPP, R.P., Jr. "The Exemplary Role of Hrothgar and Heorot", *Philological Quarterly*, 56 (1977), pp. 123–129.

TURVILLE-PETRE, E.O.G., *The Heroic Age of Scandinavia* (London, 1951).

———, *Myth and Religion of the North* (London, 1964).

TURVILLE-PETRE, J.E., "Hengest and Horsa", *Saga Book*, 14 (1958), pp. 273–290.

———, "On *Ynglingatal*", *Medieval Scandinavia*, 11 (1978–1979), pp. 47–67.

TUSO, J.F., "*Beowulf* 461b and Thorpe's *wara*", *Modern Language Quarterly*, 29 (1968), pp. 259–262.

———, "*Beowulf*'s Dialectal Vocabulary and the Kiernan Theory", *South Central Review*, 2 (1985), pp. 1–9.

ÞÓRÓLFSSON, B.K. (ed.), *Gísla Saga*, in *Vestfirðinga Sögur*, Íslenzk Fornrit, 6 (Reykjavík, 1943).

VAUGHAN, M.F., "A Reconsideration of 'Unferð' ", *Neuphilologische Mitteilungen*, 77 (1976), pp. 32–48.

VIGFÚSSON, G., and F. YORK POWELL (ed.), *Corpus Poeticum Boreale*, 2 vols (1888; repr. New York, 1965).

———, and C. UNGER (ed.), *Flateyjarbók*, 3 vols (Copenhagen, 1860–1868).

de VRIES, J. (ed.), *Altnordisches Etymologisches Wörterbuch* (Leiden).

WADSTEIN, E., *On the Origin of the English* (Uppsala, 1927).

WARDALE, E., *"Beowulf:* the Nationality of *Ecgðeow"*, *Modern Language Review*, 24 (1929), p. 322.

WARNER, P., "Pre-Conquest Territorial and Administrative Organisation in East Suffolk", *Anglo-Saxon Settlements*, ed. D. Hooke (Oxford, 1988), pp. 9–34.

WEBSTER, L., "Stylistic Aspects of the Franks Casket", *The Vikings*, ed. R.T. Farrell (London and Chichester, 1982), pp. 20–31.

———, and J. BACKHOUSE, *The Making of England: Anglo-Saxon Art and Culture AD 600–900* (London, 1991).

WERNER, K.F., "Important Noble Families in the Kingdom of Charlemagne", *The Medieval Nobility: Studies on the Ruling Classes of France and Germany from the Sixth to the Twelfth Century*, ed. T. Reuter (Amsterdam, 1978), pp. 137–202.

WEST, S.E., "The Gold Bracteate from Undley, Suffolk", *Frühmittelalterliche Studien*, 17 (1983), p. 459.

———, N. SCARFE, and R. CRAMP, "Iken, St Botolph, and the Coming of East Anglian Christianity", *Proceedings of the Suffolk Institute of Archaeology and History*, 35 (1984), pp. 279–301.

WESTPHALEN, T., *Beowulf 3150–55: Textkritik und Editionsgeschichte* (Munich, 1967).

WHITBREAD, L., *"Beowulf* and Archaeology: Two Footnotes", *Neuphilologische Mitteilungen*, 68 (1967), pp. 28–35.

WHITELOCK, D., "Anglo-Saxon Poetry and the Historian", *Transactions of the Royal Historical Society*, 4th Series, 31 (1949), pp. 75–94.

———, *The Audience of Beowulf* (Oxford, 1951).

———, "The pre-Viking Church in East Anglia", *Anglo-Saxon England*, 1 (1972), pp. 1–22.

———, "Fact and Fiction in the Legend of St Edmund", *Proceedings of the Suffolk Institute of Archaeology and History*, 31 (1973–1974), pp. 217–233.

WHITTOCK, M.J., *The Origins of England 410–600* (London, 1986).

WIERSMA, S.M., "A Linguistic Analysis of Words referring to Monsters in *Beowulf"*, unpub. Ph.D. diss. (Wisconsin, 1961).

WILSON, D.M., *Anglo-Saxon Ornamental Metalwork (700–1100) in the British Museum* (London, 1964).

———, "Sweden-England", *Vendel Period Studies*, ed. J.P. Lamm & H-Å. Nordström (Stockholm, 1983), pp. 163–166.

WILSON, R.M., *The Lost Literature of Medieval England* (London, 1952).

WINTERBOTTOM, M. (ed.), *Three Lives of English Saints* (Toronto, 1972).

WOOLF, H.B., *The Old Germanic Principles of Name-Giving* (Baltimore, 1939).

WORMALD, P., "The Uses of Literacy in Anglo-Saxon England and Its Neighbours", *Transactions of the Royal Historical Society*, 7th Series, 27 (1977), pp. 95–114.

———, "Bede, *Beowulf* and the Conversion of the Anglo-Saxon Aristocracy", *Bede and Anglo-Saxon England*, ed. R.T. Farrell, British Archaeological Reports, British Series, 46 (Oxford, 1978), pp. 32–95.

WRENN, C.L., "The Value of Spelling as Evidence", *Transactions of the Philological Society* (1943), pp. 14–27.

———, "Sutton Hoo and *Beowulf"*, in the supplement to the 3rd edition of Chambers's *Introduction to the Study of the Poem* (Cambridge, 1959), pp. 508–523.

———, *A Study of Old English Literature* (New York, 1967).

WRIGHT, C.E., *The Cultivation of Saga in Anglo-Saxon England* (Edinburgh, 1939).

WRIGHT, J., (ed.), *The English Dialect Dictionary*, 6 vols (New York, 1898–1905).

WYATT, A.J. (ed.), *Beowulf with the Finnsburg Fragment* (Cambridge, 1914).

YORKE, B., "The Kingdom of the East Saxons", *Anglo-Saxon England*, 14 (1985),
    pp. 1–36.
——, "The Jutes of Hampshire and Wight and the Origins of Wessex", *The
    Origins of the Anglo-Saxon Kingdoms*, ed. S. Bassett (Leicester, 1989), pp. 84–94.
——, *Kings and Kingdoms of Early Anglo-Saxon England* (London, 1990).

ZUPITZA, J. (ed.), *Beowulf: Reproduced in Facsimile from the Unique Manuscript,
    British Museum MS. Cotton Vitellius A.XV*, rev. N. Davis, Early English Text
    Society, original series, 245 (London, 1959).

INDEX OF LINES

Index of lines from *Beowulf* (Klaeber edition) cited or discussed

l.2603^b 121; cited 112
l.2605^a 33
l.2612^a 28
ll.2612^b–2619 (Eanmund slain by
   Wihstan) 102, 121
l.2661^b 33
ll.2703^b–2704 38
ll.2802–2807^b (Beowulf's specifies the site
   of his burial-mound) cited 44
ll.2813–2816 (Beowulf's kinship with the
   Wægmundings) cited 121

ll.2890^b–2891 cited 118
ll.2910^b–2921 (fall of Hygelac) 27
l.2916^a 119
ll.2922–2998 (fall of Ongenþeow) 25, 29,
   111
l.2928^b 28
l.2932^b 28
ll.3134–3155 (Beowulf's funeral-rites) 43
ll.3137–3148^b (Beowulf's cremation) 43
ll.3156–3162 (building of Beowulf's
   burial-mound) cited 44

GENERAL INDEX

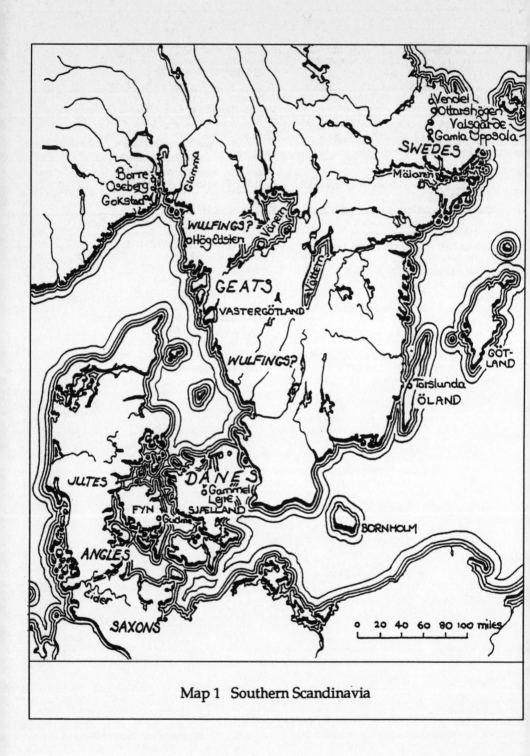

Map 1 Southern Scandinavia

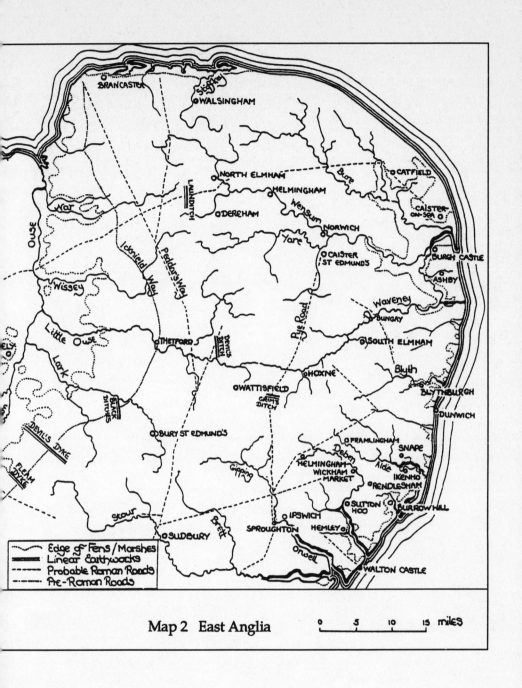

BRANCASTER

Stiffkey

WALSINGHAM

CATFIELD

NORTH ELMHAM

Bure

HELMINGHAM

CAISTER-ON-SEA

LAUNDITCH

DEREHAM

Wensum

NORWICH

Yare

CAISTER ST EDMUNDS

BURGH CASTLE

ASHBY

Ouse

Wav

Icknield Way

Peddars Way

Wissey

Waveney

BUNGAY

SOUTH ELMHAM

Little Ouse

Lark

THETFORD

DEVILS DITCH

Rye Road

HOXNE

Blyth

BLYTHBURGH

WATTISFIELD

GRIMS DITCH

DUNWICH

BLACK DITCHES

BURY ST EDMUNDS

FRAMLINGHAM

SNAPE

DEVILS DYKE

Debe

HELMINGHAM

IKENHO

FLEAM DYKE

Gipping

WICKHAM MARKET

Alde

RENDLESHAM

SUTTON HOO

BURROW HILL

Stour

IPSWICH

HEMLEY

SUDBURY

Brett

SPROUGHTON

Orwell

WALTON CASTLE

Edge of Fens/Marshes
Linear Earthworks
Probable Roman Roads
Pre-Roman Roads

Map 2 East Anglia

0   5   10   15 miles